Florence
and Tuscany

Florence and Tuscany

A Phaidon Cultural Guide

with over 260 color illustrations
and 5 pages of maps

PRENTICE HALL PRESS
NEW YORK

Editor: Dr Marianne Mehling

Contributors: Joachim Hertlein, Dr Marianne Mehling, Dr Albin Rohrmoser

Photographs: Fotostudio Camilla; Norbert Dallinger; Fratelli Fabbri Editori S.p.A., Milan; Ernst Höhne; Löbl/Schreyer, Ellbach/Obb.; Maria Paukert; SCALA Istituto Fotografico Editoriale, Florence

Maps: Huber & Oberländer, Munich

Ground-plans: Herstellung + Grafik, Lidl

Library of Congress Cataloging in Publication Data

Knaurs Kulturführer in Farbe. Florenz und Toskana.
English.
    Florence and Tuscany: a Phaidon cultural guide.

    Translation of: Knaurs Kulturführer in Farbe.
Florenz und Toskana.
    Includes index.
    1. Art—Italy—Florence—Guide-books. 2. Architecture
—Italy—Florence—Guide-books. 3. Florence (Italy)
—Description—1981—Guide-books. 4. Art—Italy—
Tuscany—Guide-books. 5. Architecture—Italy—
Tuscany—Guide-books. 6. Tuscany (Italy)—Description
and travel—Guide-books. I. Mehling, Marianne.
II. Hertlein, Joachim. III. Rohrmoser, Albin.
IV. Title.
N6921.F7K63   1986   914.5'504928   85-25775
ISBN 0-13-322512-7

This edition published in the United States and Canada in 1986 by
Prentice Hall Press Travel Publishing
A division of Simon & Schuster, Inc.
Simon & Schuster Building
Rockefeller Center
1230 Avenue of the Americas
New York, New York 10020

PRENTICE HALL PRESS is a trademark of Simon & Schuster, Inc.

Originally published as *Knaurs Kulturführer in Farbe, Florenz und Toskana*
© Droemersche Verlagsanstalt Th. Knaur Nachf. Munich 1983
Translation © Phaidon Press Limited, Oxford, 1986

ISBN 0-13-322512-7

Translated and edited by Babel Translations, London
Typeset by Hourds Typographica, Stafford
Printed in West Germany by Druckerei Appl, Wemding

Cover illustration: Florence, the Baptistery and Campanile from the west
(photo: A.F. Kersting, London)

Preface

Tuscany is the region in the middle of Italy, south of Milan, north of Rome and bordered by the sea in the west. Visitors to this fertile yet austere land, which, with its green hills, displays the loveliest countryside in the whole of Italy, will never forget it. Once they have come to know the charms of its pines, cypresses and olive trees glimmering in the haze, its half-ruined, lonely courtyards, the beauty of its towns, its villainous history, and the perfection of its culture, then they will never be free from the love of Tuscany and one day must return.

The mild climate of Tuscany has always provided man with a favourable habitat, as the area's ancient history bears witness. It was inhabited by the Etruscans in 800 BC and traces of their highly developed culture still remain. Such towns as Pisa, Volterra, Arezzo and Fiesole were important even in those days. Tuscany came under Roman rule after 280 BC. Julius Caesar founded the colony of Florentia in 59 BC. The Goths and Byzantines ruled here in the fourth century AD and in the sixth century the territory was invaded by barbarians. Charlemagne made Tuscany a Frankish province in 774.

In the Middle Ages, the Pope, the aristocracy and wealthy merchants struggled for power. The Medici ruled from 1434 to 1737, although their power was repeatedly contested. Often ruling with a cruel hand, they were nevertheless probably the greatest artistic patrons in history. It was in the Middle Ages that Tuscany, and especially the city of Florence, began its rise to become the intellectual and cultural centre of Italy. In the fifteenth and sixteenth centuries the development of Florence reached such a peak that it became a model for the whole of Europe. The Renaissance was created here, prepared by Giotto and perfected in the harmony of the dome of Florence's cathedral by Brunelleschi, in the reliefs of Ghiberti, the sculptures of Donatello and the paintings of Masaccio. The finest achievements of classical times were born again in a new form through the work of Leonardo da Vinci and Michelangelo, the greatest artists of the day.

Where else in Europe, or in the whole world, can one find such towns as Florence, Siena, Volterra, Pisa, Lucca, Fiesole, Arezzo, Pistoia and San Gimignano, and all in such a small area? The present cultural guide attempts to accompany the traveller in the exploration of this region of unsurpassed cultural significance.

As with other guides in this series, the text is arranged in alphabetical order of place names. This gives the book the clarity of a work of reference and avoids the need for lengthy searching. The link between places which are geographically close, but which are separated by the alphabet, is provided by the maps on pages 134–8. This section shows all the places mentioned which are within a short distance from any given destination and which, therefore, it might be possible to include in a tour.

The heading to each entry gives the post-code and name of the town, and, below, the name of its geographical region and a reference to the map section, giving page number and grid reference. Within each entry the particular sites of interest are printed in bold type, while less significant objects of interest appear under the heading **Also worth seeing** and places in the immediate vicinity under **Environs.**

An index of all the towns and places of interest mentioned in the text is included at the end of the book.

The publishers would be grateful for notification of any errors or omissions.

53021 Abbadia San Salvatore
Siena   p.138☐F 7

A popular holiday resort on the E. slope of the extinct volcano Amiata (5,700 ft. high). The rich deposits of mercury on Monte Amiata were known even to the Etruscans and the mines still provide work for people today.

Abbey: Formerly the richest abbey in Tuscany. Rachis from Lombardy founded it as a Benedictine monastery in 743. The monastery had been in the possession of Camaldolese monks for only a few years when the Cistercians took it over in 1228, remaining until its dissolution in 1782 by Leopold I. All that survives of what was probably the first church, an 8C pre-Romanesque building, is the crypt, which has a nave, twelve aisles and 36 columns which are all different. The two-towered façade (only the body of the right-hand tower survives) is part of the Romanesque church consecrated in 1036. The single-aisled interior (altered in 1229 & 1590 and restored in 1971) has a raised apse, a 12C wooden cross and 15C choir stalls with inlaid work. The monastery buildings no longer survive.

Also worth seeing: The *Borgo*, a castle built in trachyte, is an impressive feature of the medieval town centre.

Environs: Piancastagnaio (4.5 km. S.): The *castle* (Rocca) was enlarged by the Aldobrandeschi in the 13&14C. Today it has been partially restored and it now houses a *museum*

Abbadia San Salvatore, abbey church

Piancastagnaio, castle

with a collection of weapons and furniture. The *Palazzo del Marchese* (1611) and the *Palazzo Pretorio* are also interesting. *Santa Fiora* (12 km. W. of Piancastagnaio): This picturesque town was the feudal seat of the Aldobrandeschi from the 11C onwards. The Romanesque *church* (Renaissance portal) has terracotta altars by G. della Robbia (15&16C). The *Palazzo Sforza*, a battlemented *clock tower*, and the medieval *castle hamlet*, are also to be seen.

Arcidosso (7.5 km. NW of Santa Fiora): *Castle ruins* in the middle of the medieval town centre; 2 km. outside the town there is an 11C Romanesque *church* which has a nave, two aisles and an elevated choir.

Roccalbegna (17 km. SW of Arcidosso): A picturesque town 1715 ft. above sea level with the Romanesque church of *SS.Pietro e Paolo*, (13C, Piazza Sorge), which has two panels

from Lorenzetti's late period ('Madonna and Child', part of a Maestà, and 'St.Peter and St.Paul'), a painted crucifix by Luca di Tommè (in the Oratorio del Crocifisso), and a lofty campanile.

Seggiano (11 km. N. of Arcidosso): The *parish church* has an 11C triptych. The *Chapel of S.Rocco* has frescos from *c.* 1450.

52100 Arezzo

Arezzo   p.138□G 5

Arezzo is in E. Tuscany and occupies the slope of a hill amidst fertile and beautiful countryside. From the highest point, where the cathedral and the Medici fortress are to be found, the streets run in a fan shape to the city gates. While the upper city, whose walls surround it in an irregu-

Piancastagnaio (Abbadia San Salvatore), view of the town

lar pentagon, has retained its medieval appearance, the lower city looks very modern. Arezzo's origins go back beyond the 7C BC, when it was an important member of the Etruscan confederation of twelve cities. Well known works of art from this period are the Chimaera and the statue of Minerva, both of which are in the Archaeological Museum in Florence. *Arretium* allied itself with Rome in the 4C BC and thereby avoided devastation. Arezzo is famous for the 'Terra sigillata' (crockery with coral-coloured glaze) which was manufactured from the 2C BC to the 1C AD and used all over the Roman world. Governed by bishops in the early Middle Ages, the city became a free and prosperous community. Arezzo, supported the Ghibellines and thus the Emperor and was defeated at Campaldino in 1289 by Florence, ruled at the time by the Guelphs. Independence

was regained under Bishop Guido Tarlati (1312–27) but Arezzo was finally incorporated into the Grand Duchy of the Medici after they bought it in 1384.

Cathedral of S.Donato (Via Ricasoli): Work on building the Romanesque-Gothic cathedral began in 1277. Additions were made in 1313 & 1510 and in 1900–14 the façade was restored and finally completed. The three portals and the rose-window are 15C; the round-arched portal with the pointed-arched tympanum and the terracotta by Niccolò d'Arezzo (in the right aisle) are 14C. The bell tower was not built until 1859. The interior has a nave and two aisles subdivided by pillars and pointed arches. Behind the high altar is the marble *shrine of St.Donatus* (Arca di S.Donato) with reliefs; the work of several artists, it dates from 1369. The stained-glass

Arezzo, Pieve di S.Maria Assunta

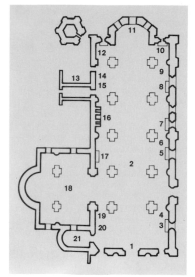

Arezzo, cathedral, W. portal, tympanum

Arezzo, cathedral of S.Donato 1 Stained-glass window by de Marcillat, 1518-24 (Descent of the Holy Ghost) **2** Nave vaulting with frescos by S.Castelucci (1668) and G. de Marcillat (1520-6) **3** Stained-glass window by de Marcillat (1520, 'Calling of Matthew') **4** Monument to Pope Gregory X (c. 1325) **5** Stained-glass window by de Marcillat (1519, 'Baptism of Christ') **6** 14C frescos, probably by Buffalmacca **7** Stained-glass windows by de Marcillat (1520); fresco by Lippo Fiorentino (early-14C, '6 scenes from the life of Christ and James', 'Madonna and Child') **8** Cappella di Guido Tarlati by Giovanni d'Agostino (1334); Sienese frescos (c. 1380); Roman marble urn from the 4C **9** Stained-glass window by de Marcillat (1520, 'Driving the money-changers from the Temple') **10** Chapel with 15C stained-glass window **11** Sanctuary; Arca di S.Donato by Giovanni and Betto di Francesco and others (the reliefs show scenes from the life of St.Donatus) **12** Cappella del B.Gregorio; stained-glass window by de Marcillat (1518-24, 'St.Lucy and St.Silvester') **13** Sacristy with small collection of paintings, including a detached fresco by B. della Gatta ('St.Jerome'); 14C Florentine terracotta ('Annunciation') **14** Fresco by Piero della Francesca (c. 1460, 'Magdalene') **15** Monument to Bishop Guido Tarlati (d. 1327) to a design by Giotto, by Agostino di Giovanni and Agnolo da Siena (1330) **16** Organ gallery by G.Vasari (1535); wood carving (late-13C, 'Madonna and Child'); base of Roman column on which St.Donatus was allegedly beheaded **17** Altarpiece by P.Benvenuti (1794, 'Martyrdom of St.Donatus') **18** Cappella della Madonna del Conforto (1796-1817); decoration by G. del Rosso; 18C wrought-iron grille; terracotta by A. della Robbia (Madonna); at the right altar: 'Crucifixion' and 'St.Donatus and St.Fran-

cis' by A. della Robbia **19** Tomb of Francesco Redi (late-17C); 13C wooden crucifix **20** 17C altar **21** Baptistery, hexagonal marble font

windows (1518–27) and the *frescos* in the first three vaults of the nave (1520–6) are the work of the French monk G.de Marcillat. Other frescos are by S.Castelucci (1668). The monument to Bishop Guido Tarlati who died in 1327 (built in 1330 to designs by Giotto de Bondone) is in the left aisle, and to the right of it is a beautiful *fresco of St.Mary Magdalen* by Piero della Francesca. Features in the right aisle include the Tarlati chapel (1334) and the monument to Gregory X (14C). There are also terracottas by A.della Robbia and his pupils in the *Cappella della Madonna del Conforto* and a hexagonal font (15C) in the baptistery, a Renaissance organ on marble supports by Giorgio

Arezzo, cathedral, high altar

Arezzo, Pieve di S.Maria Assunta

Vasari (1535), the fresco of St.Jerome by B.della Gatta and a 14C terracotta Annunciation (both in the sacristy); Outside the cathedral stands the marble statue of Ferdinand I by Giambologna.

Pieve di S.Maria Assunta (Piazza Grande): The oldest church in the town and one of the finest Romanesque structures in Tuscany, thanks mainly to its Romanesque-Pisan façade. Building began some time after 1140 and the building was dedicated to St.Mary of the Assumption and to St.Donatus (the latter's *relics* are in a gilded silver bust dating from 1346 in the crypt). This massive façade with its cornice makes a great impression owing to the three sets of arcades above the three portals and their flanking five blind arcades. The number of columns in each storey of open arcades increases storey by storey (12 columns in the 1st storey, 24 in the 2nd, 32 in the 3rd). The middle portal has depictions of the twelve months in four archivolts (by an unknown 13C artist). The *campanile* on the right side of the façade, completed in 1330 and known as the 'tower of the hundred holes', owing to its 40 double-arched windows, is one of Arezzo's landmarks. The interior of the church, with its nave and two aisles, has an irregular layout. The sanctuary, which survives from the original structure, is elevated above the crypt and has 18 two-arched windows. The finest feature internally is the high altar *polyptych* by P.Lorenzetti (1320–4) with a Madonna and Child, Annunciation and Saints.

S.Francesco (Piazza S. Francesco): It was probably in the late 13C that Fra Giovanni da Pistoia began building this Franciscan Gothic church,

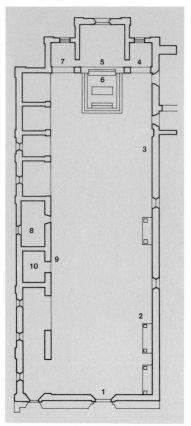

Arezzo, S.Francesco 1 Stained-glass window by G. de Marcillat (1524, 'Francis before Honorius III'); above the portal, a fresco by an unknown artist (15C, 'Betrothal of St.Catherine of Alexandria'); other frescos on the inner façade by d'Agnoli, Pecori and others (14-15C) **2** Fresco from the succession of A. del Castagno (late-15C, 2 Saints) **3** Fresco by Spinello Aretino ('Annunciation', c. 1400) **4** Cappella Guasconi; frescos by Spinello Aretino (c. 1400, 'Scenes from the life of St.Egidius'); 14C triptych **5** Axial chapel; fresco cycle by Piero della Francesca (1452-64, 'Scenes from the legend of the Holy Cross'); the cycle consists of the following scenes: 'Death and Burial of Adam' (right wall above; Seth plants the twig of life in Adam's mouth; after an enormous tree has grown from the twig, King Solomon orders a bridge to be built from the tree), 'The Queen of Sheba acknowledges the holiness of the wood from which the bridge is built, and tells Solomon of her vision that a Jew (Christ) will one day hang from this wood' (middle of right

wall); 'Solomon orders the wood to be buried' (window wall, centre right); 'Dream of Emperor Constantine: You will be victorious under this sign (the Cross)' (window wall, bottom right); 'Constantine's victory over Mexentius' (bottom of right wall); 'Levite Judas confesses to Constantine's mother Helena where the Holy Cross is' (window wall, centre left); 'Three crosses are excavated and the Holy Cross is identified' (middle of left wall); 'Emperor Heraclius conquers the Persian king Chosroes, who had carried off the Holy Cross in a military campaign' (bottom of left wall); 'Emperor Heraclius brings the Cross back to Jerusalem' (top of left wall); the 'Annunciation' (bottom left) and 'Prophets' (above, left and right) are also depicted on the window wall **6** Above the choir arch are frescos by L. di Bicci (1373-1452), 'Hell, Purgatory, Paradise' **7** Cappella Tarlati; altarpiece by Neri di Bicci (1419-91, 'Annunciation'); on the right wall, a fresco by Spinello Aretino (c. 1400, 'Crucifixion'); on the left wall, a fresco by L.Signorelli ('Annunciation', c. 1460) **8** Monument to F.Roselli by Michele da Firenze **9** Painted Crucifix with St.Francis (13C) **10** Frescos by Lorentino d'Andrea (c. 1480, 'Stories from the life of St.Anthony')

Built in brick, it measures some 174 ft. The side chapels are 15C; the campanile 16C. The single-aisled interior is simple and spacious and thus very Franciscan in style. The walls have a large number of *frescos* which were uncovered during 1900–11. The right wall has a late-15C fresco from the school of A.del Castagno and an Annunciation by Spinello Aretino, who also painted the frescos in the Cappella Guascani (to the right of the choir) in *c.* 1400. The Cappella Tarlati (to the left of the choir) contains an Annunciation (*c.* 1460) by the young L.Signorelli, who was much influenced by Piero della Francesca, and another fresco by Spinello Aretino. More frescos by L. d'Arezzo (*c.* 1480) and Margaritone (13C) are to be found in another chapel, and above the choir arch there are frescos by L.di Bicci (1373–1452). Arezzo's finest treasure, Piero della Francesca's fresco cycle *Leggenda della Croce*, covers the walls of the choir. Painted 1452–66 the frescos bear witness to Piero della Francesca's great talent, especially his mastery of perspective, his clarity of line, and clever handling of light effects. The legend consists of 16 parts, beginning with the death and burial of Adam (right wall, top), continuing with Emperor Constantine's dream of the Cross and the victory of Heraclius over the Persian king Chosroes (left wall, bottom), and ending with the return of the Cross to Jerusalem (left wall, top).

S.Domenico (Piazza S.Domenico): According to Giorgio Vasari this Gothic building founded by the Tarlati family in 1275 was built to the plans of N.Pisano. The irregular façade is original and has pillars, a Romanesque portal and bell tower. The best of the decorations is a painted *wooden crucifix* above the high altar which is thought to be one of Cimabue's earliest works dating from c. 1265. There are also several frescos by 14&15C painters from Arezzo and Siena (Spinello Aretino, Donato d'Arezzo), and a Gothic chest by Giovanni di Francesco dating from 1368.

SS.Annunziata (Via Garibaldi): Work on this Renaissance church began in 1490–1 on the site of a 14C oratory. A. da Sangallo completed the church in 1517. The right portal and a fresco by Spinello Aretino (1370) survive from the oratory. The interior has nave and two aisles, 16C stained-glass windows by G.de Marcillat and a terracotta Madonna (1433–8) by Michele da Firenze on the marble high altar (1599).

S.Flora e Lucilla in Badia (Via Cavour): This former Benedictine church was founded in the 13C and extended by G.Vasari in c. 1550. The side on the Via Cavour and part of the portal are original; the bell tower was built in c. 1650. The Renaissance interior has a nave, two aisles, a painted wooden cross (c. 1320) by Segna di Bonaventura (beneath the crossing) and a fresco of St. Lawrence by B.della Gatta (1476); the high altar by G.Vasari was originally intended as a tomb monument for himself and his family.

S.Francesco, fresco by Piero della Francesca

S.Maria in Gradi (Piaggia del Murello): This late Renaissance church was built by B.Ammannati in 1592 on the site of a Romanesque church of which only the 11C crypt has survived. In the single-aisled interior large chapels are in each case followed by small chapels. A terracotta by A.della Robbia can be seen on the first altar.

S.Maria della Grazie (Viale Mecenate, outside the city wall): Single-aisled Renaissance church built by D.Faltore in 1435–44 on the site of a reputedly miraculous spring in a forest. St.Bernardine destroyed the spring in 1430 and entrusted P.di Spinello with the task of painting the 'Madonne delle Grazie'. The marble and terracotta altar on which the image of the Madonna was placed is by A. della Robbia (late-15C). The

Arezzo, Palazzo Pretorio

splendid portico was built by B.da Maiano 1478–82.

Palazzo Comunale (Via Ricasoli): This two-storeyed building with Ghibelline battlements was erected in 1333 for the Priori family. The sturdy, battlemented tower dates from 1337. After rebuilding, mainly in the 15&16C, the building lost some of its original features.

Palazzo Pretorio (Via dei Pilesti): Originally three 14C palaces. The façade has numerous stone coats-of-arms from the old Podestà (dating from 1434). 1404–1926 it was a prison. Today the town library is housed here.

Palazzo Bruni-Ciocchi, also known as **Palazzo della Dogana** (Via S.Lorentino): An immense Renaissance structure built by B.Ros-sellino for Donato Bruni in 1445 and extended later. The town's *picture gallery* and the *museum of medieval art (Museo Medioevale e Moderno)* have been housed here since 1958. The magnificent collection includes works by Margaritone d'Arezzo (13C), Spinello Aretino, L.Signorelli, Rosso Fiorentino, A.della Robbia and G.Vasari.

Palazzo della Fraternità dei Laici (Piazza Grande): Begun by Baldino di Cino in 1375–7 in high Gothic style. 1434–5 B.Rossellini built the upper storey in the Renaissance manner (the relief of the Madonna is also his work). In 1460 G. da Settignano built the loggia and completed the building. Gothic and Renaissance forms have been most successfully combined in the façade. The early baroque clock tower was designed by G.Vasari in the early 16C.

Other palaces: In addition to the palazzi described above, three other palazzi in the Piazza Grande are: the 17C *Palazzo del Tribunale* with its circular staircase, the *Palazzo delle Logge* designed by G.Vasari in 1573–81, and the 15C *Palazzo Cafani* with Faggiola tower (13C). Mention should also be made of the Palazzo Albergotti (Via dei Pilesti) built in the 14–16C and next to it, 'Della Bigazza', a tower dating from 1351.

Casa di Giorgio Vasari (55 Via XX. Settembre): In 1540, G.Vasari, architect, painter and art historian (often called the father of art history), purchased this house which was in the process of being built at the time. By 1548 he had decorated some of the rooms himself with his own frescos (mainly on the 1st floor) and today the house contains the *Museo e Archivio Vasariano*. The collection includes frescos by Vasari (mainly portraits of contemporary artists) and letters from Michelangelo, the Medici Cosimo I and Francesco I, various Popes, etc.

Casa Petrarca (Via dell'Orto): The house in which Francesco Petrarca the poet and scholar (1304–74) was born has been destroyed. The present building dates from the 16C and was erected on what were probably the remains of the walls of the house. Restoration was necessary in 1948 after it was damaged in the war. Today the building houses the Accademia Petrarca devoted to art, literature and science.

Fortezza Medicea (Viale Buozzi): In the 16C Cosimo I commissioned the architects A. and G.Sangallo to build a fortress on the site of an old Etruscan-Roman castle. Today only a few remains survive of this structure which was razed to the ground in *c.* 1800.

Roman amphitheatre (entrance: 12 Via Margaritone) and **Museo Archeologico Mecenate** (entrance:

Arezzo, S.Francesco

10 Via Margaritone): This elliptical theatre (400–550 ft.) was built in the late 1C BC and had seats for some 8000 spectators. The Olivetans built the monastery of San Bernardo in *c.* 1550 from the ruins of one of the stands. Since 1934 this former monastery has housed the Museo Archeologico. Apart from Etruscan finds (statues, tombstones, terracotta reliefs) and Roman items (mosaics, parts of tombs, statues), there are Umbrian, Etruscan, Roman and Greek objects including coins and gold objects, finds from the Neolithic period and the Bronze Age, and above all, the world-famous collection of 'vasi arretini', coral-coloured vases dating from the 1C BC to the 1C AD.

Also worth seeing: *14C Lappoli tower* in the Piazza Grande. The *parks* (Passeggio del Prato) between the cathedral and the Fortezza Medicea.

55051 Barga

Lucca   p.134☐C 2

This city in the valley of the river Serchio was fortified under Barbarossa in 1186. Conquered by the Republic of Lucca in 1298, Barga was finally sold to Florence in 1341. An opera festival is held here in July of each year.

S.Cristofano: Work on construction of the massive Romanesque cathedral began in the 9C. It occupies the highest point in the town, the Piazza L'Arringo, from which there is a splendid view of the Serchio valley, the Apennines and the Apuan Alps. Later building is mainly 12C (façade) and 14C; only the side chapels are more recent. Brackets with human figures and fabulous beings are to be found on the two rows of arches in the Lombard-Romanesque façade. The portal is decorated with lions and the architrave depicts a wine harvest. The 12C Romanesque *lion pulpit* decorated with reliefs is the finest work inside the cathedral, which has two rows of pillars.

Also worth seeing: The *convent of San Cassiano (Barga), parish church*

Barga, cathedral of S.Cristofano

St.Clare, founded in 1456, has a large Assumption by the della Robbia school and 17C choir stalls. Some old *patricians' houses* in Barga's narrow alleyways are adorned with coats-of-arms and decorative motifs.

Environs: Bagni di Lucca (6.5 km. NE of Borgo a Mozzano): A spa whose waters have been known since the 11C but which became popular in the 19C. The main waters are the *Bagni Caldi* with their well-known salty sulphurous springs. The picturesque *Ponte a Serraglio* spans the bend of a stream.

Borgo a Mozzano (17 km. S. of Barga): The *parish church* houses carved wooden figures from the 15&16C. The so-called *devil's bridge* (Ponte del Diavolo) a little outside the town is probably 11C; its curved arch spans the river Serchio—a technical masterpiece of the early Middle Ages.

Castelnuovo di Garfagnana (12 km. NW): The best building in the old capital of N. Garfagnana is the *castle, La Rocca* which is built on an irregular ground plan and has both round and square towers. Ludovico Ariosto, the poet, lived here in 1522–5. The fortress belonged to the Este, Dukes of Ferrara. Ariosto was governor of Ferrara. Fulvio Testi resided here 1640–2.

Castelvecchio Pascoli (5 km. N.): The country house of the poet Giovanni Pascoli (1855–1912) contains a small *museum* and the poet's tomb.

Castiglione de Garfagnana (8 km. N. of Castelnuovo di Garfagnana): The picturesque *surrounding wall* dating from 1371 has survived in very good condition and can be walked along. The façade of the *church of S.Pietro* is early 13C.

Diecimo (4 km. S. of Borgo a Mozzano): The Romanesque *church* dates

Barga, cathedral of S.Cristofano.

Barga, cathedral, portal

Barga, cathedral, St.Christopher (11C)

Bibbiena, S.Lorenzo

from the 13C. In the bell tower, windows increase in number with each storey; Romanesque sculptures.
San Cassiano (9 km. NE of Bagani di Lucca): The *parish church* has an ashlar tower dating from the 11 or 12C. The façade was rebuilt in the 13C.
La Villa, (8 km. NE of Bagni di Lucca): The Romanesque *church of S.Pietro* with its sturdy bell tower can be found in the old part of town known as Corsena.

52011 Bibbiena

Arezzo   p.138□G 4

This town, under the name of *Vipena*, existed as long ago as Etruscan times. It occupies a site protected by the surrounding mountain ranges (in the E.,

a spur of Monte Falterone and in the W., the slopes of Pratomagno). The soil is very fertile. Bibbiena belonged to the Bishop of Arezzo in the early and high Middle Ages before falling to Florence in 1360. Today it is still the centre of the valley of the upper Arno, known as Casentino. The countryside here, with its olive groves, sloping vineyards, and beautiful woods, is among the most idyllic areas in Tuscany and is therefore much frequented, especially in summer.

SS.Ippolito e Donato (near the Piazza Tarlati): The *church* was built in the 12C and altered several times over the following centuries. In the choir there is a painting, 'Madonna with Angel' by Arcangelo di Cola da Camerino, and also a triptych by Bicco di Lorenzo (1453).

Caprese Michelangelo (Bibbiena), house where Michelangelo was born

S.Lorenzo (Via Dovizi): The most valuable treasures in the 15C *church* are the terracotta reliefs from the della Robbia school.

Palazzo Dovizi (Via Dovizi): The *palace*, which dates from the 16C, was the residence of the humanist Bernardo Dovizi, a cardinal from Bibbiena who made his name with the Renaissance comedy 'La Calandra'.

Environs: Caprese Michelangelo (16 km. S. of La Verna): Michelangelo, the son of the Florentine official Ludovico Buonarroti, was born here on 6 March 1475. The two-storeyed 14C house has been restored several times; the upper storey has rooms decorated in the style of the 15C; a small *museum* with photographs and copies of Michelangelo's sculptures occupies the lower storey.

La Verna monastery (25 km. E.): In 1213, Count Cattani made St.Francis of Assisi the present of an eyrie-like residence in the Verna. This rock covered with beech and pine forests is visible throughout much of Casentino. St.Francis lived here with his followers and received the stigmata here on 14 September 1224. Since that time the site has become an important place of pilgrimage for the Franciscan order. The monastery consists of several buildings, mainly from the 13–16C.

50032 Borgo San Lorenzo

Florence   p.134□E 3

A little agricultural town at the centre of the Mugello, the wide valley of the wild and frequently very torrential

Cafaggiolo (Borgo San Lorenzo), villa

river Sieve, and an area also subject to earthquakes. The town has become increasingly industrialized in recent years. It has often been necessary to alter, or even to tear down and completely rebuild, the medieval buildings.

S.Lorenzo: This 11C Romanesque church was rebuilt in Gothic style in the 16C. The Romanesque bell tower dates from 1213. The church has a painting from the Perugia school depicting St.Sebastian between St.Macarius and St.Vincent.

Environs: Barberino di Mugello (6 km. N. of Cafaggiola): This town was used as the Florentine border fortress from 1313 onwards. The *Palazzo Pretorio* and the *Medici-Palazzetto* date from the 15C.
Cafaggiolo (6 km. NW of San Piero a Sieve): This *villa*, which resembles a

castle with its tower, battlemented gateways and wall passages, was a popular summer residence of the Medici and the Grand Dukes of Tuscany. Fine view of the Chianti region.
Convento Monte Senario (21 km. S.): This monastery stands at a height of 2674 ft. in an isolated site on a hill. It was founded by seven Florentines who withdrew into solitude and lived as hermits. The entire monastery, including the church, was rebuilt in the 16–18C.
Dicomano (8 km. SE of Vicchio): The *church of S.Maria* dates from the 12C but had to be rebuilt after an earthquake. Fine reliquary in the sacristy. **Pieve S.Cresci** (6 km. S.): This *church*, some 1332 ft. up, has a Romanesque bell tower; restored after an earthquake.
San Godenzo (10 km. NE of Dicomano): It was here, in 1302, that the 'White Guelphs' who had been

Scarperia (Borgo San Lorenzo), church of Sant'Agata, tympanum

banished from Florence concluded an alliance with the Ubaldini Ghibellines against the 'Black Guelph' city of Florence. The only building of interest in what is today a health resort is the *monastery church* of the Benedictine abbey founded by the Bishop of Fiesole in 1029; 20C restoration.

San Piero a Sieve (4 km. W.): This town is overlooked by the imposing *Medici fortress* which has several bastions and was built in 1571 to a design by Buontalenti.

Sant'Agata (4 km. N. of Scarperia): Beside the font of the 8C *Pieve* there are reliefs which date from 1175 and came from a dismantled pulpit. The Pieve also contains a tabernacle by G. della Robbia.

Scarperia (4 km. N. of San Piero a Sieve): In 1306 this town was expanded to form the military base of the Guelph Florentines in Mugello.

The *Palazzo Pretorio*, built in 1306, with Guelph battlements on the palace and on the tower was built in imitation of the Palazzo Vecchio in Florence; numerous coats-of-arms of the town governors.

Trebbio (4 km. SW of San Piero a Sieve): Michelozzo built a villa for Piero de' Medici here in 1461; 16C garden.

Vicchio (7 km. SE of Borgo San Lorenzo): Fra Angelico, monk and painter, was born here in 1387.

53022 Buonconvento
Siena   p.136□F 6

Buonconvento, a picturesque town in the Arbia valley, owes its fame to the fact that Emperor Henry VII of Luxembourg died here on 24 August 1313 during his imperial campaign. The town walls are set back from the towers; 14C medieval alleyways. The commanding Porta Senese is the finest of the three gates.

Parish church: Built in the 14C and last restored in the 17C. Inside, Virgin Mary with Saints by Matteo di Giovanni.

Also worth seeing: A small *museum* has been set up in a house near the parish church. Paintings by Tuscan artists of the 14–16C, and religious objects in gold from the 15–17C, are on display here. The *Palazzo Pretorio* is decorated with several coats-of-arms of Sienese and Tuscan officials.

Environs: Abbazia di Monte Oliveto Maggiore (9 km. NE): In 1313 three Sienese noblemen—the law teacher Bernardo Tolomei and his two friends A.Piccolomini and P.Patrizi—retired to a hill 896 ft. high, covered in olive trees and cypresses and located amidst the barren 'Crete' (clay). It was on this site, on 26 March 1319, that B.Tolomei founded the Monte Oliveto monastery (Mount of Olives), the motherhouse of the Olivetan order. This new congregation, which lived according to the strict rules of the Benedictine order (ora et labora = pray and work), was finally acknowledged by Pope Clement VI in 1344. In the 15&16C the monastery was a most important centre of humanist learning. Today the Olivetans in their motherhouse are mainly engaged in renewing and compiling old, damaged books and scrolls of parchment and also in manufacturing liqueur. The brick-red complex of buildings (14–18C) makes a very well-fortified impression and is located in

Scarperia, Palazzo Pretorio

Buonconvento, town gate

the middle of a large park on a slope. There are terracottas by A.della Robbia (Virgin Mary and St.Benedict) on both sides of the battlemented gatehouse tower (1393). A route leads from here past fish ponds and herb gardens down to the domed church (1400–17) where the Gothic portal and the Romanesque-Gothic campanile both date from the first phase of construction. Some alterations were made in 1722, mainly to the apse. The reading desk and the choir stalls are the work of Fra Giovanni da Verona (1503–05). The *frescos* of Christ bearing the Cross and the Scourging of Christ in the passage leading to the church are by G.Bazzi (known as Sodoma; 1477–1549). 1505–08, he also painted 27 of the 36 well-known frescos of scenes from the life of St.Benedict in the large cloister (Chiostro Grande). The other frescos

(scenes 20–28) were painted by L.Signorelli in 1497–8. There are more frescos in the atrium where there is a marble statue by Fra Giovanni da Verona dating from 1490; the refectory dates from 1387–90. Two further rooms, reached through the middle cloister, are the library (a hall with prayer books from the 14–15C) and the pharmacy with a collection of vessels from the 15–17C.

Asciano (9 km. N. of Abbazia di Monte Oliveto Maggiore): This medieval town was given a Sienese wall in 1351. The Romanesque *Collegiata S.Agata* is 11C and has an octagonal dome. The 14C *church of S.Francesco* has a terracotta altar from the della Robbia workshop; font and frescos by Giovanni d'Asciano (14C). Works of the Sienese school are on display in the *museum of religious art* near the Collegiata.

Abbazia di Monte Oliveto Maggiore, abbey

Abbazia di Monte Oliveto Maggiore, gate-tower

Carrara, cathedral, rose-window

Carrara, cathedral, portal

54033 Carrara

Massa-Carrara   p.134□B 2

Carrara, which developed from the village of Kar (kar was a pre-Roman word for stone), is located inland from the the green Versilia coast and at the foot of the Apuan Alps from whose flanks the famous Carrara marble has been quarried for over 2000 years. Michelangelo used the dense white marble (the so-called Statuario) for some of his finest sculptures and frequently stayed in one of the old houses in the cathedral square. Today Carrara possesses the largest marble quarries in the world and produces several different varieties. In the 14&15C the town frequently changed hands. It belonged to the Malaspina family during 1473–1790, then for some decades it was a possession of Modena until it became part of the Kingdom of Italy together with Tuscany.

Cathedral of S.Andrea (cathedral square): The long building period (11–14C) means that both Romanesque and Gothic elements are present although they co-exist outstandingly

Carrara, cathedral

well. The white and grey marble facing along the side aisles and on the lower part of the façade (frieze of round arches and the frame of the portal) are Romanesque; the upper parts of the nave, apse and façade (with columns and large rose-window) are Gothic The bell tower, which was built in the 13C on a Ligurian model, is crowned by five pyramids (a larger pyramid with four smaller ones). Inside there are nave and two aisles and two rows of columns, some of whose capitals are ancient. The marble furnishings by local artists include the hexagonal font (16C) in the baptistery, the marble sculptures ('Angel and Virgin', 14C) in the left aisle, and a niche with the Virgin and Saints (1464) in the left side aisle.

Accademia del Marmo (Piazza Risorgimento): In 1805 Elisa Baciocchi-Bonaparte (Grand Duchess of Tuscany from 1809) moved the gallery of marble exhibits (set up in 1769) into the Palazzo Cybo Malaspina, built in the 16C around the medieval castle or Rocca. Collections of Roman sculptures and finds from Luni are housed here. From the tower there is a splendid view of the sea and the Apuan Alps.

Also worth seeing: The *Neptune fountain* (cathedral square) with the Andrea-Doria statue built in the 16C by B.Bandinelli. Fine 17&18C *baroque palaces* in Piazza Alberica.

Environs: Campo Cecina (20 km. NW): From this plateau some 4430 ft. up among the marble quarries there is a wonderful view of the peaks of the Apuan Alps and the Versilia coast.
Fosdinovo (15 km. NW): Built on a rocky projection, the town has a very

picturesque 13&14C Tuscan castle, the *Malaspina castle,* which has survived in very good condition (probably built above a previous building).

Marble quarries of Colonnata (8 km. E.): The marble for Michelangelo's David (now in the Accademia in Florence) was quarried here.

58043 Castiglione della Pescaia

Grosseto   p.136☐D 7

A picturesque resort with a harbour known in ancient times, it nestles at the foot of the rocky spur Poggio Petriccio (1122 ft. high) which is crowned by an imposing castle. The long sandy beach and pines along both sides of the harbour have made Castiglione della Pescaia a popular holiday resort.

Castiglione Castello and walls: 14C castle; the massive walls with defensive towers still enclose the old medieval town on the rocky spur.

Carrara, Neptune fountain and cathedral

Environs: Punta Ala (20 km. NW): A new tourist centre is being built on this rocky cape overrun by scrub and pines. There is a small castle on a rocky point on an island.

Vetulonia (19 km. NE): Vetulonia joined the Etruscan confederation in the 7C BC. In the 6C BC its deposits of gold, silver and ore enabled it to develop into one of the confederation's most important cities. The great importance of Vetulonia at that time is attested not only by the numerous gold objects found in the tombs (most of these are today in the Archaeological Museum in Florence), but also by the symbols used by the Etruscan-Vetulonian magistrates (war trumpet, toga, lictor's bundle of rods), symbols later adopted by Rome. Ancient authors frequently mentioned the area although it was not discovered by archaeologists until the late 19C. After the city's destruction by the Saracens, a new settlement arose on the old castle hill and the inhabitants used the ruins of the old Vetulonia as a quarry.

3 km. NE of the village is an area of

Vetulonia, Etruscan settlement

widely scattered excavations dating from the 8–2 BC.

The *Tomba della Pietrera* (7C BC) is the most important tomb in Vetulonia. The grave is of particular interest because there are two tombs with identical ground plans built in different types of stone one above the other. The lower tomb, with its central pillar 9 ft. 6 in. tall, was banked up because the stone was thought not to have been sufficiently strong. The upper chamber, approximately square, was built with harder, chalky sandstone.

The *Tomba del Diavolo*, also dating from the 7C BC, testifies to the magnificent vaulting and building techniques which the Etruscans used in their tombs. The domed tomb chamber is approached by a long passageway.

57023 Cecina

Livorno   p.136☐C 5

The alluvial lands of the Maremma ran wild in the Middle Ages and were drained in the 19C, at which time avenues between the newly founded villages were laid out; yet other avenues led to the Via Aurelia. Peasants settled here on the site of a former Roman horse station where there was a bridge over the Cecina. The impressions recorded by the 19C Macchiaioli painters (G.Fattori, G.Abbati and others) are witness to the wildness of the Maremma at that time. A bustling town has developed here in recent decades, and the area is favoured both by manufacturing industry and agriculture; long sandy beaches stretching some 2 km. have also contributed to the town's development.

Museum (near the town hall): Archaeological finds from the vicinity are on display here.

Environs: Castagneto Carducci (11 km. SE of S.Guido Bolgheri): This town is named after the poet Carducci, an Italian Realist who spent part of his youth in Castagneto, where

Vetulonia (Castiglione della Pescaia), Etruscan tombs

S.Guido Bolgheri (Cecina), wayside chapel

S.Guido Bolgheri (Cecina), wayside chapel

his father was for a time doctor. Ruins of the old *Gherardesca castle* are 3 km. outside the town.

Castiglioncello (6 km. W. of Rosignano-Marittimo): This town on a cape with numerous pine trees is a popular holiday resort. The *Archaeological Museum* has finds from the 3–1C BC. Old *coastal watch-tower*.

Marina di Cecina (2 km. W. of Cecina): This popular seaside resort with a fine sandy beach and in an area of dense pine forest developed around an old coastal tower which belonged to the Medici.

Rosignano Marittimo (15 km. N. of Cecina): The old core of the settlement and the remains of a 12C *castle* have survived.

S.Guido Bolgheri (11 km. S. of Cecina): This octagonal wayside chapel, built in 1703 on the Via Aurelia, opposite the turning to Bolgheri, was

praised by Giosuè Carducci (1825–1907) in one of his poems.

Suvereto (20 km. S. of Castagneto Carducci): 15C *Palazzo Comunale* and the Romanesque church of *S.Giusto*.

50052 Certaldo

Florence   p.134☐D 4

The town developed from the 10C onwards around a castle on a hill above the Elsa. From then on Certaldo was in the possession of the Counts Alberti of Prato, before it was handed over to Florence in 1293. The old medieval town, built in red brick on top of the hill, is still known as 'Castello' today. The new town is separate from the old, and was built in the valley of the Elsa about the turn of

View of Certaldo

the present century. This strict separation of the old town from the new is frequently to be observed in the small towns on the S. tributaries of the Arno. Apart from its excellent wines, Certaldo is probably mainly known for its association with Giovanni Boccaccio, author of the 'Decameron', who spent the last years of his life in the town and died here.

SS.Michele e Iacopo (old town): This church was built in the 13C and later restored. Boccaccio's cenotaph is by G.Rustici (1503); his tombstone dates from 1954 and is by the sculptor M.Moschi. The church has two ciboria with terracottas by della Robbia and a 14C fresco of the Virgin Mary. Cloister.

Casa di Boccaccio (Via Boccaccio 18): Boccaccio (1313–75) spent the last years of his life in this brick house which dates from the late 13C (much restored since then).

Palazzo Pretorio (at the end of Via Boccaccio): A brick palace crowned with battlements at the highest point of the old town. Until 1293 it was the residence of the Counts Alberti. After this it was occupied by the governors of Florence, who ordered that it should be enlarged in the 15C; the loggia dates from 1475. Numerous coats-of-arms belonging to governors adorn the façade and the inner courtyard. Frescos from the 15&16C, some of which are by P.F. Fiorentino, decorated rooms, courtyard and stairway.

Also worth seeing: The 'tabernacle of the sentenced' (15C) by B.Gozzoli and G. d'Andrea in the *church* beside

Castelfiorentino (Certaldo), San Verdiana

Certaldo, SS.Michele e Jacopo, cloister

the Palazzo Pretorio came from a chapel in which those sentenced to death were permitted last prayers. The restored Romanesque *cloister* of the *church of SS.Iacopo e Filippo* can be found on the Via Rivellino.

Environs: Castelfiorentino (9 km. NW): As with Certaldo the old town of Castelfiorentino sits on a hill, while the new settlement was built in the Elsa valley. However, unlike Certaldo the town did not develop from the castle, which was known as *Timignano* and belonged to the Counts Alberti. Only remnants of the castle walls survive. From 1149 onwards Timignano was one of the most important of the Florentine border fortresses involved in the struggle against Siena. Fine 15C frescos in the *Cappella della Visitazione* (Via Gozzoli) are by B.Gozzoli and his assistants.
Convento S.Vivaldo (15 km. SW of Castelfiorentino): A Franciscan monastery dating from 1513 built in the middle of a forest. The church is surrounded by 20 small Renaissance chapels (1515), some of which have colonnaded porticoes. Carved scenes from the life of Christ are by an unknown artist.

53043 Chiusi
Siena   p.138☐G 6

This city on a tufa hill in the S. of the Valdichiana (valley of the Chiana), one of the most important of the twelve cities of the Etruscan confederation, was known as *Chamars* and founded in the 8C BC. The city experienced a heyday in the 6–4C BC from which time various valuable works of art (some still in Chiusi itself, others in museums in Florence and Siena) have survived. The legendary King Porsenna allied with

Castelfiorentino (Certaldo), Madonna and Child by Cimabue in S.Verdiana ▷

young Tarquinius Superbus and in 520 BC attacked Romne. There was an alliance with Rome in the 4C BC and in 98 BC the inhabitants of the city, which the Romans then called *Clusium*, were granted Roman citizenship. Chiusi was an episcopal city from the 4C AD until 1561. It was occupied by the Goths in *c*. 500 and incorporated into Lombardy in the late 6C. Malaria broke out as a result of marshes encroaching up the Chiana valley and from the 10C onwards medieval Chiusi consequently lost many of its inhabitants and thereby also declined in importance. Chiusi fell to Florence in 1556 along with Siena, to which it had belonged since 1416. The town was built on the site of the Roman military post dating from the 1C BC. Parts of the Etruscan tunnels beneath private houses are today used as cellars. Remains of the Etruscan ring of walls from the 5C BC were discovered in 1967 on the hill occupied by the city.

Cathedral of S.Secondiano (Piazza del Duomo): Although founded in the 6C, the cathedral was completely rebuilt in the 12C on the remains of ancient buildings. The interior of the basilica, which has a nave, two aisles and a timber roof, is impressive for its 18 Roman columns and 15C chapels. The right aisle has an *alabaster font* with a figure of John the Baptist by A.Sansovino and a 15C Nativity by B.Fungai.

In the 19C, in order to emphasize the basilican character, walls were decorated with paintings and other changes were made; these are at present being removed. The free-standing campanile, the main body of which is Romanesque, was built in the 12C from stone taken from old Roman buildings; 16C rebuilding.

Museo Nazionale Etrusco (Piazza del Duomo): This museum houses Greek ceramics and Roman art (e.g. statuettes, glass, mosaics, etc.), as well as Etruscan finds from nearby (tomb furnishings, sarcophagi, sphinxes). The large sculptures were made of a calcareous stone and these include sphinxes, female half-statues on pedestals (most of which were found in pairs beside the entrance to the

Chiusi, museum

Chiusi, cathedral, apse mosaic

tomb) and the so-called Cippi (tomb-stones from the 6&5C BC decorated with very flat reliefs). There are numerous urns, some terracotta, one travertine, the best known of which are the so-called Canopic urns (with heads for lids and arms; 7&6C BC).

Etruscan tombs: The three most important of the numerous tombs in the vicinity of Chiusi are quite close to one another (2 km. N. of the town, on the Via delle Tombe Etrusche). The *Tomba della Pellegrina* from the 3&2C BC was only discovered in 1927 and it still contains several sarcophagi and cinerary urns decorated with reliefs in the niches and cells of the long corridor (dromos). An oval tomb chamber (near the end of the corridor) formerly contained a large sarcopha-gus and an alabaster urn with the like-ness of Larth Sentinales Caesa; these are now on display in the museum. The *Tomba della Scimmia* (or *di Poggio Renzio*) from the 1st half of the 5C BC is the most interesting of the tombs because of the fine condition of its wall paintings. Discovered in 1846, it opened to the public in 1873. 27

steps lead down to a door which opens into the main room (9 ft. high); off this there are three side rooms. The tufa walls are painted throughout and include scenes depicting competitions, a leave-taking, and also a monkey (Ital.: scimmia) tied to a tree, hence the name of the tomb. The draughtsmanship of these paintings is very fine—in contrast with Tarquinia—and paintings of naked youths in a side room are surprising for their well-preserved colours. A Gorgon's head is attached to the ceiling of each of the side chambers. The *Tomba del Granduca* (tomb of the Grand Duke) dates from the 3&2C BC. It was so named because of its discovery on Grand Ducal lands in 1818.

The *Tomba del Colle* above Chiusi is situated below the graveyard. This tomb dates from the 5C AD and was formerly known as *Tomba Casuccini* because it was discovered on the private grounds of Bonci Casuccini. The two leaves of the travertine door have survived in fine condition. A depiction of a banquet to the left of the entrance in the large hallway had to be replaced (to the right of the

entrance it is preserved). A chariot race is depicted on the rear and right side walls, and there are various games shown on the left side wall. The small tomb chamber shows scenes with musicians, dancers and contestants. The ceilings are splendid.

Also worth seeing: 1 km. to the E. of Chiusi we find the *catacomb of Mustiola,* an early Christian burial site from the 3–5C.

Environs: Cetona (10 km. SW): This town boasts a collection of *Etruscan finds* from the tombs nearby; these are housed in the Palazzo Terrosi. 1 km. to the W. there is a *Franciscan monastery* whose walls are decorated with 14&15C frescos. Near the monastery there are some prehistoric *caves.*
Sarteano (9 km. SW): The centre of this town founded by the Etruscans is the *castle* which dates from the 15C. An Annunciation by G. del Pacchia (1477–1535) can be seen in the *church of S.Lorenzo.* Various Etruscan finds are preserved in the *Palazzo Bargagli.*

Chiusi, Etruscan tomb

52044 Cortona

Arezzo   p.138☐G 5

Cortona occupies a spur of the Alta S. Egidio, high above Lake Trasimene which lies not far away to the S. and is the place where the army of the Roman consul Flaminius suffered a devastating defeat at the hands of Hannibal. The valley of Chiana (Valdichiana) opens towards the W. The city, originally an Umbrian foundation, is one of the oldest in the whole of Italy. Conquered by the Etruscans, the city became one of their military bases. However, it is still unclear whether *Corita* was one of the Etruscan confederation of twelve cities. Various finds, and also the walls which are 8,500 ft. long and date from the 5C BC, bear witness to the size of the city at that time. Etruscan sandstone ashlars which formed the foundation of the medieval ring of walls can still be made out today. The present system of streets in the old walled city is almost identical to that in the Etruscan settlement. The inhabitants of Cortona, like almost all

Chiusi, Etruscan necropolis

Chiusi, wall painting in Etruscan tomb from 5C BC

Chiusi, amphora from Etruscan period

Cortona, cathedral portal

Cortona, S.Maria Nuova

the inhabitants of Italy, were given Roman citizenship in 89 BC, but the city was never able to play a particularly important role within the Roman Empire. Cortona completely disappeared from historical record after being destroyed by the Goths in *c.* 450. There is no further documentary record of it until the 11C. Only after being sold to Florence in 1411 did it enjoy a new heyday. Cortona was the home town of Luca Signorelli (1441–1523), who was among the most important of Italian Renaissance painters and the fatherly friend of Michelangelo. The town was also home to the painter and architect Pietro da Cortona (1596–1669).

A famous antique fair (Mostra Mercato Nazionale del Mobile Antica) is held every year from 25 August until 25 September.

Cathedral of S.Maria (on the NW city wall, cathedral square): Of the 11C Romanesque church only part of the façade has survived the Renaissance rebuilding (*c.* 1480 by Giuliano da Sangallo or his followers). The bell tower with its double-arched windows extending through two storeys was built by F.Laparelli in 1556. The portal by Cristofanello is also 16C.

S.Domenico (Via Nazionale, a little way outside the city wall to the S.): The church, which has a plain façade and a Gothic portal, was built in the early 15C. The single-aisled interior boasts fine *paintings*, like the Coronation of the Virgin (1402) by L. di N.Gerini at the high altar (1402), and an Assumption by B. della Gatta (1480–5) on the left wall. Next to this we see the detached fresco of the Madonna with two Dominican monks by Fra Angelico, a Virgin with Angels

Cortona, Palazzo Comunale, fresco

and Saints by L.Signorelli and an Annunciation by Palma il Giovane.

S.Francesco (Via Berettini, E. of the Piazza della Repubblica): The building, begun by Fra E. Coppi in 1245, is one of the first Franciscan churches in Italy. After 17C reconstruction all that survives of the original building is the left side wall and the portal. The most valuable treasure in the single-aisled interior with three Gothic chapels is the 10C *reliquary of the Holy Cross*, a Byzantine ivory kept in the marble tabernacle on the high altar. The Romanesque-Gothic *monument* to Bishop Ranieri Ubertini (14C) in the apse, and an Annunciation by P. da Cortona in the 2nd altar on the right, are also worth noting.

Santuario di S.Margherita (in a car park behind the Via S.Margherita, below the fortress): This completely new building was erected on the ruins of a 13C church in 1856–97 to the plans of G.Pisano. Only the bell tower is older (1650). In the sanctuary there is the *monument* to St.Margherita who died in 1297. Excellent reliefs (1362) by A. and F. di Pietro showing scenes from the lives of saints can be seen on a sarcophagus. 14C *wooden cross* just to the right of the sanctuary.

S.Maria Nuova (a little way outside the N. city wall): Cristofanello began this square Renaissance church in the mid 16C. It was altered by Vasari who modelled it on the church of the Madonna del Calcinaio. 17C hemispherical dome.

S.Nicolò (above the Via S. Nicolò): A small church built in the 15C; 18C coffered ceiling. Fine *paintings* on the high altar—Entombment and the Virgin Mary by L.Signorelli.

*Castiglion Fiorentino (Cortona),
S.Francesco*

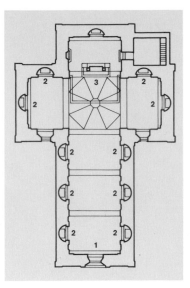

Cortona, Madonna del Calcinaio 1 Stained-glass window by G. de Marcillat (1516, 'Madonna della Misericordia') **2** Altarpieces by 16-18C artists **3** Main altarpiece by Covatti (1519, 'Madonna del Calcinaio')

Madonna del Calcinaio (3 km. below the town, on the road to Camucia): This elegant Renaissance church was built 1484–1513 to a design by F. di G.Martini to house a miraculous image of the Virgin Mary which originally hung in a limestone pit (= Calcinaio) and is today at the high altar. The ground plan takes the form of a Latin cross, with three short aisles and the nave extending from the central crossing over which there is an octagonal dome. The inside exudes a sublime and solemn aura being simple and clear in design. The stained-glass window 'Madonna della Misericordia' (1516) is a masterpiece by the monk G. de Marcillat.

Fortezza Medicea/city wall: The Medici fortress of Girifalco was built in the mid-16C on the ruins of an older 13C castle at the highest point of

the town (2,130 ft.). Remains of the ancient acropolis can still be seen in the E. From here there is a splendid view of Lake Trasimene, Monte Cetona, and the Talebene of the Chiana.

The 13C city wall was built on the foundations of the Etruscan wall and is some 8500 ft. long. The Etruscan remains are particularly visible in the Piazza del Mercato, the Porta S. Maria and near the Porta Colonia (to the right of the cathedral).

Museo Diocesano (Piazza del Duomo): The diocesan museum is housed in the former Chiesa del Gesù (two churches; one above the other and connected by staircases). The lower church was painted throughout in 1555 to a design by Vasari and has stalls decorated with inlay work by V. da Cortona (1517). The finest works

Castiglion Fiorentino (Cortona), S.Francesco, cloister

of art in the church include an Annunciation by Fra Angelico along with scenes from the life of St.Domi nic, a triptych by Sassetta, a Crucifixion and a Virgin Mary by P.Lorenzetti, and a Deposition, and a Mother of God, and a Communion of Apostles by L.Signorelli.

Museo dell'Accademia Etrusca (Palazzo Pretorio, Piazza Signorelli): A 13C palace and seat of the Casali family. 16C alterations include the façade by B.F. Berettini. The library of the Accademia Etrusca, the municipal archive, and the Etruscan museum are housed here. Apart from a collection of Roman busts (1–3C AD), the museum also has amphoras, Bucchero vessels, ivories, bronzes, Etruscan bronze statuettes, Etruscan and Roman coins, medieval and modern paintings (Pinturicchio, L.Signorelli and others), and even

various Egyptian objects (mummies and a ship of the dead from the 12th dynasty). The most valuable item is the world-famous sixteen-armed Etruscan *bronze candle holder* (Lampadario) dating from the 2nd half of the 5C BC, probably unique among ancient works of art. Interesting large statuette of a young god with a two-faced head.

Tanella di Pitagora (S. of the Porta S. Agostino): The small rectangular tomb with six niches dates from 4C–1C BC. The name Pitagora is the result of confusing the name of the town Croton, where Pythagoras lived, with the name Cortona.

Also worth seeing: The numerous Palazzi include the 13C *Palazzo Comunale* (on the Piazza Signorelli), the medieval *Palazzo Mancini* (Via Dardano) altered in the 16C, and the 15C

Castiglion Fiorentino (Cortona), Collegiata

Castiglion Fiorentino (16 km. NW): A hillside town with an 11C *castle* and turreted *town wall* built on Etruscan-Roman foundations. The Romanesque-Gothic *church of S.Francesco* (*c.* 1280) has a 13C painting of St.Francis by Margaritone d'Arezzo and some 14C frescos. 15C cloister. 15C *parish church* with a 15C font and a fresco depicting the Lamentation by Luca Signorelli painted some time after 1502. 19C *collegiate church* with a terracotta by della Robbia and 16C choir stalls. The *loggias* of the Piazza del Municipio are decorated with coats-of-arms and were built by Vasari in 1560. The *Pinacoteca Comunale* with its 13–16C paintings (T.Gaddi, B. della Gatta, Giovanni di Paolo and others) occupies the 16C *town hall* (restored) in the same square.
Montecchio Vesponi (12 km. NW): 13C *castle* with battlemented towers and walls rises impressively on a hill.

Palazzo Fierli-Petrella (on the Piazza Signorelli). 2 km. N. of the railway station (on the road to Arezzo) there is an enormous *tumulus* from the 7C BC; the so-called Melone del Sodo is a symmetrical structure with dromos (corridor), square vestibule and five chambers opening off the corridor.

Environs: Abbazia di Farneta (11 km. SW): Built in the 9C and extensively altered. Only parts of the abbey *church* (apse) date from this time.
Camucia (5 km. S., at the feet of Cortona): The Melone di Camucia, a *tumulus* from the 7C BC is to be found in the middle of the town. The most interesting of the burial objects (e.g. a large bowl), which are now in the Archaeological Museum in Florence, were found in three attached chambers, the discovery of which was only made in 1842.

51024 Cutigliano

Pistoia   p.134☐D 2

This town above the Lima valley in the Apennines was important in the Middle Ages as the headquarters of seven mountain villages which had united to form an alliance. Today Cutigliano is a popular holiday resort and a departure point for mountain walks.

Palazzo Pretoria: This stately 14C palace bears the coats-of-arms of the Podestà and Capitani of the seven united mountain villages. The Florentine Marzocco lion and the open courtroom loggia also survive.

Also worth seeing: The *Casa Lazzerini* (17&18C) is a fine late-Renaissance house in the mountains.

Environs: Abetone (14 km. NW): A holiday resort in the midst of thick pine woods and mixed forests on the

Gavinana (Cutigliano), view

border between Tuscany and Emilia.
Gavinana (3 km. E. of San Marcello
Pistoiese): This holiday resort is sur-
rounded by chestnut groves. In the
main square, outside the church (of
Romanesque origin) stands the *eques-
trian statue* in memory of Francesco
Ferucci who fell here in the battle

between Florence and Imperial
forces. A small museum is devoted to
Ferucci.
San Marcello Pistoiese (7.5 km. SE
of Cutigliano): A town at the centre of
the Pistoia mountains, and the starting point of many mountain tours into
the Apennines.

Elba/Isola d'Elba

Livorno   p.136□B 7

Elba, an island some 6 miles from the
Italian mainland, has an area of 86
square miles, making it the largest
island in the Tuscan archipelago
which includes Capraia, Giannutri,
Giglio, Gorgona, Montecristo, Pia-
nosa as well as numerous smaller
islands. The Etruscans knew of the
island's rich iron deposits and called it
Ilva (iron). Elba was the cause of
much dispute because of its iron and

the consequent connection with arms manufacture and also by reason of its strategic location. The island frequently changed– hands. Sicilian Greeks from Syracuse occupied the island in the 5C BC and in 264 BC it was conquered by the Romans. At various times it belonged to the Genoese, Lombards, Pisans and Spaniards, until the treaty of Amiens in 1802, when it became a French possession. Napoleon spent his period of banishment in Elba from 4 May 1814 until 26 February 1815, having himself selected the island as a place of exile. The ex-emperor of the French enjoyed all the rights of sovereignty and, during the ten months of his stay, established a modern administration and gave the island's economy a tremendous impetus, partly by expanding the system of roads. In 1815 Elba fell to the Grand Duchy of Tuscany, along with which it finally became part of the Kingdom of Italy in 1860. Many blast furnaces belonging to the ore factories were destroyed in heavy attacks during World War 2. Until the mid 20C the island was almost exclusively used as a supplier of raw materials, and for this reason there are very few historical remains. Over the last few decades the delightful island of Elba, with its rocky and sandy coast 91 miles long and high mountains (the highest is Monte Capanne, 3,345 ft.), has become a popular tourist centre.

Portoferraio: The main town of the island (12,000 inhabitants) was founded by the Greeks in the 4C BC and called *Argoos*. Framed by crags and mountain chains, it lies on the tip of a neck of land on the N. coast. In 1548, Cosimo I de' Medici built the two fortresses that overlook the town. *Forte della Stella* is roughly star

Portoferraio (Elba), panorama

shaped; *Forte del Falcone* is roughly square. Cosimo I also ordered the octagonal *Torre del Martello* to be built beside the sea.

Access to the old town, which is surrounded by the 17C town wall, can only be gained through two gates. The *Chiesa della Misericordia* built in 1556 preserves a copy of Napoleon's sarcophagus (the original is in Paris) and a bronze copy of the death mask of the famous Corsican. A requiem for Napoleon is said in this church on 5 May of each year. The *Casa di Napoleone*, in the upper part of town between the two fortresses, is also known as the Villa dei Mulini, as J.D. de' Medici had it built on the site of some ruined mills (milini). Napoleon occupied this palace (central section with two wings) when he was not staying in one of his other two villas. The upper storey of the central section, with several rooms and a ban-

queting hall, was built on Napoleon's orders. Furniture, caricatures and portraits of the Emperor dating from this time along with other mementoes, are on display here today. There is a bust of Napoleon by F.Rude and a painting, 'Napoleon on horseback', by J.L. David.

Environs: 6 km. to the SW is the *Villa Napoleonica di S.Martino*. Workrooms, several bedrooms and some halls (including the Egyptian Hall and the Hall of Grapes) can be visited.

Marciana (Alta): This village 22 km. W. of Portoferraio on the slope of Monte Capanne is overlooked by the ruins of the castle built by Pisa in 1015.

Environs: Madonna del Monte (1 km. W. of Marciana): The *mountain chapel* some 2,055 ft. up has a miraculous image of the Virgin from the 15C. The marble altar dates from 1661.

Marciana (Elba), view

San Piero in Campo (16 km. SE of Marciana): The remains of a Roman temple and 14C mosaics can be seen in the church of *S.Niccolò*.

Sant Ilario in Campo (10 km. SE of Marciana): *Parish church* with five-sided bell tower.

Marciana Marina (17 km. W. of Portoferraio): This picturesque town lies on the N. coast, with Monte Capanne in the background. The so-called *Saracen tower*, which is cylindrical, was built by the Pisans in the 12C.

Porto Azzurro (14 km. SE of Portoferraio): In 1603, Philip III of Spain built a massive fortification for this little fishing town in the SE of the island in order to protect it against continual raids by pirates.

Rio nell'Elba (17 km. E. of Portoferraio): One of the first places to be settled in Elba because of the nearby ore mines which were exploited at a very early date. 5 km. to the W. are the ruins of the massive castle of *Volterraio*.

Environs: Capraia (an island 45 km. NW of Elba): This picturesque and very mountainous 'island of goats' can be reached from Portoferraio twice a week.

Montecristo (an island 40 km. S. of Elba): This almost circular granite island is probably best known from the novel 'The Count of Monte Cristo' by Alexander Dumas.

50053 Empoli
Florence   p.134☐D 4

Empoli, to the W. of Florence on the left bank of the Arno, was a fortress in the 8C, although it was not until 1119 that the city developed around S.Andrea. Guelph Florence was defeated by the Ghibellines at Montaperti in the autumn of 1260 and it was in the Palazzo Ghibellino (unfortunately completely altered today) that Manfred, the Hohenstaufen leader, demanded the complete destruction of Florence. However, Farinata degli Uberti, the Ghibelline leader banned from Florence, so energetically advo-

Elba, Roman walls opposite Portoferraio

cated the preservation of his native city that it was decided not to destroy it.

Collegiata di S.Andrea, cathedral (Piazza Farinata degli Uberti): This church was built in 1093 above a late-5C church. The geometrical white-and-green marble façade is in imitation of the Romanesque-Florentine style of the church of S.Miniato al Monte in Florence.

S.Stefano (Via dei Neri): 14C church badly damaged towards the end of World War 2. Inside (nave, two aisles) there are frescos painted by Masolino da Panicale in 1424.

Museo della Collegiata (beside the Collegiata di S.Andrea): The first room which the visitor enters is the baptistery, where there is a font in the form of a marble vase from the Donatello school (1447). The baptistery also houses a marble holy-water stoup (1557), several 15C statues, and a bronze eagle lectern (1520). Art from the 14–16C can be seen in the halls on the first floor, including the Annun-ciation by A. and B.Rossellino (1447), a Pietà by Masolino da Panicale (1425), a Madonna and Child triptych by L.Monaco, an Annunciation by F.Botticini (1447), a depiction of St.Nicholas by Bicci di Lorenzo, a marble Virgin Mary by Mino da Fiesole, and a 15C St.Sebastian tabernacle built by A.Rossellino and painted by A.Botticini.

Also worth seeing: A 15C image of the Virgin Mary is preserved in the *Santuario della Madonna del Pozzo* (Piazza della Vittoria), which is surrounded by a loggia.

Environs: Cerreto Guidi (8 km. NW): The *Medici villa* was built by B.Buontalenti (1536–1608) on the orders of Cosimo I.
Montelupo Fiorentino (7 km. E.): This hill town, located where the Pesa flows into the Arno, was the home town of Baccio da Montelupo, the architect (1469–1535). The square *Medici villa of Ambrogiana*, with its four corner towers, was built in the 16C.
Vinci (11 km. N.): This picturesque

Empoli, Porta Pisana

town on the SW slope of Montalbano is framed by vineyards and olive groves and was the home town of Leonardo da Vinci (1452–1519). Leonardo was born the illegitimate son of a maid called Caterina and the Florentine notary Ser Pietro. He was born at the notary's country seat in Anchiano, 3 km. outside Vinci. Leonardo was probably the most versatile genius of the Italian High Renaissance, being an artist, architect, astronomer and mathematician among other things. The house in Anchiano where he was born can still be visited today. The medieval appearance of the town of Vinci itself comes from the restored 11C *Guidi fortress* and by the houses surrounding it. Numerous drawings and other mementoes of Leonardo are preserved in the *Museo Vinciano* housed in the fortress. The Biblioteca Leonardiana on the first floor is the research centre for Leonardo studies and has documents relating to Leonardo's life and work. Leonardo was baptized in the *church of S.Croce*. The font dating from that period still survives.

50053 Fiesole

Florence   p.134☐E 3

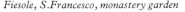

Fiesole is picturesquely sited on a hill to the NE of Florence, of which there is an incomparable view. It was founded by the Etruscans as long ago as the 7C BC and is thus older than Florence. Fiesole played a not insignificant role in Etruria without ever being a member of the Etruscan confederation of twelve cities, the source of important cultural and political

Empoli, cathedral portal

Fiesole, S.Francesco, monastery garden

influences. A few remains of the walls have survived; originally 2 miles long they surrounded the city which at that time lay mainly on the N. side of the hill (the side facing away from Florence). In 225 BC, the city—now known to the Romans as *Faesulum*—became a federal ally of Rome. In 90 BC it joined the Italic revolt which led to Roman citizenship being granted all over Italy. Some 10 years later, Sulla severely punished the city for the assistance given to his opponent Marius. Building a theatre within the temple precinct, Sulla secularized this sacred site; he also humiliated Facsulum, making it a Roman colony. After the Goths had devastated Faesulum in 405, it was besieged and starved into submission by the Lombards (539–40). An increasing number of inhabitants left the city (the seat of a bishop from 492) in the following centuries settling in Florence down in the valley. In 1125, Fiesole was destroyed by Florentine troops for no clear reason (only the cathedral and the bishop's palace were spared), and from that time on it progressively declined in importance while Flor-

ence correspondingly increased. From the 15C onwards, rich Florentine citizens built their grand summer villas on the side of the hill facing Florence and thereby helped Fiesole flourish once again. A drama festival, held in the Roman theatre in July of each year, is worth visiting.

Cathedral of S.Romolo (Piazza Mino da Fiesole): Work on this Romanesque cathedral began under Bishop Jakob of Bavaria in 1028. The bell tower was built in 1213. After being extended in the 13C and in 1348 the cathedral was restored, although not very successfully, in 1878–83. Two rows of ancient columns subdivide the basilican interior into a nave and two aisles. To the right of the elevated choir is the Cappella Salutati with the monument to Bishop Leonardo Salutati (1464) by Mino da Fiesole. The triptych on the high altar is by Bicci di Lorenzo (*c.* 1440), and a statue of St.Romulus in the niche above the main portal is the work of G. della Robbia (1521).

S.Allesandro (Via S.Francesco): In

Fiesole, Roman theatre

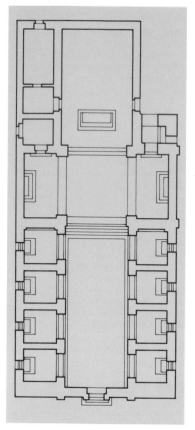

Fiesole, Badia di Fiesole This building was the cathedral of Fiesole until 1028, and was rebuilt by the Rossellino workshop in 1458-66; the nave has 8 side chapels; compact tunnel vault in the early Renaissance style

the 6C, the Gothic king Theodoric built a Christian church on the site of a Roman temple of Bacchus. However, this church was much altered in the 11C. The basilican interior has a nave, two aisles and 16 ancient columns which have Ionic capitals and may have come from the temple of Bacchus.

S.Francesco (Via S.Francesco):

This monastery built in 1030 on the site of the ancient acropolis has been occupied by Franciscans since 1399. The Gothic church is 15C. Monastery and church were largely rebuilt in 1905. The church's most valuable art treasures are the late-15C Annunciation by R. del Garbo at the high altar, and a Virgin Mary by Piero di Cosimo (c. 1480) on the right side altar. The idyllic 15C cloister and a small missionary museum are also visible.

S.Domenico (Via S.Domenico): Below Fiesole, half way to Florence, this church dates from 1406–35. 17C bell tower and portico. The single-aisled interior was altered in baroque style in the 17C. In the first chapel, the altarpiece of the Virgin Mary between Angels was painted in c. 1430 by Fra Angelico, who lived in the monastery. Fra Angelico originally chose a gold background, but this was altered in 1501 by L. di Credi.

Badia di Fiesole (near S.Domenico): The cathedral, which was probably torn down in the 11C, stood on this site until 1028 when the Camaldolese built a new church and monastery. Benedictines took over the complex in the 13C, and in 1439 it finally passed to the Augustinian canons. The present structure was erected in 1458–66 by order of Cosimo de' Medici; the Romanesque marble façade was retained.

Roman theatre (behind the cathedral): Built in the 1C BC and rediscovered in 1809. After rebuilding under Claudius (AD 41–54) and Septimius Severus (193–211), it had 24 rows of seats and space for 3,000 spectators. The remains of *thermal springs* enlarged under Hadrian (117–138) are to be found not far away. To the left of this and behind it there was an Etrusco-Roman *temple*, the ruins of which were not completely excavated until 1918. Remains of the massive *Etruscan city wall* with Etruscan gate

Fiesole, Roman remains

arc to be found between the temple and the thermal springs.

Museo Civico (at the entrance to the theatre): This small museum set up in 1912–14 mainly contains local finds.

Also worth seeing: Inside the medieval *oratory of S.Maria Primerano* (Piazza Mino da Fiesole) are 14C frescos and a wooden cross. Palazzi include the *Palazzo Pretorio* (14C, and altered several times since), which is decorated with coats-of-arms and stands in the Piazza Mino da Fiesole, and the 11C *Palazzo Vescovile* (to the W. of the cathedral and behind it). The *Villa Medici*, built by Michelozzo for Cosimo il Vecchio in 1458–61, stands on the Via Vecchia Fiesolana, a little way outside Fiesole. This villa with its beautiful terraced garden is a fine example of Tuscan early Renaissance.

Firenze/Florence

Florence   p.134☐E 3/4

Traces of Italic colonization in the area where the Mungone flows into the Arno suggest that the area around Florence was settled continuously from the time of the Villa-Nova culture (10–9C BC) onwards. However, the Etruscans who followed chose a protected, elevated location as the site for their city of *Faesulae* (Fiesole); preferring such a position to the valleys of the Arno which were still marshy at that time. Fiesole became Florence's strongest rival in the high Middle Ages, mainly as a result of Fiesole's powerful position in church politics (it was the seat of a bishop directly subordinate to the Emperor with the biggest diocese in Italy). However, the settlement on the bank of the Arno must also have continued to develop, because Sulla destroyed a 'municipium splendidissimum' which had sided with Marius, Sulla's opponent. Roman *Florentia* first achieved prominence under Caesar whose agrarian reform made the city a veterans' colony.

When the Corrector Italiae, an administrator for Tuscany and Umbria, was installed under Marcus Aurelius or Diocletian, the city came to occupy a position it was not to hold again until the Middle Ages when control over Tuscany was regained. The square Roman settlement—expanded in the 8/9C by the addition of the triangle facing the bank of the Arno—is composed of a system of streets running parallel to the former Decumanus and Cardo; today this is still an integral part of the city.

The Roman bridge, the Ponte Vecchio, provided the only link with the other side of the Arno until the Ponte Nuova was built in 1218–20; the Ponte di Rubaconte (1237) and the Ponte S.Trinità (1252) followed shortly thereafter.Like most towns, Florence experienced turbulent times during the barbarian invasions. After the Ostrogoths and Visigoths, it was twice conquered by Byzantium (541 & 551). In 570 it was occupied by the Lombards, who founded the duchy of Tuscia. Charlemagne converted it into a Frankish margraviate in *c*. 774.

Gerhard, a native of Burgundy who supported the Cluniac reform, became Bishop of Florence in 1045. When he was Pope Nicholas II, he laid the foundation stone for the baptistery which, together with the church of S.Miniato al Monte, built about the same time, introduced the first flourishing of Florentine art. The memory of Italy's great political past, and the artistic heritage of the Roman Empire united to produce in Florence an early form of the Renaissance consisting of a revival of classical forms and known as the Proto-Renaissance. Countess Mathilda of Tuscia, who acted as a mediator in the investiture dispute between Pope Gregory VII

and Emperor Henry IV in Canossa in 1077, finally bequeathed her extensive estates to the church. The only exceptions she made were the cities of Florence, Siena and Lucca. She granted Florence the status of an autonomous city in 1115. The undesirable competition of Fiesole, the sister city, was eliminated by pillage in 1125. Under the aristocracy, and with support from the city of Lucca, Florence became one of the leading powers in Tuscany. The *popolo*, the people of Florence, who in 1244 had organized themselves into guilds under Ghibelline protection, profited from the internal dispute between the Guelphs (loyal to the Pope) and the Ghibellines (loyal to the Emperor). In September 1250, the Guelphs and the Ghibellines confronted one another outside the city ready to do battle. The people of Florence now seized the opportunity to carry out a revolt, and they proclaimed democratic rule with a constitution of their own. The podestà was now joined by a captain (Capitaneus popoli), supported by a council of elders (12 ancients) which represented the people's rights. The city itself was divided into 20 districts whose leaders (gonfalonieri) were elected annually. The Capitaneus and the council of elders were granted rights previously only enjoyed by the podestà.

The people also set up a council consisting of thirty 'buonomini'. This, the third constitution since autonomy, was known as the 'primo populo' ('first democracy') in the history of Florence. It succeeded in strengthening hegemony within Tuscany. San Gimignano, Poggibonsi and Volterra were occupied and Arezzo was compelled to maintain friendly relations.

The victory gained by King Manfred of Sicily at Montaperti on 4 September 1260 over the citizens' army which had united with the Guelph nobles led to the loss of the

Florence, cathedral ▷

freedom gained; democratic rule was largely abolished and the Guelphs went into exile. Ater the death of King Manfred in 1266, the guilds attempted to take over the government through their priori (leaders). This attempt failed. Pope Clement was requested to mediate in order to restore order and he brought about a reconciliation between the Ghibellines and Guelphs. Howver, this did not last long. The Ghibellines were driven out of the city in 1267. Continuing tensions, intensified by social disputes, necessitated a further Papal intervention which finally led to a renewal of the democratic constitution, a 'secondo popolo'.

The renewal of the constitution at the turn of the years 1282–3 manifested itself in the 'Ordinamenti di Giustizia' issued in 1293. The number of 'arti maggiori' ('large guilds') was increased from seven guilds to twelve, while the number of 'arti minori' ('small' or 'low' guilds) was reduced to nine. The two groups together had six priori (leaders of guilds) representing them in the Priorato, which replaced the council of elders and which together with the Gonfaloniere di Giustizia, formed the city's government. The position of the 'Difensore delle arti', who soon advanced to be the Capitano del popolo, remained as it was in 1282, and so did that of the Podestà (which frequently sympathized with the aristocracy) in spite of the attempt to break its power. There was great disunity within the aristocracy, which had split into the party of the 'Blacks' and that of the Ghibelline 'Whites', but the influence of the aristocracy remained unchecked. Their internal dispute led finally in 1305 to the expulsion of 600 'Whites', including Dante Alighieri. However, development continued with the guilds, whose position was stabilized by the Ordinamenti. Depending on their interests, the guilds were divided into 'grassi' (= the 'fat ones', i.e. the rich members of the Great Guilds, whose

expansionist interests coincided with those of the magnates) and 'popolo minuto' (= the 'little people', who needed internal peace for their daily work).

The active part the people of Florence played in the political events of their city finds its expression in great building projects of public interest. The city began by coining a gold ducat in 1252. This was the *fiorino* or *florinus* (cf. the English word florin), a coin which was to be one of the economic foundations of the city's increasing prosperity. Work on building the *Bargello*, a 'symbol of the victory over the aristocracy' (Georg Kauffmann), began in 1255. From 1261 onwards the Bargello was the seat of the Podestà. The *3rd city wall* (begun in 1284, completed in 1333) is over 8 km. long, and has over 70 towers and a number of fortresses over the gates. The building of this wall was much more a demonstration of the city's claims to power than a fulfilment of practical necessities. Work on reconstructing the *cathedral* began in 1296. Its huge dimensions enabled it to compete with cathedrals in the rival

Florence, panorama

cities of Pisa and Siena. But even this massive structure had to play second fiddle to the demonstration of fortified power which is the 3rd city wall. Interestingly, it was planned by Arnolfo di Cambio, cathedral architect.

There is no better demonstration of the impetus which the city experienced under the guildsmen's constitution than the immense building projects which had a decisive influence on the future appearance of the city. Hardly had the foundation stone of the cathedral been laid than work commenced (1299) on erecting the defiant-looking government building which was to provide accommodation and protection for the Signoria.

The first church to belong to a powerful order of monks, the Franciscan church of *S. Croce*, was built in the same period. The population increased enormously by medieval standards (the number of inhabitants was some 40,000 in *c.* 1200, and about 100,000 in *c.* 1300). This provided a rich field of activity for the Franciscan order, concerned as it was with people's spiritual welfare. The Dominicans had settled in Florence in 1221, earlier than the Franciscans (1226). Then followed the Servites (1248), the Augustinians (1250) and the Carmelites (1268). The subsequent vigorous church-building and the numerous donations relating to the embellishment of the churches internally meant that the climate in the city was not conducive to artistic flowering.

Church architecture was characterized by the infiltration of Gothic style, with a local change. Painting went through a development of similarly epoch-making dimensions. Cimabue, who perfected the 'maniera greca', was still at work when Giotto, born nearby, began to give European painting a new look. Pisan and Sienese inspiration made themselves felt in the shape of Arnolfo di Cambio, pupil and colleague of Nicola Pisano.

The first half of the 14C brought a number of internal and external political setbacks accompanied by the natural disaster of the flooding of the Arno in 1333 and epidemics: more than half the inhabitants died in two

waves of pestilence in 1340 and 1348. Even the hallowed 'ordinamenti' were in danger of being abolished in favour of the aristocracy. In this critical situation, the 'popolo minuto' took up arms, successfully defended the 'ordinamenti', put the city's disastrous economic situation in order and even achieved territorial expansion (Prato, Pistoia and San Miniato; an advantageous peace was concluded with Pisa) by military means. Another people's uprising (revolt of the wool-carders, 1378) brought Michele di Landi, a wool-carder, to power. By creating three new guilds of the 'arti minori' he temporarily broadened democracy; his attempts, however, foundered on the massive resistance offered by the 'popolo grasso'. Landi was forced into exile and Salvestro de' Medici, the rich merchant who sympathized with the common people, went with him.

The people, led by the Medici, opposed the creation of an oligarchy. However, Rinaldo degli Albizi eventually succeeded in gaining power with the aid of a Signoria which was favourably disposed towards him; furthermore Cosimo de' Medici, Salvestro's successor (1433) was banished. A year later the tables were turned; Rinaldo degli Albizi was expelled and Cosimo was recalled from exile in Padua. On 1 October 1434 Cosimo ceremoniously entered Florence which he subsequently ruled with extreme political tact until his death in 1464. He allowed the honourable republican institutions to continue, but appointed men whom he trusted to fill the posts. Celebrated as 'pater patriae', he led Florence to the zenith of its power and the arts went through a brilliant period of development under his rule. Scholars fleeing from the Turks in Byzantium (1453) strengthened the reputation of Florence as a centre of knowledge. Wool and silk factories ensured the city's economic welfare in the 14C and provided employment for about a

S.Miniato, choir mosaic ▷

third of the city's inhabitants. Apart from this, trade was flourishing and the crafts were operating productively.

14C architecture owed much to a feeling for design which was strongly characterized by the Gothic style. S.Croce and Orsanmichele (built to serve as the city's granary; begun in 1337) are good examples of this. The first indication of the architectural change came with the construction of the Loggia dei Lanzi (begun in 1374). Artists born over the following twenty-five years brought about this transformation. By the late 1420s, the 'Patres' generation of the Renaissance (Brunelleschi, b. 1377; Ghiberti, b. 1381; Nanni di Banco, b. *c.* 1380; Donatello, b. 1386; Fra Angelico, b. 1387; Uccello, b. 1397; Luca della Robbia, b. 1399; Masaccio, b. 1401; Leon Battista Alberti, b. 1406) had given a clear outline of its objectives in all fields of art. An architecture which was marked by its rational clarity and looked to the classical period for its forms and standards stood side by side with a new image of man in sculpture and a style in painting which was based on the discovery of central perspective (Brunelleschi, 1410). A kind of intermediate balance, showing the early Renaissance on its way towards the high Renaissance, is to be seen in the Pazzi chapel by Brunelleschi, the bronze David by Donatello, and the Trinity fresco by Masaccio in S. Maria Novella. Works such as those mentioned also formed the preliminary stage of an intermediate period which was rich in individual talents and was characterized by a new conception of the personality. The increasing autonomy enjoyed by the artist can be understood from this conception. The intellectual centre for further development towards a social system based on humanistic ideals was the 'Platonic Academy' founded under Cosimo the Elder in 1459, which believed it could achieve a balance between the classical mind and Christianity.

After the death of Cosimo and Elder and the brief interlude during which his son Piero il Gottoso (= the palsied one) was in power, Lorenzo il Magnifico (= the Magnificent) continued the splendid tradition of his grandfather Cosimo. During his rule (1469–92) the people carried out their revolt against the conspiracy led by the Pazzi. Giuliano de' Medici died in this revolt (1478). Lorenzo's successor, his son Piero (II), was expelled from Florence in 1294 along with his family after he had, without the knowledge of the other members of his government, submitted to Charles VIII of France who was invading Italy at that time. The Dominican priest Fra Girolamo Savonarola, who worked in Florence as a preacher of penitence from 1482 onwards, took this opportunity to establish a theocratic state. His insistent appeals for penitence, self-communion and Christian asceticism induced some artists, including Botticelli, to burn some of their secular works on the 'pyre of vanity'. A governmental reform finally took Pier Soderini to the head of the government 'for the rest of his life' in the capacity of a gonfaloniere. Savonarola was finally burned at the stake in 1498 as a result of the intervention of Pope Alexander Borgia VI. The Medici returned to Florence in 1512; they were in exile again from 1527–30. After conquering the city in 1530, Charles V appointed Alessandro de' Medici (murdered in 1537) hereditary Duke. His successor, Cosimo I, was confirmed as Grand Duke of Tuscany by Pope Pius V in 1569. After the Medici family had died out, the dukedom passed to Francesco of Lorraine. At the time when the new Italy was in the process of formation, Florence was temporar-

Baptistery, 'Paradise door' ▷

ily (1865–71) the capital of the young kingdom.

Leonardo da Vinci (1452–1519) was in his youth when he created his first independent works which pointed the way to the coming High Renaissance. The 'Adoration of the Magi' (Uffizi) was incomplete when he moved to Milan in 1482. He was in Florence again from 1500 to 1506, at about the time (1501–05) when Michelangelo was also once again in that city. They competed with one another in painting the frescos in the 'Hall of the Five Hundred' (now lost) which was built in the Palazzo Vecchio during the rule of Savonarola. It was during this period in Florence that Michelangelo sculpted his 'David' (the original is in the Galleria dell' Accademia, q.v.) and painted the 'Holy Family' tondo in the Uffizi (q.v.). Raphael was in Florence in 1504, studied the works of Florentine art, and produced a number of paintings of the Madonna among other things. It was in the Florentine works of Leonardo, but especially in the later works of Michelangelo (the latter was in Florence several times between 1520 and 1534, worked on the Medici tombs and built the Biblioteca Laurenziana), that doubt was cast on the ideality of the High Renaissance and a tendency became noticeable which art historians describe as 'Mannerism'. The creative power of the city wilted after Rome had become its cultural successor.

Arciconfraternità della Misericordia (arch-confraternity of mercy): See under Cathedral district.

Badia Fiorentina: The Benedictine abbey (= Badia) was founded in 978 by Willa of Tuscany (mother of Duke Ugo who was wrongly described as founder by Dante in the 'Paradiso'). It is the oldest monastery within the city walls and the only imperial abbey in Florence. The Ottonian church (969–78) was rebuilt by A. di Cambio (1284–1310) and decorated with frescos by Giotto (now lost). From 1627 onwards, the church was enlarged to the plans of M.Segaloni and the old church became the transept. The monastery was dissolved in

Baptistery, door, detail

SS.Annunziato, atrium frescos

1810. Inside the church near the entrance, a fine early work of Filippino Lippi's, the 'Vision of St.Bernard' (c. 1480), has a portrait of the founder and possibly also of other members of the family (Virgin Mary and angels). Combining the grace of Botticelli with Verrocchio's approach to reality, the painting is one of the most important examples of Florentine quattrocento painting.

Bargello → Palazzo del Bargello.

Battistero S.Giovanni: The baptistery stands on the site of earlier buildings (including Roman), one of which was mentioned in 897. It is known that in 1060 Pope Nicholas II consecrated a foundation stone for today's domed 8-sided building, which Dante refers to as 'bel S.Giovanni'. By 1128 it was already in use and it was completed c. 1150.
Exterior: This is original except for the square choir chapel dating from 1202 (originally semicircular) and the marble facing of the corner pillars by Arnolfo di Cambio (1296). The architecture of the building manifests an interest in things ancient (in addition to the use of spoils, ancient structural elements are also imitated) viewed through medieval eyes and as such it is a model of the Proto-Renaissance. The three-storeyed building is totally covered with a geometric pattern of green and white marble resulting in a rich visual interplay of proportional relationships. Round arches alternate with aedicule windows—the earliest example of the Tuscan window arrangement which became fashionable again in the Renaissance. The rich external decoration culminates in the bronze doors on the S., N. and E. sides. The oldest door, the *S. door,* has 2 × 14 reliefs in quatrefoil frames by A.Pisano (1330–6). These were cast by Leonardo d'Avanzo the Venetian and mounted on the door opposite the cathedral façade in 1338. In 1452 they were moved to the S. portal (the Renaissance frame is by V.Ghiberti, 1453–61). Except for the two lower compartments, this door depicts scenes from the life of St.John the Baptist, patron saint of the baptistery, in Giottesque style. Above the portal there is a group of sculptures

by V.Danti (Beheading of John the Baptist, 1570). The designs for the N. door, (1403–24) were chosen by competition in 1401. Seven artists, including L.Ghiberti and Brunelleschi, took part and the best of the entries can be seen in the Bargello. Ghiberti's designs were chosen for reasons of both economy (he understood how to cast the individual panels as one whole) and style—Ghiberti's decorative and narrative talent obviously impressed his contemporaries. The quatrefoil frames, though stylistically outmoded, were obligatory. The Church Fathers, the Evangelists and the New Testament are shown on the doors, which should be read as continuous horizontal lines beginning from the bottom. The sculpture (John the Baptist teaching the Pharisees and Levites) above the gate is by F.Rustici (1506–11). The famous *E. door* (facing the cathedral façade) is the most mature work L.Ghiberti (1425–52) produced and Michelangelo called it the 'gate of paradise'. The Old Testament programme set out for the gate had to be contained within the ten individual panels, and this forced Ghiberti to combine several subjects in a single panel. In order to do this he employed architecture and landscape to the full to separate the narrative. Ghiberti also put to work the new possibilities of perspective foreshortening so that the reliefs are fully three-dimensional in the foreground and bas-relief in the background, the eyes being drawn along the lines of perspective (Donatello had been the first artist to employ this technique).

The chronological succession of the panels can be read in lines starting from the top left:

Content of the pictures:

1) Paradise: creation of Adam, creation of Eve, Fall of Man, and expulsion from Paradise.

2) Cain and Abel: Cain pulling the plough; Abel as a herdsman and, to the left, Adam and Eve with Cain and Abel; Cain and Abel sacrificing, and Cain slaying his brother Abel; God calling Cain to account.

3) Noah: Mount Ararat with the survivors from the Flood; Offering; the drunkenness of Noah, whose sons attempt to cover his nakedness.

4) Abraham and Isaac: the appearance of the three angels to Abraham; sacrifice of Isaac.

5) Jacob and Esau: birth of Jacob and Esau; sale of the birthright; Isaac sending Esau hunting; the hunt; Rebecca advising Jacob to practise deceit; Isaac is deceived.

6) Joseph: sale of Joseph to the merchants; the golden cup is discovered in Benjamin's grain sack; Joseph revealing his identity to his brothers.

7) Moses: Moses receiving the tablets of the law on Mount Sinai.

8) Joshua: the Israelites crossing the Jordan; siege of Jericho.

9) Saul and David: the battle against the Philistines; David slaying Goliath.

10) Solomon receiving the Queen of Sheba.

In the frame, figures in niches alternate with portrait medallions. (Self-portrait of 60-year old Ghiberti can be seen on the left inner strip, 3rd head up.) Horizontal strips show the recumbent figures of Adam and Eve (above) and Noah with his wife (below). The frame of the portal itself comes from Ghiberti's workshop. Above the portal there is a baptism of Christ by A.Sansovino (1505) except for the angel, which is by Spinazzi (1792), a substitute for a clay figure by V. Danti.

Interior: The double-shelled dome consists of eight sections braced against each other, making it possible to pierce the wall extensively. The dome, 84 ft. in diameter, is very much in the spirit of late classical buildings, and indeed the 14 columns of the lower order (the 4 exemplary capitals of the N. and S. wall are Roman spoils) are in imitation of classical

Cathedral, W. front ▷

style. In contrast to this, the spatial effect is medieval in character because of the proportions and the mystical semi-darkness (some light enters through the lantern). The *floor* (much restored) resembles a carpet and is a fine example of Tuscan inlay work of the Middle Ages. The rich *marble facing* of the walls culminates in the splendour of the enormous mosaic vault (early 13C until *c.* 1330). This vault is much dependent on Venetian Byzantine models. Above the apse is the Last Judgement with Christ Pantocrator, then there is a ring in which Christ with Seraphim and the heavenly hierarchy appear. The final 4 bands of the dome illustrate: 1. Story of Creation, 2. Story of Joseph, 3. Life of Christ and 4. Life of John the Baptist. The best of the other decorations (to the right of the choir chapel) include the tomb monument to Anti-Pope John XXIII (Cardinal Baldassarre Coscia, deposed by the Council of Constance, d. Florence 1419) by Michelozzo (*c.* 1425); Donatello's Mary Magdalene is in the Museo dell'Opera del Duomo.

Biblioteca Laurenziana → S.Lorenzo.

Brancacci chapel → S.Maria del Carmine.

Campanile → Cathedral of S.Maria del Fiore.

Capelle Medice → S.Lorenzo.

Casa Buonarroti (Michelangelo's house, Via Ghibellina 70): The small museum has Michelangelo's drawings, models and copies of his works. Particularly interesting are: the marble relief of the battle of the Centaurs (carved by Michelangelo at the age of 17 in 1492); a marble relief of the Madonna and Child (Madonna della Scala; his earliest surviving work from 1490–92, which shows the influence of Donatello); wooden crucifix for S.Spirito (1494).

Cenacoli: The Cenacoli (refectories) of monasteries often had their walls painted with elevating religious subjects, in particular the Last Supper. *Cenacolo di Foligno* (Via Faenza 42): The refectory of the former Franciscan convent of S.Onofrio has a painting of the Last Supper, a delightful work by Perugino (*c.* 1490) which has similarities to the work of A. del Castagno and Ghirlandaio, although the idyllic view of the Umbrian landscape, including 'Christ on the Mount of Olives', is typical of Perugino.

Cenacolo del Ghirlandaio → Ognissanti.

Cenacolo di S.Salvi (Via di S.Salvi 16): The refectory of the former Vallombrosan abbey of S.Salvi (founded in 1048), with a Last Supper by Andrea del Sarto (begun in 1519). The 'pittore senza errori', Vasari's 'painter without errors', depicts the scene with the highest dramatic tension; elegant composition, harmonious use of both space and colour. Other works include Sarto's 'Pietà'.

Cenacolo di S.Apollonia (Via XXVII Aprile 1): The refectory of the Benedictine convent which was dissolved in 1808. Subsequently a military store and then part of the university, today it houses the Castagno museum. The 'Last Supper' is not only one of Andrea del Castagno's finest works, it is also one of the most interesting Florentine paintings from the middle of the century and it became the model for the later paintings of the Last Supper, with its scientific realism and dramatic sensitivity. Above this there are some further scenes from the Passion. Castagno's paintings of 'Famous Men and Women' were removed from the Villa Pandolfini-Carducci in Lignaio (Dante, Boccaccio and Petrarch).

Chiostro dello Scalzo (cloister of the Discalced Friars, Via Cavour 69): An elegant cloister decorated by Andrea del Sarto for the brotherhood of John the Baptist with frescos

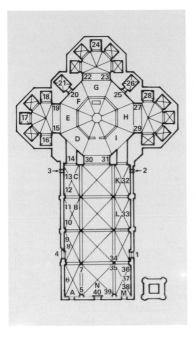

Cathedral, portal

Florence, cathedral 1 Porta del Campanile with Annunciation **2** Porta dei Canonici **3** Porta della mandorla with the Virgin Mary bestowing the Girdle on St.Thomas (masterpiece of Nanni di Banco) **4** Porta della Balla **5** panel painting of St.Catherine, school of Bernardo Daddi **6** statue of Joshua (probably a portrait of the humanist Poggio Bracciolini; the head is by Donatello) **7** niche with St.Zenobius (trampling on Pride and Cruelty) by G.del Biondo **8** bust of the organist Antonio Squarcia by Benedetto da Maiano **9** Niccolò da Tolentino on horseback, fresco by Andrea del Castagno **10** Giovanni Acuto (John Hawkwood) on horseback, fresco by P.Uccello **11** statue of King David by B.Ciuffagni **12** panel with St.Cosmas and St.Damian by Bicci di Lorenzo **13** Dante and the 'Divine Comedy', design by Baldovinetti, execution by Dom. di Michelino **14** ascent to the dome **15** St.Thomas by Vinc. de'Rossi **16** panel with St.Joseph by L.di Credi **17** marble altar by Buggiano, 1447, with bronze grille by Michelozzo **18** incomplete Pietà by Michelangelo, see Cathedral Museum **19** statue of St.Andrew by A.-Ferrucci **20** door lunette with terracotta of the Resurrection by Luca della Robbia, 1444; the bronze door, 1445–69, is partly the work of Michelozzo and Maso di Bartolomeo **21** Sagrestia Nuova (or 'delle Messe') with splendidly inlaid cupboards (G. and B.da Maiano and others), fine marble lavabo by Buggiano, 1440 **22** statue of St.Peter by B.Bandinelli **23** statue of St.John by Ben. da Rovezzano **24** bronze shrine to St.Zeno-

bius by Ghiberti under the altar, 1432–42; candlestick angel by Luca della Robbia, c. 1450 **25** door lunette with Ascension by Luca della Robbia, c. 1450 **26** Sagrestia Vecchia (or 'dei Canonici') **27** statue of St.James the Less by G.Bandini **28** Giottesque fresco fragment of 'Madonna del Popolo' **29** statue of St.Philip by G.Bandini **30** statue of St.James the Great by J.Sansovino **31** statue of St.Matthew by Vinc. de' Rossi **32** bust of the philosopher Marsilio Ficino by A.Ferrucci, 1521 **33** niche figure of Isaiah by B.Ciuffagni, 1427 **34** descent to the Cripta di S.Reperata **35** Gothic holy-water stoup, c. 1380 **36** Tondo with a half-figure of Giotto by Benedetto da Maiano, 1450 **37** statue of a prophet by Nanni di Banco, 1408 **38** bust of Brunelleschi by his pupil A.Cavalcanti, known as il Buggiano, 1466 **39** tomb of Antonio d'Orso by Trino di Camaino **40** clock with prophets painted by P.Uccello **Stained-glass windows** (designers): **A** St.Stephen, flanked by two angels (L.Ghiberti) **B** window dating from 1395; **C** (Agnolo Gaddi) **D** Nativity of Christ (Paolo Uccello) **E** Lamentation (Andrea del Castagno) **F** Resurrection (Paolo Uccello) **G** Coronation of the Virgin Mary (Donatello) **H** Prayer on the Mount of Olives (Ghiberti) **I** Presentation in the Temple (Ghiberti) **K** (Agnolo Gaddi) **L** window with six Saints (Agnolo Gaddi) **M** St.Lawrence with angels (Ghiberti) **N** Assumption of the Virgin Mary (Ghiberti)

(1514–26) of scenes from his life; barefooted friar bearing cross at the head of the brotherhood's processions.

Cathedral district: The cathedral and free-standing bell tower, both in the Cathedral Square, and the baptistery in the Piazza S.Giovanni form the religious centre of the city. The two squares actually form a single unit, bounded in the W. by the *Palazzo Arcivescovado*. In 1895 the Palazzo was moved back 164 ft. and lengthened towards the S., increasing the number of bays from 8 to 11, rear and side façades being completely rebuilt in the process. The courtyard is a high baroque imitation of Mannerism by Ciurini, who completed the palace (begun in 1582) in 1727. In the courtyard there is the entrance to the church of *S.Salvatore nell'Arcivescovado*, first mentioned in 1032. Encrusted façade on the Piazza dell'Olio. Interior decoration dating from 1737 with architectural painting by D.Ferretti and V.Meucci. To the S., on the right by the entrance in the Via Calzaiuoli, is the *Loggia del Bigallo*, which was built in the mid

13C as the original seat of the Misericordia and from 1425 onwards was the seat of the Compagnia di S.M. del Bigallo. Founded by St.Peter the Martyr, this was a charitable community caring for the sick. Some of the frescos are old; on the loggia there is an early-16C tabernacle with a statue of the Madonna (1359–64) flanked by angels. To the left is the *Misericordia* (Arciconfraternità della Misericordia).

Cathedral of S.Maria del Fiore with campanile: In order to counterbalance the massive new monastery buildings, the cathedral of S.Reparata, itself only 12C, was pulled down, and work on a new building began under Arnolfo di Cambio in 1296. Work proceeded slowly as a result of interruptions, with a side-glance at the massive cathedrals of the competing cities of Pisa and Siena. Giotto, when working as architect from 1334–7, was mainly concerned with the campanile. The nave vault was finished in 1378, aisle vaults date from 1380; the tribune was built in 1380–1421, which is probably also the date

Cathedral, tympanum by L. della Robbia

of the dome. The competition for the dome was won by F.Brunelleschi in 1420 and it was completed in 1436; the lantern was finished in 1461, after his death. The cathedral was consecrated on 1 January 1436 by Pope Eugene IV. The cathedral façade, which had become out of date, was torn down in 1587, and only replaced in 1871–87 (E. De Fabris).

Outside: Lavish façade in Gothic style designed by Emilio de Fabris and built in 1871–87 with a series of statues and mosaics. The cathedral's massive exterior—the portals and the E. end in particular—became the place where the dramatic developments made by Renaissance sculptors were most clearly documented. The gable of the *Porta della Mandorla* (see ground plan: 3) has an alto relievo of the Virgin Mary presenting her girdle to St.Thomas, a masterpiece by Nanni di Banco (1414–22). The lunette has a mosaic of the Annunciation by Domenico and Davide Ghirlandaio (1491). On either side there is a statuette of a prophet; that on the right has strong Gothic characteristics and is regarded as the earliest definite

work of the youthful Donatello. The octagonal dome over the crossing is interesting, having two shells and rising to an overall height of 351 ft. (steps at the end of the left aisle). Note the 'exedrae' (also by F.Brunelleschi and typical of Renaissance architecture), the magnificent drum, most of which is clad in marble, and the lantern buttresses (pierced by arches) which continue the ribs of the dome. The rich marble facing of the cathedral exterior as a whole (green 'verde di Prato', red 'rosso di Maremma' and white 'bianco di Carrara'), together with the theme of the decorations, date from the initial phase of building under A. di Cambio.*Inside and decoration:* Basilica (nave, two aisles) in the form of a Latin cross (length 502 ft., maximum width about 295 ft.). The nave, airy with four widely spaced pillars, leads to the octagonal area beneath the dome, from which transept and choir extend, each with 5 chapels and ending in an apse (five sides of an octagon, and five chapels). The simple vertical arrangement of the Gothic nave is enriched by the presence of a gallery—instead of a tri-

Cathedral museum

forium—which continues beneath the dome. Domed sacristies lie between transepts and choir, with organ lofts above their entrances. The inlaid marble pavement was completed by G. and F. da Sangallo to a design by Baccio d'Angolo. The stained-glass windows were designed by Ghiberti (some were executed by the German artist Nicolò di Piero Tedesco), Donatello, Uccello and others.

Campanile: The slim tower, 278 ft. high and with octagonal clasping buttresses, was begun by Giotto in 1334 (lower part of the 1st double storey), continued by A.Pisano after Giotto's death in 1337, and completed by F.Talenti in 1359 after Pisano's death (1348). With its coloured marble facing, it is one of the finest bell towers in Italy.

Cathedral museum (Museo dell'Opera del Duomo): In the 15C, this was the site of the cathedral stonemasons' studios and workshops. The exhibits, which have accumulated over the centuries, have been accessible to the public since 1891. They include not only liturgical utensils but also sculptures from the old cathedral façade (torn down in 1587) and more recent additions of sculptures which have been replaced by copies to save their further erosion by the elements and pollution.
Main works: The *main sculpture room* (Sala dell'antica facciata del Duomo) has a late-16C drawing of the façade before it was torn down in 1587. Other exhibits include works by Arnolfo di Cambio (Enthroned Madonna with the Christ-child blessing; Boniface VIII Enthroned; St.Reparata). St.Luke by Nanni di Banco, and St.John by Donatello are powerful figures and outstanding testimonies to the new spirit of the early Renaissance.
Moving from the hall of sculptures, to the right is the *Saletta* with interesting choir-book stands, antiphonals, and a large 15C processional cross.

Ponte Vecchio

These are followed by the *octagon* displaying the art of the goldsmith (decorated in 1954), which has numerous 13–18C reliquaries and a retable by B.Daddi (1334).
On the *landing* there is a Pietà by Michelangelo (formerly in the cathedral). A late work, it was among his most dramatic achievements and was intended for his own burial chapel. He was dissatisfied with the piece, however, and broke it up. His pupil, T.Calcagni, restored it and completed Mary Magdalene.
A room on the upper storey has the two famous 'cantorie'. Built in marble they were originally located above the entrances to the sacristies but were removed in 1686 on the occasion of the marriage of Ferdinando de' Medici to Violante Beatrix of Bavaria. The reliefs illustrate Psalm 150. That by Luca-della-Robbia (1431-8) consists of ten reliefs in classical style,

with angels dancing, singing and playing musical instruments. The Donatello cantoria (1433–9) depicts putti packed tight in a dance of bacchanalian exuberance; both architecture and decorations were influenced by Donatello's journey to Rome in 1431. Underneath the Donatello cantoria stands his Mary Magdalene from the baptistery, a late work of touching humanity and frail worldly beauty, carved when Donatello was 69. Of the 16 statues from the niches in the campanile, the oldest are attributed to A.Pisano and his workshop (prophets, sibyls, Solomon, David), while the others are by Donatello (the impressively realistic signed statue of the prophet Habakkuk dating from 1434–6 and known as 'Lo Zuccone', the pumpkin) and Nanni di Bartolo.

To the left is the *room containing the reliefs from the campanile*, exhibited in two rows, one above the other, in accordance with the original arrangement. Their themes reveal the concerns of the medieval mind: man's creation; man's self-realization through the arts and sciences; his destiny's dependence on the planets; the virtues and sacraments as his mainstay. These reliefs are by A.Pisano and his school (1337–48), except for that of the sacraments which is possibly by Arnoldi [?]), and the five of the Liberal Arts by L. della Robbia. The final room is devoted to the sumptuous silver-gilt baptistery altar, a splendid Florentine Gothic work (begun in 1366 and completed in the early 15C with additions from the late 15C). Statuettes by A.Pisano. Numerous gold on silk embroideries. Two 12C Byzantine mosaic miniatures in rich silver frames with scenes from the life of Christ and the Virgin Mary.

Fortifications: In contrast to the medieval city wall, which demonstrated Florence's power to enemies from the outside, fortifications were also built to protect the Medici against internal enemies of their state (the Fortezza di S.Miniato is an exception).

Forte di Belvedere (also called *di S.Giorgio* after its location at the → Porta di S.Giorgio): Possibly built by B.Buontalenti in 1590–5 by order of Grand Duke Ferdinand I to the plans of Giovanni de' Medici. This stellar complex has at its centre the elegant *Palazzetto* which is now used for temporary exhibitions.

Fortezza da Basso (di S.Giovanni Battista, Viale Filippo Strozzi, near the main railway station): Built by Alessandro de' Medici after his entrance into Florence in 1530 and the proclamation of the dukedom. Plans for the impressive pentagonal fortress with bastions at the corners were drawn up by A.Sangallo the younger, while Piero Francesco da Viterbo and A.Vitelli supervised building (1534–5).

Fortezza di S.Miniato: These fortresses were built by Michelangelo in a few months as a temporary line of defence before the siege of the city in 1530. They secured the flank of Monte alle Croce as far up as San Miniato al Monte. They were rebuilt in a more permanent form by Francesco da Sangallo and others from 1553 onwards.

Galleries → Museums and collections.

Giardino di Boboli (Boboli garden) → Palazzo Pitti.

Loggia dei Lanzi: An airy, open, colonnaded hall built by Benci di Cione and Simone Talenti in 1374–81 for public ceremonies of State. It earned its present name under Cosimo I when it functioned as guard room for the German mercenaries (Lanzichenecchi; it was the model for the Feldherrnhalle in Munich). The arch spandrels, which have reliefs of the Virtues on a blue enamel background, date from 1384–9 and were designed by Agnolo Gaddi. The hall is rich in ancient and Mannerist sculptures. The *Rape of the Sabine Women* (under the arch to the right of the entrance), a marble group by Giov. da Bologna dating from 1583, is one of the most influential Mannerist sculptures. The 'figura serpentinata', so typical of the Mannerist style, here takes the form of a column of figures striving upwards in a complicated flow of movement; the pedestal too is outstanding with fine bronze reliefs. The bronze statue of '*Perseus with the head of the Medusa*' (1545–54) is one of B.Cellini's finest works (under the arch to the left of the entrance). The beauty of the nude figure and the artistry with which the bronze has been handled to suggest different textures are rooted firmly in Mannerism.

Loggia del Mercato Nuovo (on the corner of Via Porta Rossa/Via Calimala): This open colonnaded hall built by G.B. del Tasso in 1547–51 was originally a silk and gold market. Today typical Florentine crafts are on sale.

Loggia del Bigallo → Cathedral district.

Medici chapel (Cappelle Medicee) → S.Lorenzo.

MUSEUMS AND COLLECTIONS:

Galleria dell'Accademia (entrance in 52 Via Ricasoli): This collection of studies from the Accademia was set up by Grand Duke Pietro Leopoldo I in 1784. Under his supervision the collection, assembled from several schools of drawing, was housed in the vacant buildings of the Ospedale di S.Matteo, which included the former monastery of S.Nicolà di Caffaggio.

Another part of the former hospital is occupied by the *Opificio delle Pietre Dure* (No. 78 Via degli Alfani), an institution devoted to teaching of the techniques of stone inlay and their subsequent care, established by Grand Duke Ferdinando I de Medici in 1588. Fine examples of this craft can be seen on the fronts of the Cappella dei Principi and the Medici chapel of S.Lorenzo. Often rare and valuable stones (pietre dure) were used.

The extensive collection (mainly from the Florentine school of the 13–16C) is especially important for its works by Michelangelo. Interesting paintings from the Duecento and Trecento include: a Sienese crucifix from the 2nd half of the 13C (in the style of Duccio); a polyptych with Crucifixion and Saints, and the allegorical 'Cross' tree (inspired by St.Bonaventura) which has scenes from the life of Christ in small tondi along with paintings of historical events preceding him, both of which latter works are by Pacino di Buonaguida (one of Giotto's first pupils); a fine painting of St.Mary Magdalene with eight scenes from her life; a polyptych by A.Orcagna (Virgin Mary with Angels and Saints); a triptych of the Trinity (dated 1365) by Nardo di Cione and his workshop; an expressive Pietà, Giovanni da Milano's finest work; scenes from the life of Christ (14) and St.Francis (10) by T.Gaddi (former sacristy cupboard doors from S.Croce, they were once thought to be by Giotto).

Major early Renaissance works include: 'Job and Isaiah' by Fra Bartolommeo; 'Deposition', begun by Perugino and completed (lower section) by Filippino Lippi;

Loggia dei Lanzi, Perseus by Cellini

Loggia dei Lanzi, Rape of the Sabine Women

'Madonna and Child, with Angels and Saints' by Fra Bartolommeo; 'Visitation', attributed to Ghirlandaio; 'Adoration of the Christ-child' by Lorenzo di Credi; 'Madonna and Child with St.John as a boy and Angels' by Botticelli; 'Madonna del Mare' attributed to Botticelli.

Florentine Mannerist paintings include the work of Bronzino, A.Allori, Santi di Tito, and others.

In the *Salone*, which ends with the *Tribune*, there are two series of tapestries. The Brussels tapestries depict the Story of Creation, while Florentine tapestries tell the story of the Medici. In front of these stand Michelangelo's 'Slaves' ('gli Schiavi' or 'Prigioni')—the 'waking slave', the 'bearded slave', 'boy' and 'Atlas', known as 'Boboli slaves' after their previous location—along with the two Louvre slaves, all of which were originally intended for the unfinished tomb of Pope Julius II in Rome (S.Pietro in Vincoli). In the tribune itself stands Michelangelo's 'David' (1501–04), originally set up outside the Palazzo Vecchio in 1505 as a symbol of courage in the defence of the freedom of the Republic. Some 13 ft. 6 in. high, the figure was carved from a block regarded as unworkable.

Galleria d'Arte Moderna (museum of modern art) → Palazzo Pitti.

Galleria Corsi → Museo Bardini.

Galleria Corsini → Palazzo Corsini.

Galleria Ferroni (Ferroni collection, 40–48 Via Faenza): This collection was donated to the State by Marchese Ferroni in 1850 and comprises works from the 15–18C (not yet accessible).

La Galleria dell'Ospedale degli Innocenti → Spedale degli Innocenti.

Galleria Pitti or **Palatina** → Palazzo Pitti.

Galleria degli Uffizi and Graphic Collection (Gabinetto dei Disegni delle Stampe) → Uffizi.

Museo (dell') Angelico → S.Marco.

Museo dell'Antica Casa Fioren- tina (Medieval house of a Florentine nobleman) → Palazzo Davanzati.

Museo Archeologico: (9b Piazza SS.Annunziata) Since 1870 this museum has been housed in the Palazzo della Crocetta built in 1620 for Grand Duchess Maria Maddalena d'Austria. It is mainly of interest for its Etruscan collection. The adjoining *Egyptian Museum*, with the richest Egyptian collection in Italy apart from that in Turin, was built around the Medici's collection. On the ground floor there are of Greek, Etruscan and Roman sculptures. The **Museo Topografico dell'Etruria**, also on the ground floor, has numerous finds from Etruria with reconstructions of monuments and tombs in the garden. The **Egyptian Museum** occupies the first floor and includes among its exhibits a wooden Hittite carriage (containing bones), which came from a tomb in Thebes dating from the time of Rameses II (14C BC). The **Etrusco-Greco-Roman Museum** has a collection of Etruscan sculpture (urns from the most important sites; sarcophagus of Ramta Uzenai from Tarquinia, 4C BC, with reliefs), a collection of Etruscan, Greek and Roman bronzes, including famous items such as the so-called 'Idolino' (life-sized victor's statue of a youth offering a libation; Attic, 5C BC); a Greek horse's head from the Roman period; the 'chimera' wounded by Bellerophon (5C BC); and the 'orator' (Arringatore), a tomb figure of Aulo Metello (inscription on the robe) in orator's pose. The **coin room** has classical coins as well as more recent ones. Jewellery collection (glass, gems, gold and silver objects). On the second floor is the **Prehistoric Collection** with Italic items, mainly from Tuscany, along with examples from non-Italian prehistoric cultures. The collection of **vases** and terracottas includes the famous François vase (painted by Klitias in the

Uffizi, Raising of Lazarus by Nicolas Froment ▷

Athenian workshop of Ergotimos, 6C
BC).

Museo degli Argenti (silver collection) → Palazzo Pitti.

Museo Bardini: In 1923 the art
dealer Stefano Bardini bequeathed his
19C palazzo to the city of Florence,
along with his art collection which
comprises works of pure and applied
art dating up to the beginning of the
baroque period.

Museo del Bargello (Nazionale) →
Palazzo del Bargello.

Museo delle Carrozze → Palazzo
Pitti.

Museo della Fondazione Horne
(Horne museum, 6 Via de' Benci):
The alazzetto Horne, rebuilt in the
15C, probably by S. del Pollaiuolo
(known as Cronaca), and with a
charming entrance courtyard (two
columns with magnificent capitals) in
the manner of A.Sansovino, was
bequeathed to the Italian State by the
English art critic Herbert Percy
Horne (1864–1916) along with its rich
art collections. Exhibits include:
tondo of the 'Virgin Mary with
Angels' from the workshop of L. della
Robbia; 'Holy Family' tondo by Beccafumi; 15C inlaid sacristy bench; a
painting of the 'Allegory of Music' by
D.Dossi; fragments of a polpytych by
P.Lorenzetti; Crucifixion, Virgin
Mary and four Saints, attributed to
B.Daddi; a panel of 'St.Stephen' by
Giotto; 'Pietà' by Filippo Lippi;
'Esther' by Filippino Lippi. The
upper floor has a collection of Renaissance and baroque drawings by
Michelangelo, Raphael, Pontormo,
Carracci, Poussin, Guardi and others.

The **Museo di Dante**, devoted to the
poet and Florence in Dante's day
(Dante editions, portraits, etc.), occupies one of the houses in the
picturesque complex of the 'Case
degli Alighieri', where tradition has it
Dante was born (entrance in 1 Via S.
Margherita).

Museo Nazionale (Bargello) →
Palazzo del Bargello.

Museo dell'Opera del Duomo →
Cathedral museum.

Museo dell'Opera di S.Croce →
S.Croce.

Museo delle Pietre Dure → Galleria dell'Accademia.

Museo delle Porcellane → Palazzo
Pitti.

Museo Stibbert (Via Federico Stibbert 26): Frederick Stibbert, the Scottish collector and Garibaldi's
comrade-in-arms, left his extensive
collection to the British government
who renounced their right to it in

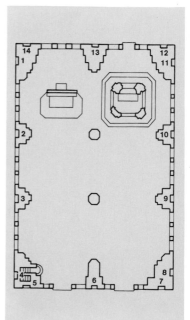

Florence, Orsanmichele, niche figures 1
Donatello, 'St.Peter' (1413) **2** Nanni di Banco,
'St.Philip' (c. 1412) **3** Nanni di Banco, 'Quattro
Coronati' (1408) **4** Donatello, 'St.George'
(1416), second bronze cast **5** Ghiberti, 'St.Matthew' (1422) **6** Ghiberti, 'St.Stephen' (1426) **7**
Nanni di Banco, 'St.Eligius' (c. 1415) **8** Donatello, 'St.Mark' (1411) **9** Pietro Lamberti,
'St.James' (later than 1422) **10** Simone Ferrucci,
'Virgin Mary with Rose' (1399) **11** Baccio da
Montelupo, 'John the Evangelist' (1515) **12** Ghiberti, 'John the Baptist' (1414-16) **13** Verrocchio, 'Christ and Doubting Thomas' (c. 1480) **14**
Giovanni da Bologna, 'St.Luke' (1562)

favour of the city of Florence. The collection, housed in the Sala della Cavalcata of the Villa Stibbert (formerly Davanzati), consists mainly of armour and weapons of Spanish, Italian, German, Oriental and Japanese origin; procession of 14 knights and 14 footsoldiers. Paintings include: 'St.Catherine and St.Dominic' by C.Crivelli and two paintings by G.B.Tiepolo. The museum also includes the splendid **porcelain collection** of Baron Marzio de' Tschudy (Chinese, Japanese and European porcelain).

Ognissanti (All Saints' Church, Piazza Ognissanti): Founded in 1256 and completely rebuilt in 1627 to a design by B.Pettirossi. The existing façade, one of the earliest examples of Florentine baroque, was built by M.Nigetti in c. 1637. Above the entrance there is a glazed terracotta of

the 'Coronation of the Virgin Mary with Saints' attributed to G. della Robbia or B.Buglione. The campanile has two- and three-arched windows (13/14C) similar to those of S.Maria Novella. Inside, the 2nd altar on the right has a painting of the 'Madonna della Misericordia' (Virgin Mary of the Protecting Cloak) shown as the guardian of the Vespucci family (the head of a youth next to the Virgin may be a portait of Amerigo Vespucci, who gave his name to America). Beneath, there is a 'Pietà' fresco by Domenico and Davide Ghirlandaio (c. 1472). In front and to the left of the altar there is a tomb slab (1471) of the Vespucci family. The 3rd altar has 'Virgin Mary Enthroned with Saints', an early work by Santi di Tito (c. 1565). The tomb of Botticelli (Filipepi) is in the 2nd chapel of the right transept.

The anteroom to the sacristy (off the

Orsanmichele, façade decorations

left transept) has a crucifix from the Veit-Stoss school. The sacristy itself has other painted wooden crucifixes, one from Giotto's workshop, the other by T.Gaddi; Resurrection and Ascension are attributed to A.Gaddi. Beyond the cloister (entrance in the Piazza Ognissanti), the visitor enters the *refectory,* where detached frescos and sinopie are on display; the (attached) fresco of the 'Last Supper' by D.Ghirlandaio (1480) shows a rhythmical arrangement of figures (in pairs in this picture) and seems to be the predecessor to Leonardo's Last Supper in Milan. 'St.Augustine in his study' by Botticelli, and 'St.Jerome in his retreat' by Domenico Ghirlandaio (both 1480) come from the former monks' choir. The former chapter-house has a small *museum* with paraments, gold objects and illuminated books.

Orsanmichele: Probably by Arnolfo di Cambio. Built as a hall for the sale of grain on the site of an 8C oratory. Destroyed by a fire in *c.* 1304, it was rebuilt to its present size from 1307 onwards. The market hall was vaulted in 1357; the open arcades were closed in 1367–80 when the building was converted into a church. The two upper storeys were intended to be a granary. The sculptured decorations, commissioned by the guilds led by the silk weavers, form an open-air museum of Early Renaissance sculpture and chart its development. This is especially true of the niche figures, the earliest of which (10 on the plan) is firmly Gothic in style. Ghiberti's figures (12, 5 and 6) clearly date from around 1400, while the 'Quattro Coronati' (3), carved by Nanni di Banco as early as 1408, visibly show the influence of classical antiquity, an influence which first found expression in a more refined manner in Donatello's 'St.George'. Verrocchio's group of figures (13) opens the path to the High Renaissance. 'St.Luke' by Giovanni da Bologna (14) replaces a figure by Lamberti (→ Palazzo del Bargello).

The interior decorations date mainly from before 1400. The stained-glass windows with the miracles of the Virgin Mary (Joachim with the herdsmen) are by L.Monaco). Frescos on

Palazzo del Bargello

the pillars show patrons of the guilds with scenes from their lives. Vault frescos, illustrating God's saving grace in the history of the world, are by the same artists as the pillar frescos. In the centre of the church stands the *altar tabernacle* from the S. aisle, built by Orcagna in 1359 to house the old, miraculous image. The altar is surrounded by a marble screen of 1366 with bronze railings. The altarpiece dating from 1347 is by B.Daddi and replaces the original miraculous image lost in the fire of 1304. A bridge (1569) leads from Orsanmichele across the Via dell'Arte della Lana to the **Palazzo dell'Arte della Lana,** built in 1308 by the rich guild of wool merchants. Since 1905 this has been the headquarters of the Dante society (fine rooms inside). At the corner of the Via Orsanmichele there is the 14C Gothic tabernacle of S.Maria della Tromba, with a panel by J.Landini dating from the 1st half of the 14C.

Palazzo Arcivescovado → Cathedral district.

Palazzo dell' Arte della Lana → Orsanmichele.

Palazzo del Bargello—National Museum (Palazzo del Podestà, Via del rocònsolo): The second most important medieval public building in Florence (after the Palazzo Vecchio), it expresses the new spirit at work in the city. Work began five years after declaration of the city's constitution and proclamation of democratic rule (1250). The core of the building is formed by the family tower of an older palazzo (the Volognana tower). The main façade, which dates from the initial phase of construction and is built of ashlars, stands in the Via del Procònsolo. Extensions to the building in rough masonry (N. and S. wings) date from *c.* 1325–46 and face

Uffizi, Botticelli, Minerva and the centaur ▷

into the Via Vigna Vecchia and Via l'Acqua. The palazzo was the residence of the Podestà from 1261 onwards, and of the police prefect (popularly known as bargello = head of police) from 1574.

The 13&14C courtyard is splendidly arcaded on three sides.

Beside the external staircase (1345–67) is the entrance to the *hall of sculptures* with works by Michelangelo and other famous Tuscan sculptors up to the beginning of the baroque. 'Drunken Bacchus', an early work by Michelangelo carved for the Roman banker Jacopo Galli, dates from 1497 and was intended to be a garden figure standing with classical figures. Michelangelo's 'Pitti Tondo' was carved in *c.* 1504–5 and was the third version on the theme of the Madonna and Child with St.John as a boy (incomplete). In the marble bust, 'Brutus', Michelangelo idealizes Lorenzino the tyrannicide who slew the hated Alessandro de' Medici and was celebrated by the patriots as 'Bruto nuovo'. Roman portrait busts were the model for this sculpture, which

dates from in *c.* 1540 and is unfinished. Michelangelo's 'Apollo' or 'David' (*c.* 1531) is one of his finest works, both as regards the contrapposto treatment reminiscent of the 'Slaves' and the richly differentiated surface modelling. The marble statue of 'Bacchus' by J.Sansovino, described by Vasari as 'molto più simile alla carne' (as if of flesh and blood), dates from the time before he moved to Rome (1520). The bust of Cosimo I (1545) is B.Cellini's first great bronze for the Grand Duke. 'Florence winning the victory over Pisa' by Giovanni da Bologna (1570), an allegorical group and 'figura serpentinata', is one of the most important examples of Mannerist sculpture. On the first floor the *Donatello room* has some of the sculptor's most important works. The marble David (1408–09), intended for the cathedral but placed in the Palazzo Vecchio in 1416 after reworking, is still clearly Gothic in style (particularly the drapery). The bronze David (*c.* 1430–2), however, shows Donatello taking a step towards regaining

Pal. Pitti, Sala dell'Iliade, ceiling by Sabatelli

Pal. Pitti, 'Love and Faithfulness' by P.Freccia

the classical ideal of beauty; it is also the first nude since classical times. 'St.George' by Donatello, carved for the armourers' guild in 1416–20 for an external niche of Orsanmichele, clearly demonstrates the new character of early Renaissance sculpture.

The second floor has a collection of small bronzes and medals and L.Bernini's bust of his friend Constanza Bonarelli.

Palazzo Corsini with the Galleria Corsini (10 Lungarno Corsini; entrance, number 11, Via di Parioni): Still owned by the Corsini family, it was built in 1648–56 in the style of a century before, but remained incomplete. The palazzo houses the collection of paintings started in 1765 by L.Corsini, nephew of Pope Clement XII. The picture gallery, still laid out in its original form, includes a 'Crucifixion' attributed to A. da Messina, 'Madonna and Child with St.John' by Pontormo, a cartoon with a portrait of Julius II from the Raphael workshop and numerous baroque paintings, including a bozzetto by L.Giordano for the dome of the Corsini chapel in S.Maria del Carmine.

Palazzo Davanzati (Museo dell' Antica Casa Fiorentina, Piazza Davanzati): A fine example of Floren-

Florence, Palazzo Pitti, 1st floor 1 Sala di Venere: Titian, Tintoretto 2 Sala di Apollo: Van Dyck, Rubens, Reni, del Sarto, Titian, Tintoretto 3 Sala di Marte: Tintoretto, Reni, Titian, Rubens, Murillo, Veronese 4 Sala di Ciove: Raphael, Bordone, Rubens, del Sarto, Perugino, Guercino 5 Sala di Saturno: Raphael ('Madonna della Seggiola') 6 Sala dell'Iliade: Velázquez, Titian, Raphael 7 Sala della Stufa: frescos by Rosselli, da Cortona 8 Sala dell'Educazione di Giove: Caravaggio, Allori 9 Saletta da Bagno 10 Sala di Ulisse: Raphael, Reni, Lippi 11 Sala di Prometeo: Signorelli, Lippi 12 Corridoio delle Colonne 13 Sala della Giustizia: Veronese, Titian 14 Sala di Flora: Canova, Bronzino 15 Sala dei Putti: Jordaens, Rubens 16 Galleria Poccetti: Pontormo, Rubens, Ribera, Dughet 17 Sala della Musica 18 Sala Castagnoli 19 Sala delle Allegorie 20 Sala delle Belle Arti 21 Salone d'Ercole 22 Sala dell'Aurora 23 Sala di Berenice A Vestibolo B Sala degli Staffieri C Galleria delle Statue D Sala delle Nicchie E Sala verde F Sala del trono G Sala celeste H Cappella J Sala dei pappagalli J Sala gialla K Camera da letto L Gabinetto da toletta M Sala da musica e da lavoro N Camera da letto O Salotto di ricevimento P Sala di Bona Q Sala da ballo R Sala della Fede S Sala della Carità T Salla della Giustizia U Cortile dell'Ammannati V Fontana del Carciofo

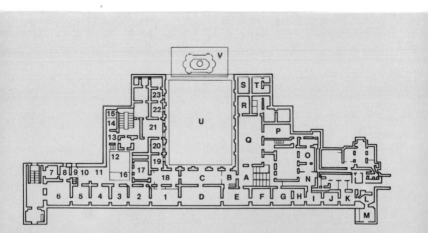

Uffizi, dome

Uffizi, 'Holy Family' by Michelangelo

tine Trecento secular architecture. The tall four-storeyed façade has a 15C loggia. Since 1950 it has been a state museum; fine furniture from a medieval nobleman's house.

Palazzo Gondi (Piazza S.Firenze 1): Built by G. da Sangallo in 1490–1501, it is one of the finest of Quattrocento palazzi. The façade appears to be structurally lighter the further it rises above the ground. The elegant court-yard is of finely balanced proportions.

Palazzo Medici-Riccardi (Via Cavour, corner of Via dei Gori): Built in 1444–52 by Michelozzo for Cosimo il Vecchio. 1459–60 B.Gozzoli fres-coed the chapel. It was sold to Fran-cesco Riccardi in 1659 and extended by seven bays, although the existing scheme in the Via Cavour was retained. The main staircase was added in 1715. State property, it has

been the seat of the prefecture since 1814. One of the Florence's finest early Renaissance palazzi it is inter-esting to look well at the three storeys. The completely independent articula-tion of the rusticated ground floor with rough bosses contrasts with the two other storeys, which are related to one another by their window arrange-ment. A massive cornice unites the whole. The square courtyard is one of the finest examples from the Renais-sance; the original statues have been replaced by antiquities from the Ric-cardi collections. The design of the ornamental garden dates from the time of Riccardi. The *Medici Museum* has been housed here since 1929. Of especial artistic importance is the *chapel*, whose interior by Michelozzo gives an impression of the original lavishness of the palace decoration as a whole. Frescos of the 'Procession of the Magi on their way to Bethlehem'

Uffizi, 'Birth of Venus' by Botticelli

are by B.Gozzoli (1459–60), the inspiration for this solemn procession being the historic equestrian procession of the Greeks entering Florence for the famous council of 1439.
The altarpiece is a copy of the 'Nativity' by Filippo Lippi. The *Galleria* has a vault fresco of the 'Apotheosis of the Medici' by L.Giordano (1682–3), who also frescoed the vault in the showpiece room of the adjoining *Biblioteca Riccardiana* ('Victory of Wisdom over Folly').

Palazzo Pandolfini (74 Via S.Gallo): Designed by Raphael for Giannozzo andolfini, Archbishop of Troia, and built in *c.* 1520 by Giovanni Francesco and Aristotele da Sangallo.

Palazzo dei Pazzi (10 Via del Procònsolo, Borgo degli Albizi):
Originally attributed to Brunelleschi, it is now thought to be the work of Giuliano da Maiano. Rebuilt in 1462–72 for Jacopo de' Pazzi (who was executed in 1478 as a result of the unsuccessful Pazzi conspiracy against the Medici). The arcaded courtyard has columns with splendid capitals.

Palazzo Pitti with museums and Boboli garden (Piazza Pitti): The central part of this splendid complex survives from the original palazzo built in 1457–66 by Luca Fancelli for Luca Pitti, son of one of Florence's richest families. It was acquired in 1550 by Eleonore di Toledo, wife of Cosimo I, and from 1560 onwards it was altered by Ammannati and the courtyard side was extended. From 1592 onwards it was extended further by G.Parigi, whose son Alfonso added three window bays to the left and right to enlarge it to its present size.

The addition of the terrace wings projecting towards the W. was begun in 1764 and completed in 1819. This step-by-step expansion is matched by the decoration, which includes Mannerist frescos (Poccetti), baroque frescos (Giovanni da San Giovanni, F.Furini, Pietro da Cortona, and others), as well as Italian Romantic works. In 1860, together with the picture gallery which had been considerably expanded since the time of the Medici, it passed to the crown of Italy. Vittorio Emanuele II resided here (1865–71), during the time that Florence was the capital of Italy. Further collections (see below) were set up in addition to the gallery of paintings. The three-storeyed, rough-hewn façade becomes progressively lighter from storey to storey. The three sides of the courtyard with their rusticated Doric, Ionic and Corinthian orders make the courtyard one of the most original pieces of Mannerist architecture, and at the same time provide a successful link with the equally Mannerist Boboli gardens.

Boboli Gardens: Laid out in 1560, they are amongst the finest gardens in Italy. Begun by Tribolo, Ammannati designed the amphitheatre which extends from the courtyard of the Pitti. The *Grotta Grande*, on which Buontalenti worked from 1556–92, consists of three chambers, the first of which has copies of Michelangelo's 'Slaves' (for the originals → Palazzo del Bargello).

The collections in the palace: *Galleria Palatina:* The exhibits are arranged in the manner of a prince's collection. The highlights of the picture gallery are 13 paintings by Raphael, 12 by Titian, 8 by Tintoretto and 16 by A. del Sarto. Also represented are Rubens, Van Dyck, Guido Reni, Bronzino, Velázquez and others. There is a *porcelain collection* on the mezzanine. The *Museo degli Argenti* (royal silver room) has valuable gold and silver objects, including the almost complete archbishop's treasury brought from Salzburg by Ferdinando III in 1814. On the 2nd floor is the *Galleria d'Arte Moderna* (founded in 1860), decorated chiefly with 19C Tuscan paintings. Some of the rooms of the *Appartamenti ex Reali* are also open to the public. Magnificently furnished, they were used as official apartments by the Medici and the Dukes of Lorraine, and later by Vittorio Emanuele II.

Palazzo Rucellai (18 Via della Vigna Nova): Probably designed 1446–1451, by Leon Battista Alberti for the rich Florentine merchant Giovanni di Paolo Rucellai; built largely by Bernardo Rossellino. The façade is articulated by pilasters in a way which was quite new.

Florence, Uffizi A Second vestibule with classical statues **E. gallery** (giving access to rooms 1 to 24): Grotesque paintings by A. Allori and others; Florentine tapestry and Brussels hangings on the walls; the classical works here include the Hellenistic group of Heracles slaying the centaur (77); statue of Proserpine, a Roman copy after an Attic original of the 4C (120); Apollo after Praxiteles (162) **Room 2:** Cimabue, Giotto, Duccio **Room 3:** Siena, 14C **Room 4:** Florence, 14C **Rooms 5 and 6:** Representatives of the International Style of the period around 1400 and thereafter **Room 7:** Early Renaissance (Uccello, P. della Francesca, Masaccio, Angelico) **Room 8:** F.Lippi (temporary location) **Room 9:** Early works by Botticelli **Room 10:** Botticelli **Room 11:** Botticelli **Rooms 12–14:** Rogier van der Weyden, Hugo van der Goes, Botticelli, Lippi **Room 15:** Leonardo, Verrocchio, Perugino, Signorelli **Room 16:** Leonardo **Room 17:** Umbrian school **Room 18:** (Tribuna): Florentine Mannerists; Medici Venus **Room 19:** Mantegna, Perugino, Signorelli **Room 20:** German Renaissance (Dürer, Cranach etc.) **Room 21:** G.Bellini, Giorgione **Room 22:** 16C, Germany and Netherlands **Room 23:** Correggio **Room 24:** Cabinet of miniatures **S.gallery:** (c. 1658), decorated with grotesque paintings; numerous classical sculptures) **W. gallery:** Access to rooms 25–44; toilet and bar with terrace **Room 25:** Michelangelo, Fra Bartolommeo and others **Room 26:** Raphael, A. del Sarto, Pontormo **Room 27:** Florentine Mannerists **Room 28:** Titian, Palma il Vecchio **Rooms 29–30:** Florentine Mannerists (including Parmigianino) **Room 31:** Dosso **Room 32:** Piombo, Bordone **Room 33:** Passage with various 16C painters **Room 34** leads past the entrance to the 'Corridoio Vasariano' and to the 16C Venetians (**Room 35**) **Rooms 36–40** are being redesigned. **Room 41:** Rubens, Van Dyck **Room 42** (hall of the Niobide): Roman marble copy to a lost model; the remaining rooms are being rearranged

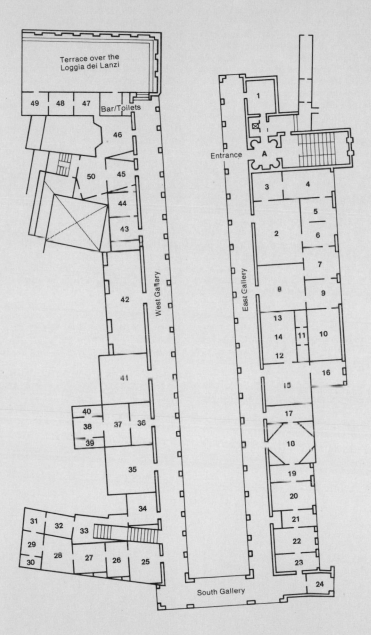

Terrace over the
Loggia dei Lanzi

49 48 47 Bar/Toilets

46

50 45

44

43

42

West Gallery

41

40
38 37 36
39

35

34

31 32 33
29
30 28 27 26 25

Entrance

1

A

3 4

5

2 6

7

8 9

13
14 11 10
12

16

15

17

18

19

20

21

22

23

24

East Gallery

South Gallery

Palazzo de la Signoria → Palazzo Vecchio.

Palazzo Strozzi (Piazza Strozzi): Built for Filippo di Matteo Strozzi by B. da Maiano, who was inspired by the → Palazzo Medici by Michelozzo. This, the most characterful Renaissance palazzo in Florence, was begun in 1489. After the death of the owner in 1491 and of the architect in 1497, Cronaca (= Simone del Pollaiuolo) continued work on the building until 1536. The splendid courtyard was designed by Cronaca.

Uffizi: In 1560 Cosimo I engaged Giorgio Vasari to build a government building for the Grand Duchy of Tuscany. Making use of older buildings, Vasari's design consists of two long, symmetrical wings ending in a portico facing the Arno and open at the other end on to the Piazza della Signorina. There are three storeys with arcades on the ground floor. It was completed in 1580 under A.Parigi and B.Buontalenti. The top storey was a sculpture gallery in Buontalenti's day, while under Francesco I the Medici's art collections were housed here, as Cosimo I had planned. Apart from the rooms used for administration ('Uffizi'), other institutions based here include judicial bodies, the state archive and a number of workshops (W. wing). Vasari also built a covered passage over the Ponte Vecchio linking the Uffizi to the Palazzo Pitti (Vasari's Corridor). Until recently the Uffizi housed both the state archive and one of the world's finest collection of paintings. The **drawing and print collection** (Gabinetto dei Disegni e delle Stampe) is also here, and comprises well over 100,000 sheets, including drawings by major Florentine Renaissance artists.

The picture galleries, the **Galleria degli Uffizi**, occupy the third floor. The Prima Galleria (E. gallery, B) has grotesque paintings by A.Allori, G.Butteri, A.Pieroni and G.Bizzelli (1581, mythological scenes, landscapes, freely invented scenes, flowers, birds, etc.). Rooms 1–24 trace the development of Tuscan painting from the end of the Duecento up until the time of Mannerism (access from the E. gallery).

Uffizi, Luther and Katharina von Bora by L. Cranach

Room 2: Cimabue's main work, 'Madonna Enthroned' or 'Madonna in Maestà' was originally the high altarpiece of S.Trinità *(c.* 1290 or just after). In this work the 'maniera greca' attains its final expression— angels are reminiscent of classical models, folds in the Virgin Mary's garment appear almost as relief, the painting is contained within an illuminated frame. By contrast, 'Madonna Enthroned' ('Madonna Rucellai', 1285, from the Rucellai chapel in S.Maria Novella) by Duccio di Buoninsegna is a later, Gothic work, advanced both in its humanization of the classical subject and in the graceful, lyrical manner of presentation; the very border of the mantle outlining the flow of the garment is firmly Gothic. This panel very clearly exemplifies the Sienese style of painting. In contrast to the latter two madonnas Giotto's 'Madonna Enthroned' (from the church of Ognissanti) shows the revolutionary new characteristics of realistic painting.

Room 3: Although the revolutionary characteristics of Giottesque style are noticeable in the 'Annunciation with

Saints' by the Sienese artist S.Martini, they seem in this case to have been employed in a Gothic framework and to have an other-worldly splendour (1333; painted for the chapel of S.Ansano in Siena cathedral). Interestingly, A.Lorenzetti, who lived in Siena from 1319–47, based himself more obviously on Giotto. The 'Presentation in the Temple', a late work, shows a use of perspective (in the complicated architectural and spatial relationship between the simultaneous exterior and interior views of the temple) which goes beyond Giotto.

Room 5/6: The work of the Sienese artist L.Monaco (in Florence 1388– 1422) is an example of the lively interest Florence displayed in the 'International Style' with its strong Gothic tendencies (*c.*1400). The 'Adoration of the Magi' by L.Monaco (*c.* 1420) shows Gothic feeling for form and Giottesque massiveness. The lyrical line of this style was later taken up by some other painters—2 of whom were incidentally monks, namely Fra Filippo Lippi and Botticelli. However, the chief representa-

Uffizi, Venus of Urbino

tive of the 'International Style' in Italy was G. da Fabriano. His polyptych 'Pala Strozzi' (painted in 1423 for the burial chapel of the Strozzi family in S.Trinità) has the Adoration of the Magi as its central image, a subject handled with courtly brilliance, and a precise attention for detail reminiscent of the splendour of Burgundian manuscripts.

Room 7: P.Uccello's 'Battle of S.Romano' (1456) once hung in Lorenzo il Magnifico's bedroom in the Palazzo Medici, together with his battle paintings now in the National Gallery in London and the Louvre. In it Uccello makes a very individual declaration of loyalty to the scientific perspective of the Brunelleschi tradition, particularly as formulated by L.B. Alberti in 1436.

In contrast, in Fra Angelico's 'Coronation of the Virgin' (*c.* 1435), the realism brought about by the use of perspective is kept in check by his revival of the medieval gold background and his use of pure clear colours.

At the court of Urbino artistic genius flourished and no paintings could be a clearer indication of this than the double portrait of Federico da Montefeltro, Duke of Urbino and artistic patron, and his wife Battista Sforza. Piero della Francesca (*c.* 1465) painted these two profiles in imitation of classical antiquity but he set them in a Tuscan landscape of fascinating perspective. Further, each painting is bathed in the glimmering silvery light so typical of Tuscany, which has the result of uniting portrait with landscape. On the reverse of the portraits, Prudence, Justice, Fortitude and Temperance, the cardinal virtues, accompany the Duke, who is being crowned by the goddess of victory. Faith, Hope and Charity, the theological virtues, accompany the Duchess, whose chariot is drawn by unicorns, the symbols of chastity.

Room 8 has paintings by Filippo Lippi and his son Filippino Lippi.

Room 9 has the work of A. del Pollaiuolo and Botticelli.

Room 10 has some famous paintings by Botticelli. 'The Birth of Venus' (1486), which along with 'Primavera' (Spring) was painted for a room in the Villa di Castello (residence of Lor-

Uffizi, tapestry of 'Henry III' by La Quintana

enzo di Pierfrancesco), shows Venus born out of the foam, a symbol of neo-Platonic beauty. The subtle beauty of the softly curving outlines of Venus, of the nymph receiving her and of the personified wind sublimates the sensuality of her appearance. The high poetic sensibility of this painting links it with 'Primavera' ('Spring'). In the latter, from right to left, a zephyr pursues the nymph Cloris, who evades him by transforming herself into Flora (the creator of flowers). Venus and Eros (contemplative and passionate love) dominate the middle of the picture. The intertwined dance of the three Graces is an allegory of giving and self-surrender. Mercury secures the spirit's domination by drivng away the clouds.

Room 12: The 'Entombment' by R. van der Weyden, painted in 1449, probably on the occasion of a pilgrimage to Rome (1450 was a holy year), formerly had a portrait of Lionello d'Este in the predella, but this has since been lost. His painting of the dead Redeemer is devoid of action and is essentially a quiet devotional picture in which the flow of the lines of composition is the most important expressive element (especially the Virgin Mary, Christ and St. John).

Room 14: The 'Portinari altar' (*c.* 1476–8) by H. van der Goes from Ghent is an outstanding Dutch painting, donated to the Uffizi by T Portinari who was the Medici's representative in Bruges until 1465 (the wing panels depict him and his family with patron Saints). The artist has made full use of a massive canvas, handling both space and the interrelation of the various groups of figures with great mastery, while at the same time producing a beautiful decorative effect and paying such an attention to detail that the still life in the foreground could stand on its own. The central panel deals with the Adoration of the Shepherds, the perspective of which, with its vigorous foreshortening, draws the viewer into the picture itself.

Room 15 has work from the Tuscan and Umbrian schools. The 'Baptism of Christ' (*c.* 1470–5) comes from A. del Verrochio's workshop (the latter was mainly active as a sculptor). Detailed scientific investigation of this painting has shown that Botticelli may have participated at an early stage and that the young Leonardo completed the work after various alterations—the angel on the left and the landscape in the background are attributed to him. Delicate glazes have given the painting a soft atmospheric effect and toned down the hard and detailed anatomic drawing of Christ's body. Perugino, Leonardo da Vinci and Raphael are said to have studied under Verrochio, who paved the way for the high Renaissance. In his late period, he was much influenced by the genius who was his pupil. The step towards classicism is marked by a balance between maximum symmetry and the asymmetries of a natural-seeming grouping. The 'Lamentation' from about 1493 is a good example of this. The tensions of the figures in the composition are resolved in the symmetry of the archi-

Uffizi, painting of H. Purrmann

tecture. Leonardo da Vinci's 'Adoration of the Magi' for the monastery of S.Donato in Scopeto (1481–2) is an incomplete work which reflects similar inclinations; essentially triangular in composition, the ecstasy and turbulence of the groups thronging in from both sides make for a dramatization extending beyond classical harmony. The incompleteness of the colouring, which is based on Leonardo's sfumato technique, contributes to the picture's mystery.

Room 16: The 'Annunciation' painted by Leonardo da Vinci in *c.* 1472, treats light and colour in a way that points ahead to the possibilities of sfumato.

Room 18: The mode of exhibition of the 'Tribuna' (completed in 1581 by Vasari's pupil Buontalenti) has been of exemplary importance for the display of objects of art in modern museums. Indirect lighting from above and uninterrupted wall surfaces for hanging the pictures (originally in close succession and above one another) are still the dream of every curator today. The room's decorations symbolize the world's domination by the four elements. Air is represented by the compass rose which is connected to a weather vane; water by the mother-of-pearl cladding of the dome; fire by the red covering on the walls; earth by the green 'Pietra dura' floor. The selection of paintings in today's decorations accords with the Mannerist language of symbols. One of the best examples of Mannerist portraiture is A.Bronzino's 'Duchess Eleonore of Toledo with her son Giovanni de' Medici'. An aloof coolness in the colouring and a strict and aristocratic love of splendour create an icy atmosphere of unapproachability.

Room 19: A.Mantegna, a passionate admirer of classical antiquity and advocate of the perspective achievements of the early Renaissance, painted the 'Virgin Mary of the Rocks' between 1488 & 1490 in Rome (according to Vasari).

Room 20: There are only a few examples of German painting, but these are of outstanding quality. A.-Dürer's 'Adoration of the Magi' (1504) came to the Uffizi in 1793 as a result of an exchange with the Vienna collection.

L.Cranach's 'Adam' and 'Eve' from 1528 (dated on the 'Adam' panel) remain intrinsically Gothic as to their anatomy, although a hint of Renaissance can be discerned.

The Uffizi possesses two outstanding examples of the Danube school in the Florian panels in *Room 22* ('Leavetaking' and 'Martyrdom of St. Florian') by A.Altdorfer (*c.* 1525–30).

Room 23: Correggio's importance lies mainly in his anticipation of the baroque, especially in his treatment of light and his diagonal composition. For example, the dynamic structural effect achieved by accentuating the diagonal transforms the subject-matter of a 'Rest during the Flight into Egypt' (*c.* 1520) into a dramatic event. The flow of the drapery in Correggio's 'Adoration of the Child by the Madonna' (*c.* 1520) creates an intimacy in the relationship between mother and child.

Room 24: Cabinet of miniatures.

Room 25: The 'Doni Tondo', painted in 1505 when Michelangelo was about 30 (dated 1508–10 by some), on the occasion of Agnolo Doni's marriage to Maddalena Strozzi, is the only painting certainly by Michelangelo. The interpretation of the picture is a matter of dispute, but it is probable that the three figures symbolize the three phases of Christian history, i.e. 'ante legem', before the law, that is to say before Moses, the figures in the background; after Moses, 'sub lege', the transitional figure of John the Baptist as a boy in the middle ground; and 'sub gratia', the age of grace, in the Holy Family.

Room 26: Raphael's 'Virgin Mary with the Goldfinch' (*c.* 1506) radiates

Ognissanti, St.Augustine by Botticelli ▷

tranquillity and classical harmony in an ideal world. His 'Pope Leo X with Cardinals Giulio de' Medici and Luigi de' Rossi' (a late work, completed in *c.* 1518 with the assistance of his pupil Giuglio Romano) is an outstanding piece of characterization, in which the politically active head of the Church and lover of the arts, is depicted not only as a man of action, but also as a clever and rather distrustful character. The Cardinals at his side intensify the impression of firm rule. The 'Madonna with the Harpies' (girls shown as the bird-like creatures, symbols of the storm in Greek mythology) by A. del Sarto has been regarded as the chief work of 16C Florentine classicism since the time of Vasari.

Room 28: Titian's two paintings of Venus in the Uffizi are among the most mature treatments of a subject which the artist had attempted several times previously. 'Venus and Cupid' (*c.* 1555; a variant of the Madrid and Berlin versions) in which the organist turns round towards the female nude, is an expression of inner tranquillity and harmony conveyed by the relaxed

Palazzo Vecchio

attitude of the beautiful female nude and by the landscape, typical of Venetian painting.

The famous 'Venus of Urbino' was painted by Titian in 1538 for Guidobaldo delle Rovere, later Duke of Urbino.

Room 29: Amongst Mannerists no one was better than Parmigianino at expressing the fundamental uncertainty of 16C man, an uncertainty which resulted from the intellectual and social upheavals of those times. The 'Madonna dal collo lungo' ('Madonna with the long neck') is a painting beautiful in detail and exciting for its tension, which comes from the direct contrast between the scale of the foreground figures and those further back (an enormous Madonna, tiny prophet in the far distance, and the towering columns deprived of function beside beside the Madonna), and from the strange light, all of which act to intensify the painting's unreal, spectral character.

Room 41: The two paintings ('Henry IV entering Paris' and 'Henry IV at the battle of Ivry') belong to the incomplete cycle of Henry IV's life, which Rubens began in *c.* 1628 for the widow of the king (who had been murdered in 1610). They are full of baroque richness of both movement and radiant colour.

Room 44: The young Caravaggio set new standards by regaining a firmness and simplicity in the composition of his paintings which had been rendered unclear by Mannerism. He did this by studying classical antiquity and recollecting the simplicity and clarity of the high Renaissance. In his 'Youthful Bacchus' of *c.* 1589, the half-figure of Bacchus (which dominates the picture) sleepily regards the onlooker while beside him is a still life painted with great realism (as is the god's crown of vine leaves). In 'Abraham sacrificing Isaac' (1591), light is the dominant force in the composition, a characteristic feature of Caravaggio's later works, the light drawing the onlooker's attention to the important elements in the story (Isaac the victim, the ram who replaced him, and the intervening angel). Caravaggio's method of composition opened up possibilities to other artists, especially Rembrandt. The high, emotionally expressive qualities which Rembrandt gave to this method are seen in the contrast between the two artists' works. In his 'Youthful Self-Portrait' (1634), Rembrandt continues, though in an independent and individual manner, this style of composition in which light is very important.

A door leads to the roof terrace of the Loggia dei Lanzi (cafeteria).

Palazzo Vecchio (Palazzo della Signoria): Tradition has it that the central section of this sturdy but elegant palazzo was built in 1299–1314 by A. di Cambio as the residence of the Priori delle Arti and the Gonfaloniere. The block-like character of the building is emphasized by a battlemented gallery atop two storeys which have regular rows of two-arched windows. The rusticated palace underwent several phases of building before attaining its present size and extent although this is not clear from the inside. The slender tower (1310), 308 ft. high and solid up to the battlements, is a landmark.

Inside: The entrance leads into the small courtyard by Michelozzo (1470). This has a *porphyry fountain basin* with the famous 'Putto with Dolphin', a cast of a masterpiece by Verrocchio (1476). Frescos showing cities of the Habsburg Empire were painted on the upper part of the wall on the occasion of Granprincipe Ferdinando's marriage to Joanna of Austria (1565). The decorations were supervised by G.Vasari, who also redesigned the *stairs* (3) to the two upper storeys (1560–3). The armoury (2) adjoining the courtyard survives in its original 14C form. On the first floor there is the *Salone dei Cinquecento* (4; 174 ft. long, 72 ft. wide, height increased by 23 ft. to 59 ft. at

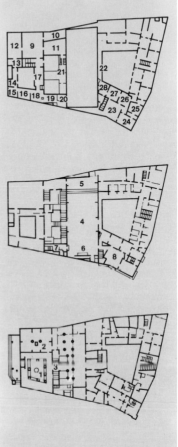

Florence, Palazzo Vecchio Ground floor: **1** First courtyard by Michelozzo with fountain **2** Armoury **3** Scalone del Vasari (Vasari's staircase) First floor: **4** Salone dei Cinquecento **5** Udienza **6** Central niche with Michelangelo's 'Victory' **7** Studiolo Francesco I de' Medici **8** Hall of Leo X Second floor: **9** Sala degli Gigli (hall of lilies) **10** Cancelleria, Machiavelli's former office **11** Cloakroom **12** Sala dell'Udienza (audience room) **13** Cappella della Signoria **14** Hall of Gualdrada **15** Hall of Penelope **16** Hall of Ester or dining hall **17** Drawing room **18** Hall of the Sabine women **19** Green hall **20** Chapel of Eleonore **21** Passage leading to the 'Quartiere di Eleonora di Toledo' **22** Gallery along the Salone dei Cinquecento **23** Hall of the elements **24** Loggia of Saturn **25** Hall of Hercules **26** Jupiter hall **27** Hall of Cybele **28** Hall of Ceres

Michelangelo's suggestion), by Cronaca, 1495. The assembly hall of the Consiglio Maggiore until the latter's dissolutiom in 1530, it is today a concert hall. Preparatory cartoons are all that remain of the original frescos by Leonardo da Vinci ('Equestrian battle of Anghiari') and Michelangelo ('Battle of Cascina'). Battle paintings by Vasari survive. The 39 compartments of the richly decorated ceiling show scenes from the history of Florence and the Medici. On the N. side is the so-called *Udienza* (5), the imposing audience hall from the time of Grand Duke Cosimo I. The statues and niche figures are by Baccio Bandinelli (Cosimo I; Leo X blessing; Giovanni delle Bande Nere; Alexander de'Medici) and G.Caccini (Pope Clement VII crowning Charles V; Grand Duke Francesco I). Above the niches there are paintings by Ligozzi (Boniface VIII receiving ambassadors from different states and noting to his astonishment that they are all Florentines) and Cigoli (Pius V presenting the Grand Ducal insignia to Cosimo). Opposite the Udienza, below a connecting loggia between the Quartiere degli Elementi and the Quartiere di Eleonora Toledo, there is a large *central niche* (6) with Michelangelo's 'Victory'—intended for the tomb of Julius II in Rome (1516–1534)—which glorifies the spirit's victory over the powers of darkness. Classical Roman statues stand in the side niches. Statues of the Labours of Hercules by V. de' Rossi are found along the walls, which are themselves hung with rare tapestries. To the right of the wall with Michelangelo's 'Victory' is the entrance to the *Studiolo* (= study room) *di Francesco I de' Medici* (7) by Vasari. Frescos by Vasari and his school depict man and nature. The corner niches have statuettes by Giov. da Bologna and others. Opposite the entrance to the Studiolo, the visitor may enter the *Quartiere di Leone X* (8). Only the Sala de Leone X is open and in it there are frescos glorifying this Pope. The 2nd storey includes the *Quartiere degli Elementi* (23–28) with five rooms and two loggias by Giov. Battista del Tasso (*c.* 1550), decorated by Vasari in collaboration

Palazzo Vecchio, detail

with Cristoforo Gherardi. The *Quartiere di Eleonora di Toledo* (14–22) for Grand Duke Cosimo I's wife was designed by Vasari (1559–62), and includes rooms originally intended for the Priori. The associated private chapel (20) has frescos by Bronzino (1540). The main room on the 2nd storey is the *Sala dell'Udienza*, (12) originally the Republic's audience chamber. G. da Maiano was amongst those who painted the ceiling, a work of unprecededented splendour; the magnificent marble portals (1476–8) are by his brother Benedetto. The Sala dei Gigli (Hall of Lilies) (9), has a screen by Benedetto da Maiano and a fresco by D.Ghirlandaio (1481–5). *The Quartiere del Mezzanino*, extended by Michelozzo for the Priori, is in the *mezzanine* and houses a splendid art collection: the delicate, rhythmic flow of the 'Madonna dell'Umiltà' by Masolino da Panicale is late Gothic in style; 'St Cecilia' and 'St.Catherine' are by B.Strozzi; 'Pygmalion and Galatea' are by Bronzino; 'Leda' is from the Leonardo school; the 'Equestrian portrait of Principe G.C.Doria' is by Rubens, as is 'Judith with the head of Holofernes'; portrait of a man by H. Memling; 'Leda' by Tintoretto.

Palazzo dei Vescovi → S.Miniato (bishops' palace).
Pazzi chapel → S.Croce.
Piazza del Duomo → cathedral district.
Piazza di S.Croce → S.Croce.

Piazza di S.Maria Novella: This piazza outside the church of the same name is the scene of the 'Palio dei Cocchi', a historical horse race held since 1563. On the S. side of this five-sided piazza is the *Loggia di S.Paolo* (1489–96), built on the model of the portico in the → Spedale degli Innocenti (F.Brunelleschi) and decorated with terracottas by G. and A. della Robbia. The garden in the piazza has two obelisks on bronze tortoises by Giovanni da Bologna (1608).

Piazza della SS.Annunziata: This spacious piazza is dominated by three porticoes, that of SS.Annunziata, that

Piazza della Signoria, Hercules and Cacus by B.Bandinelli (left), equestrian monument to Cosimo I (right)

Piazza della SS.Annunziata, equestrian statue of Grand Duke Ferdinand I by G. da Bologna

of the Spedale degli Innocenti by Brunelleschi and that of Confraternita dei Servi di Maria, which was inspired by the front of the Sepdale. The church's portico (1516–25) is by A.di Sangallo the elder, working in collaboration with Baccio d'Agnolo. On the SW of the piazza the Palazzo Riccardi-Manelli (1557–63; formerly known as Grifoni) is by Ammannati. In the middle of the square stands the splendid equestrian statue of Grand Duke Ferdinand I by Giovanni da Bologna, the fine Mannerist sculptor. His last work, it was completed by his pupil P.Tacca in 1608. The two original fountains with sea monsters (1629) are also by Tacca, to a design by B.Radi.

Piazza della Signoria: This developed into the political centre worthy of the city's increasing importance.

The *Palazzo Vecchio* or Palazzo della Signoria which dominates the square was the original seat of the former city government, the Signoria. The Loggia dei Lanzi stands on the S. side. Of the old buildings surrounding the square, the *Tribunale di Mercadanzia* (former merchant's court) of 1359 on the E. side, and the *Palazzo Uguccioni* of *c.* 1550 on the N. side have survived. The square is decorated with important pieces of Florentine sculpture, including the *Neptune fountain*, is by Bart. Ammannati and his school (1563–75) at the edge of which there are twelve fine bronze figures by Giov. Bologna.

Piazzale Michelangelo: The spacious terrace of this piazza (1865–70) has an unusual view of the city with the main buildings easily recognizable. In the piazza there are bronze

Piazza della Signoria, David by Michelangelo (left), Neptune fountain by B.Ammannati (right)

casts of Michelangelo's David and casts of his recumbent figures from the Medici tomb monuments in S.Lorenzo.

Pinacoteca dello Spedale degli Innocenti → Spedale degli Innocenti.

Ponte Vecchio: This bridge spanning a narrow part of the river deserves its name of 'Old Bridge' if the tradition according to which there was a bridge here in the Etruscan period is true. The bridge has become famous for the little houses which line it on both sides. Grand Duke Ferdinand I issued a decree ruling that only goldsmiths were permitted to trade from shops here. These houses have made the bridge famous, and the Ponte Vecchio is one of the sights which no stranger to the city should

miss. Vasari's passage leads from the Palazzo Vecchio across the bridge to the Palazzo Pitti.

Porta alla Croce (Piazza Beccaria): Built in 1218. Inside is the much damaged fresco 'Madonna and Child with St.John the Baptist and St.Ambrose'.

Porta Romana (Via Romana): The S. gate of the oldest fortification (1284–1333) on the far side of the Arno (Oltrarno). There is a 14C fresco of 'Madonna and Child with four Saints' inside the gate (1326).

Porta S.Frediana (or: Porta Pisana; Borgo S.Frediano): Built in 1332-4, probably to a design by A.Pisano.

Porta S.Giorgio (Costa S.Giorgio): A gate (completed in 1260) in the wall

Ponte Vecchio, Cellini bust

on the left bank of the Arno. There is a relief of St.George on the outside; inside, there is a fresco of the Virgin Mary by Bicci di Lorenzo.

Porta S.Niccolò (Piazza Poggi): This city gate (1324) operated in conjunction with the Zecca tower on the other bank of the Arno and made it possible to close the Arno to all traffic.

S.Ambrogio (Piazza S.Ambrogio): One of the earliest of Florentine churches lies concealed behind the Gothic-style façade which dates from 1888. This single-storeyed building has memorial stones to Renaissance artists who lie buried in the church (Cronaca, Mino da Fiesole and Verrocchio). Good decorations. The second altar on the right has frescos of the Virgin Mary enthroned with John the Baptist and St.Bartholomew,

attributed to A.Gaddi. A triptych attributed to Bicci di Lorenzo (Madonna and Child with Saints) is seen on the wall behind the third altar. To the left of the high altar is the *Cappella del Miracolo,* dedicated to a miracle (*c.*1230) in which the wine drops remaining in a chalice carelessly cleaned by a priest called Uguccione (*c.* 1230) turned into blood overnight.

S.Felice (Piazza S.Felice; opposite the Palazzo Pitti): A sober medieval building altered several times (in the 14,15&16C). The Renaissance façade (1457) is attributed to Michelozzo. Inside there is a painted crucifix from the Giotto workshop. The 5th altar on the right has a Madonna and Child with four Saints by R.Ghirlandaio and his pupils. The 2nd altar on the left from the choir has a triptych of 1467 by Neri di Bicci, above which there is a 14C fresco.

S.Felicità (Piazza S.Felicità): Probably the second oldest church in Florence, it occupies the site of a previous building and an early Christian graveyard. Rebuilt in 1736 after much alteration; Vasari's portico survives. Inside there two galleries in which the Grand Dukes and their families sat when attending divine service.

S.Gaetano (Piazza Antinori): This church stood here in the 11C, but was completely rebuilt from 1604 onwards. The façade by G.Silvani (1648) is one of the finest 17C church façades in Florence. The *Cappella Antinori,* which adjoins the first chapel on the left, has a Crucifixion with St.Mary Magdalene, St.Francis and St.Jerome by Filippo Lippi.

S.Leonardo in Arcetri (Via di S.Leonardo, near the Porta S.Giorgio): A single-aisled 11C church with a famous 13C pulpit (from which St.Antony preached) transferred from a church now demolished. Numerous

15C paintings include some by Neri di Bicci.

S.Lorenzo (Piazza S.Lorenzo): The present building, the plans for which existed in 1419, was erected on the site of the early Christian basilica of Ambrosiana (consecrated by St.Ambrose in 393) and of the subsequent 11C Romanesque building. Giovanni de' Medici originally employed the young and still unknown Brunelleschi to build the sacristy, but he was finally given the commission for the entire building (*c.* 1419/20), along with the chance to redesign it. The *Old Sacristy* and the *choir chapel* were completed in 1428. On Brunelleschi's death in 1446 his pupil Manetti undertook the completion of the nave; the dome was built to his own plan and completed in 1469. The façade designed by Michelangelo (the model dates from 1517) was left unexecuted. However, in 1521 Pope Leo X commissioned Michelangelo to complete the *New Sacristy* and furnishings as a burial chapel. From 1524 onwards he worked on installing the *Biblioteca Laurenziana* in the monastery cloister built by Manetti in 1457. The *Cappella dei Principi* adjoining the church's choir was planned by Vasari in 1561-8. The foundation stone was not laid until 1605. The dome was completed in the 19C.

Church of S.Lorenzo: Simple exterior with façade left in the rough. The *interior* was conceived as a flat-roofed columned basilica in strict application of the metrical system. The articulation of the choir is repeated in the aisle walls and the front elevation. This articulation, combined with the balanced proportions, makes the church a model of Renaissance architecture. The two *pulpits* by Donatello and his pupils (see plan 3, 15) are as important as the architecture; the *cantoria* (1) is attributed to Donatello.

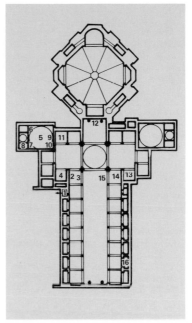

Pulpit by Donatello, c. 1460, and his pupils Bellano and Bertoldo (first provisionally erected in 1515) **4** Chapel of the Martelli with monument to Donatello (1896) above his tomb in the floor; altar diptych with predella by Filippo Lippi, c. 1440; sarcophagus by Niccolò Martelli. Donatello school **5** Sagrestia Vecchia, designed by Brunelleschi, 1420-9, with decoration by Donatello (4 stucco medallions from the story of John the Evangelist; 4 painted terracottas with the Evangelists; at the altar designed by Donatello, is a triptych from the Taddeo Gaddi school, and in the middle of the sacristy is the sarcophagus of the parents of Cosimo il Vecchio (Giov. Bicci de'Medici and Piccarda Bueri) **6** Porta degli Apostoli; bronze door with 20 figures by Donatello **7** Porta dei Martiri (bronze door with pairs of martyrs) in 10 panels by Donatello; above the two doors are painted terracotta reliefs showing the patrons of the Medici family **8** Marble basin from the Donatello workshop **9** Terracotta bust of St.Lawrence (or St.Leonard), attributed to Donatello **10** Monument to Piero and Giovanni de' Medici (sons of Cosimo il Vecchio) by A.Verrochio, 1472 **11** Altar from the Ghirlandaio school **12** Crucifix by Baccio di Montelupo **13** Altar, late-15C; Roman sarcophagus used as the tomb of Niccolò di Tommaso **14** Marble tabernacle by Desiderio da Settignano **15** Pulpit by Donatello, c. 1460, and his pupils Bellano and Bertoldo (first temporarily erected in 1515) **16** Altarpiece showing the Marriage of the Virgin Mary by R.Fiorentino, 1523 - Newly discovered fresco sketch(es) by Michelangelo in the basement of the Medici chapel. Can only be viewed by special permission.

Florence, S.Lorenzo **1** Marble cantoria to a design by Donatello (attributed) **2** Fresco of martyrdom of St.Lawrence by A.Bronzino 1565-9 **3**

Filippo Lippi's altar diptych (4) is *c.* 1440. The altarpieces by R.Fiorentino (16) and A.Bronzino (4) are important Mannerist paintings. The *Old Sacristy*, a key work of the early Renaissance, is a square domed room with an adjacent altar. Original twelve-sided dome. The decoration (see plan), executed by Donatello in 1435 when the building was already finished deserves particular attention. The monument to the sons of Cosimo il Vecchio Medici (10) is an early masterpiece by Verrocchio. The *New Sacristy* is by Michelangelo but was completed with alterations. He was responsible for the dome (modelled on the Pantheon) and the twelve-sided lantern above it. The monumental figures by Michelangelo are among the most important accomplishments of European art: the tomb of Giuliano de' Medici, Duke of Nemours (d. 1516), son of Lorenzo il Magnifico, has the recumbent figures of Day and Night. The tomb of Lorenzo de' Medici, Duke of Urbino (d. 1519), grandson of Lorenzo il Magnifico, displays the recumbent figures of Morning and Evening.

Fresco sketches by Michelangelo were discovered near the New Sacristy in 1976. The *Cappella dei Principi* (Chapel of the Princes) is the third Medici funerary chapel, and six of the Grand Dukes of Tuscany are interred here; two of the tombs have colossal figures by P.Tacca. The richly articulated domed building is inlaid with precious stones (Pietre Dure; see also under Galleria dell'Accademia: Opificio delle Pietre Dure). *Biblioteca Laurenziana:* Founded in 1444 with Cosimo I's extensive library, it was finally housed in the building begun by Michelangelo, in 1524 above the W. side of the two-storeyed cloister built by Manetti.

S.Marco (church and monastery, Piazza San Marco): Originally a Vallombrosan monastery taken over by the Sylvestrines. In 1436 it was transferred to the Dominicans of Fiesole and in 1437–52 Cosimo il Vecchio had it rebuilt by the architect Michelozzo. Subsequently the monastery became one of the most important spiritual centres in Florence; the religious

San Lorenzo, Cappella dei Principi, dome

reformer Savonarola was one-time prior. Fra Angelico (in whose memory a special museum was set up in 1919, using works from Florentine collections) was the monastery's most famous member. Archbishop Antoninus, a Dominican from S.Marco, was canonized in 1526. Giovanni da Bologna built a fine burial chapel for him in 1578–9. The façade dates from 1777/8 in its present form. The interior is still Gothic and has a massive Giottesque cross on the inner wall of the façade, a Virgin Mary (1509) by Fra Bartolommeo, a number of late Mannerist Florentine paintings, as well as paintings by Giovanni da Bologna and his followers. The *Chapel of St.Antoninus* has frescos by A.Allori; the antependium and bronze candelabra are by Giovanni da Bologna. The *sacristy* (1437–43) by Michelozzo shows Brunelleschi's influence. The recumbent bronze figure of St.Antonino in the choir chapel is by Giovanni da Bologna (the casting is by Dom. Ortigiani). The *monastery* was restored and partly extended by Michelozzo (1437–52).

Frescos by Fra Angelico date from the time the church was rebuilt.

S.Miniato al Monte: Occupies a splendid position on a hill high above Florence. A masterpiece of the Florentine Proto-Renaissance, it was mentioned in Carolingian times. It was originally built as a shrine above the tomb of Minias a Christian beheaded in *c.* 250 under Emperor Decius. In 1018 it was a Cluniac abbey; the abbey church was probably completed in 1207. The monastery and church passed into the possession of the Olivetans in 1373. In 1460 Manetti built the burial chapel of Cardinal Jacob of Portugal, a member of the Portuguese royal family, who died in Florence in 1459. The church, which suffered in the wars of the 16C, was subject to 18&19C restorations. The campanile fell down and was rebuilt in 1524–7. The splendid *façade* is faced in white and green, the richness of the decoration progressively increasing from the lowest of the three zones to the topmost. This lessening of the decorative weight

San Lorenzo, tomb with figures by Michelangelo

San Marco, façade

accords with the progressive flattening of the façade relief, which begins with sculptured supports on the ground floor, continues with pilasters, and ends in a gable surface with a pattern consisting merely of the green of Verde di Prato and the white of Carrara marble.

The *interior* takes the form of a basilica with alternating columns and pillars dividing nave and two aisles (some of the capitals are ancient spoils); splendid timber roof. The choir, partitioned off by an arch and transenna, lies above the 11C hall crypt, which projects like a stage. The crypt has seven aisles with groin vaults, some ancient columns and good capitals; vault frescos by T.Gaddi depict Saints and Prophets. The splendid, Cappella del Crocifisso (1448) by Michelozzo stands at the end of the nave, with steps to the crypt to each side. This chapel has a barrel vault with a glazed terracotta coffered ceiling by L. della Robbia. Originally built by Piero de' Medici to house the famous Cross of S.Giovanni Gualberto (now in S.Trinità) today it has a much-restored 13C cross; painted panels of St.Miniato, St.Giovanni Gualberto, the Annunciation, and scenes from the Passion are by A.Gaddi (1394–6). The floor of the nave has marble intarsia (signs of the zodiac, doves, lions, etc.) dating from 1207. The choir has three aisles and, because of the projecting crypt which raises the choir, resembles a tribune. The choir meets the nave with a magnificent marble screen (1207). The richly decorated pulpit is joined to the choir; the lectern, supported by a small figure, rests upon the outstretched wings of the eagle of St.John. The apse has intarsia work, with embedded window niches closed off by transparent stone slabs. The calotte has a mosaic (1297) of Christ Pantocrator flanked by the Virgin Mary and St.Miniato surrounded by the symbols of the Evangelists (restored by Baldovinetti in 1491). On the right is the sacristy, a large square room dating from 1387 with rich fresco decorations by Spinello Arentino and his workshop (later than 1387).

The chapel of Cardinal Jacob of Portugal, by A.Manetti and modelled on

San Marco, fresco by Fra Angelico in the monastery   *San Miniato al Monte* ▷

the Old Sacristy of San Lorenzo, was added on the left aisle. The fine architecture has equally fine decorations: vault panels by L. della Robbia (glazed multicoloured terracottas depicting the Holy Ghost, the cardinal virtues, and Angels); frescos by A.Baldovinetti (Evangelists, Church Fathers, Prophets); the monument to the Cardinal of Portugal (nephew of King Alfonso, Archbishop of Lisbon) by A.Rossellino (1461). The altar panel is a copy of the original (→ Uffizi) by A. and P. del Pollaiuolo (1467). To the right of the church stands the massive **Palazzo dei Vescovi,** begun under the Florentine bishop Andrea dei Mozzi (mentioned in Dante, 'Inferno', XV). Completed in 1320 and later extended, this was the summer residence of the Florentine bishops. After sustaining damage during wars, it was restored in 1903–22. Today the palace is frequently used as a concert hall.

S.Trinità (Piazza S.Trinità): Built by Vallombrosan monks in the 2nd half of the 11C; rebuilt in the 14C, when it was redesigned in Gothic style. The façade is by B.Buontalenti (1593–4). There are a nave, two aisles and a square apse. Frescos by Lorenzo Monaco (c. 1420–25) in the *Bartolini* chapel in the right aisle. To the right of the choir is the Sassetti chapel with frescos by D.Ghirlandaio (1483–6); the altarpiece (1485) of the Adoration of the Shepherds is also by Ghirlandaio.

S.Niccolò sopr'Arno (Via S.Miniato): A 12C church largely rebuilt in the 15C. The sacristy has an aedicule in the manner of Michelozzo, with a fresco of 1450 by Baldovinetti or P. del Pollaiolo depicting the Virgin Mary presenting her girdle.

S.Pancrazio and Cappela Rucellai (Via della Spada): The deconsecrated church of S.Pancrazio has a fine

San Miniato, crypt ▷

Santa Croce

Dante monument by Santa Croce

14C façade (*c.* 1375). The *Cappella Rucellai* next door is a model of the temple of the Holy Sepulchre (1467) built by L.B. Alberti for Giovanni Rucellai.

S.Salvatore al Monte (also known as S.Francesco al Monte alle Croce; near S.Miniato al Monte): The monastery and church were built for the Franciscans by the Della Tosa family on the site of an oratory to St.Cosmas and St.Damian. The present church was begun in 1499 to a design by Cronaca.

S.Croce (Piazza S.Croce): The expansive *Piazza di S.Croce* (monument to Dante dating from 1865), which dates from the Middle Ages and has from time immemorial been the unofficial meeting place of the people of Florence, occupies the site of an ancient amphitheatre. On its E.

side is the church of S.Croce, the greatest church of the Franciscan order. According to Vasari, it was begun by A. di Cambio in 1294 on the site of an earlier building dating from 1228. The transept was completed about 1300, but the church was only consecrated in 1443 in the presence of Pope Eugene IV. The door to the sacristy corridor, and the *Medici chapel* at the end of it, are early masterpieces by Michelozzo (*c.* 1455). The façade dates from 1853–63; the campanile from 1847. Vasari made radical alterations to the decorations (stone altar tabernacles in the aisles and the removal of choir stalls from the nave). Simple *exterior;* at the E. end of the N. side there is a portico with a marble tomb from the school of Tino da Camaino (*c.* 1330). The clearly designed, broad *interior*, is basilican with a nave, two aisles, and transept at the end surrounded by chapels.

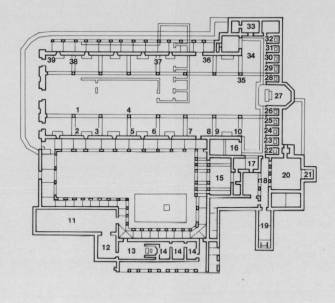

Decorations: S.Croce has become a pantheon for notable Florentines and as such has numerous *tombs* and *cenotaphs*, and 276 memorials in the floor. The tomb carved by B.Rossellino in 1444–5 for *Leonardo Bruni* (1369–1444), humanist, historian and chancellor of the Florentine Republic, is of particular interest as it became the prototype Florentine Renaissance tomb. Other important monuments include one of the most beautiful of Renaissance tombs—that of Carlo Marsuppini (1398–1453), humanist andb Chancellor—by D. da Settignano (in 1455–66). The *tomb of Michelangelo*, designed by Vasari, was completed in 1573. There are also the tombs of *Galileo Galilei* dating from 1737, that of *Machiavelli* (1787), and also that of *Gioacchino Rossini*, the

Florence, S.Croce 1 'Madonna col Bambino', relief by A. Rossellino **2** Monument to Michelan-

gelo by Vasari (1570) **3** Cenotaph to Dante Alighieri by S.Rica (1829) **4** Marble pulpit by B. da Maiano (1472-6) **5** Monument to Vittorio Alfieri by Canova (1010) **6** Monument to Niccolò Machiavelli by Spinazzi (1787) **7** Niche by Donatello with alto relievo of 'L'Annunziazione' (1435) **8** Tomb of Leonardo Bruni **9** Monument to Gioacchino Rossini by G.Cassioli **10** Tomb of the poet Ugo Foscolo **11** Former refectory **12** Former Little Refectory **13** Former Cappella Canigiani **14** Collection with significant paintings **15** Cappella de' Pazzi by Brunelleschi **16** Cappella Castellani with frescos by A.Gaddi **17** Cappella Baroncelli with frescos by T.Gaddi **18** Sacristy passage by Michelozzo **19** Novices' or dei Medici chapel (1445) **20** Sacristy **21** Cappella Rinuccini with frescos by G. da Milano and the artist of the Cappella Rinuccini **22** Cappella Velluti, followers of Cimabue **23** Cappella Calderini **24** Cappella Giugni **25** Cappella Peruzzi with frescos by Giotto **26** Cappella Bardi with frescos by Giotto **27** Cappella Maggiore with altar cross by the di Figline artist **28** Cappella Tosinghi/Spinelli **29** Cappella Capponi **30** Cappella Ricasoli **31** Cappella Pulci e Beraldi with frescos by B.Daddi (c. 1330) **32** Cappella Bardi di Vernio, story of St.Silvester by Maso di Banco (c. 1340) **33** Cappella Bardi with crucifix by Donatello **34** Monument to Luigi Cherubini by O.Fantacchiotti **35** Monument to Leon Battista Alberti by L.Bartolini **36** Monument to Carlo Marsuppini by D. da Settignano **37** 'Pietà' by Bronzino **38** Monument to Galileo Galilei by G.Foggini **39** 15C frescos

Galilei monument in Santa Croce

of the early Renaissance. The simple paintings on the spandrels of the E. chapels in the transept chapels are the oldest frescos. A follower of Cimabue (or Cavallini) painted frescos of scenes from the legend of St.Michael in the *Cappella Velluti*, the altar of which has a polyptych by Giotto (one of the earliest works from his late period). The frescos in the *Peruzzi chapel*, with scenes from the life of the two Saints John, are from Giotto's middle period (later than 1320), while frescos in the *Bardi chapel*, which are a little later, show scenes from the legend of St.Francis (the altar panel is attributed to Barone Berlinghieri). Frescos in the *Baroncelli chapel* are by T.Gaddi, Giotto's most loyal pupil, and date from 1332–8; the Presentation of the Girdle is by B.Mainardi (1480); the monument to the Baroncelli family is by G. di Balduccio from Pisa (the workshop companion of T. di Camaino). Roughly similar in date with the last-mentioned are frescos by B.Daddi (*c.* 1330) in the *Pulci-Beraldi chapel*, and also those by Maso di Banco (*c.* 1340) in the second *Bardi chapel*. The development of frescos in the second half of the century can be observed in the frescos of A.Gaddi (*c.* 1385) in the *Castella chapel* (also known as *Sacrament chapel*) and in the *choir chapel*, where the legend of the Holy Cross is depicted. The 14C *sacristy*, is like a small church and has fine 15&16C cupboards and a terracotta bust of Christ by G. della Robbia. The *Rinuccini chapel* adjoins the sacristy as a choir would a church, and contains frescos (the finest work by G. da Milano (*c.* 1366). A beautiful wrought-iron railing has an inscription commemorating the consecration. The altarpieces in the aisles are good examples of Florentine Mannerists' painting at the time of Vasari: Santi di Tito (Crucifixion, Resurrection, Emmaus); J.Coppi del Moglio (Ecce homo); B.Naldini (Deposition).

composer. One of the most important sepulchral monuments of Italian classicism is that carved by A.Canova in 1810 for Vitt. Alfieri. A cenotaph to Dante was built in 1829. Major pieces of *Florentine Renaissance sculpture* include the marble relief of the Madonna and Child in a mandorla of angels by A.Rosselino (1478), a graceful and delicate relief on the tomb of Francesco Nori. In 1435 Donatello produced one of his best works, a tabernacle of the Annunciation for the Cavalcanti family. He is also the artist of the wooden crucifix in the *Bardi chapel* at the N. end of the transept. B. da Maiano's octagonal *marble pulpit* with five reliefs showing scenes from the legend of St.Francis dates from 1472–6. The extremely fine collection of *frescos* from the Duecento makes it possible to study the development of Florentine painting from the generation before Giotto up to the stirrings

The first cloister, which is an irregular shape, was formed from the fusion of two Trecento cloisters and is enclosed by arcades (that joining the church dates from the early 14C). Opposite the entrance is the **Pazzi chapel**, the chapterhouse and burial chapel of the Pazzi, built by Andrea de' Pazzi. Begun by Brunelleschi in 1430, this is an important early Renaissance work of perfect harmony; terracottas by L. della Robbia, wooden doors carved by G. da Sangallo (1470–8). The entrance to the **monastery museum**, the former refectory (= Museo dell'Opera di S. Croce) is in the first cloister. The main works of the collection are: six fresco scenes (about 1290 sq.ft.; detached as one unit) by T.Gaddi; the large painted wooden crucifix, a later work by Cimabue; and the gilded bronze statue of St.Louis, one of the first figures by Donatello which already shows his commitment to the ideas of the Renaissance (*c.* 1423). The second cloister *(Chiostro Grande)*, is another beautiful work by Brunelleschi (finished in 1453 after his death, probably with the assistance of B.Rossellino). The portal is by B. da Maiano (*c.* 1450).

S.Maria del Carmine: The church of the former Carmelite monastery was largely destroyed by fire in 1771 and rebuilt in 1782. Fortunately the *Brancacci chapel* with the outstanding frescos by Masolino and Masaccio (1424–7) has survived. The chapel, which dates back to some time before 1386, was decorated with frescos at the expense of Felice Brancacci, rich merchant, politician and diplomat (who among other things was the ambassador of Florence in Egypt) after 1424. The decoration was begun by Masolino, who had undertaken the commission on his own, but he was soon assisted by Masaccio and came under the latter's influence. During a two-year stay in Hungary (1425–7) Masolino left it to Masaccio (18 years younger) to continue the work. Both painters were in Rome in 1428, and the frescos remained incomplete when

Masaccio died during this visit. Filippino Lippi (1481/2) finished the painting. The vault was not painted until much later (baroque). These frescos are of particular interest for in them the origins of early Renaissance painting can be traced. Masolino was born in 1383 and by training was committed to Gothic tendencies in the International Style, a lyrically delicate narrative style of art. Masaccio, who had absorbed new thinking and sought for greater realism in his painting (Brunelleschi had discovered linear perspective) was a follower of Giotto, even more than a century after the latter's death and with him he shared an approach to figure painting and an ability to depict human emotions.

Other things of interest in the church include frescos of 1394 by Bicci di Lorenzo, a crucifix by followers of Cimabue in the sacristy and the dome fresco (1682) by L.Giordano in the Corsini chapel.

S.Maria Novella (church and monastery): The Dominicans' most important church in Florence. The present church, on the site of a 10C oratory, was begun in 1246 and largely completed in 1360. The lower part of the façade dates from 1350; the upper part by Alberti from 1456). The 'avelli' or family tombs are to the right of the church. The choir is particularly beautiful. The interior, which takes the form of a pillared basilica with rib vaults and transept choir chapels in the Cistercian tradition, has a simple solemnity which makes it one of the finest Gothic church interiors in Italy. Among the best decorations is the *fresco* paid for by Gonfaloniere and painted by Masaccio in 1425, which depicts the founders kneeling in front of a tunnel-vaulted Renaissance room. The beautiful wooden *crucifix* by Brunelleschi (designed by G.da Sangallo in 1508) can be found in the *Gondi chapel*, beside and to the left of the main choir. The ceiling frescos dating from *c.* 1270 are related to the mosaics in the baptistery dome. In the *Strozzi chapel* (front wall of the left transept), are the frescos painted by Nardo di Cione in *c.* 1357; the altar by Andrea di Cione (known as Orcagna) dates from 1357. An important early work by Giotto (a painted crucifix above the entrance door) is to be found in the sacristy by J.Talenti. The wall fountain is by G. della Robbia (1498). The main choir chapel has a famous fresco cycle by D.Ghirlandaio dating from 1485–90 (the young Michelangelo was among the pupils who participated.) Mannerist paintings include the last work of A.Bronzino, altarpiece in the Gaddi chapel. The *Chiostro Verde,* built later than 1350, possibly by J.Talenti, is known as the *Green Corridor* after the frescos painted by P.Uccello and assistants in 'Terra Verde' in the E. wing (most of the frescos have been detached and are exhibited in the refectory). These frescos painted some time after 1447 are outstanding examples of the new style of the early Renaissance. On the N. side of the Chiostro Verde is the so-called *Spanish Chapel,* which is

both the chapterhouse and at the same time the burial place of the founding family (Buon Amico di Lapo Guidalotti). Begun in 1348, it was completed in 1355. The wall paintings by Andrea da Firenze were finished in 1365 and are a fine example of Trecento Florentine painting. The other cloister, the *Chiostro dei Morti* has the burial chapel of the Strozzi decorated with frescos by the Orcagna circle of artists.

Church of SS.Annunziata (Piazza della SS.Annunziata): Built in 1250 as the oratory of the Servites living in the settlement founded on Monte Senario in 1234. The miraculous completion by an angel (1252) of the fresco begun by Bartholomew the monk made the oratory into a popular shrine. After some extentions which quickly became necessary, the building was redesigned in 1444 by Michelozzo, beginning with the laying of the foundation stone of the circular tribune, which was completed in 1477 with the assistance of L.B.Alberti. The church and atrium date from

Santa Maria Novella

1453, and the portico was completed in 1604. Rich baroque decoration. Behind the portico with its seven bays is the *atrium* (Chiostrino dei Voti; roofed in 1833) with excellent High Renaissance and early Mannerist *frescos* by A. del Sarto and his school: Pontormo, 'Visitation' (1516); Franciabigio, 'Marriage of the Virgin' (1513); 'Nativity of the Virgin Mary' by A. del Sarto (signed); 'Coming of the Magi' (1514) and scenes from the life of St.Filippo Benizzi (left side wall) of 1509–10 (except 'Vision and Investiture' of the Saint, by C.Rosselli, 1475). The oldest fresco is the 'Nativity of Christ' by A.Baldovinetti (1460–2). *Church:* The side aisles of this 14C basilica were subdivided into chapel-like units by Michelozzo. The rich baroque flat ceiling dates from 1669. The original choir section was demolished and, with the assistance of L.B.Alberti, was replaced by a rotunda on the model of the classic Minerva Medica in Rome. To the left of the entrance is the *Cappella dell'Annunziata* with a marble tempietto (1447–61) in honour of the miraculous 14C Annunciation fresco. Note

also: the marble Pietà by B.Bandinelli (chapel in right transept); Trinity with Saints, detached fresco by A. del Castagno (1454–5; on the altar of the second chapel on the left); 'Resurrection' by A.Bronzino (*c.* 1550; first chapel to the left of the E. chapel of the rotunda). The former *chapterhouse*, the 'painter's chapel, has works by Michelangelo's followers and is notable for its unique decoration. The ceiling has the 'Vision of St.Bernard' by L.Giordano (*c.* 1650). The lunettes of the *cloister* (Chiostro dei Morti), which is entered from outside the church, are frescoed with scenes from the history of the Servite order. These frescos are leading works of the early-17C Tuscan school (Mascagni, Poccetti, Rosselli and others). Above the door to the church is the *Madonna del Sacco*, a masterpiece by A. del Sarto (1525).

S.Spirito (Piazza S.Spirito): A splendid example of Renaissance architecture. It was completely rebuilt by Brunelleschi on the site of an Augustinian church which existed in 1250 and has been altered several

Santa Maria Novella

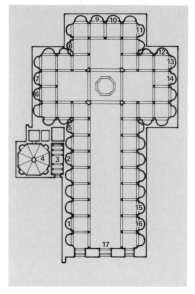

mythological figures and scenes; some of the capitals are attributed to A.Sansovino, 1489-92, to plans by G. da Sangallo; the dome and lantern are to a model by A. da Pollaiuolo and Salvi d'Andrea, 1495-6; capitals by A.Sansovino; altar by A.Allori, 1596 **5** Madonna Enthroned with Saints, school of Fra' Bartolomeo; on the right a bust of G.Montorsoli by Tom. Cavalcanti, c. 1560 **6** Trinity, revered by St.Catherine and Mary Magdalene, by Franc. Granacci **7** Cappella Corbinelli; architecture and rich sculptured decorations are an early work by A.Sansovino, 1492; the best of the decorations is **8** Nativity, school of Dom. Ghirlandaio **9** Adulteress, by A.Allori, 1577 **10** Altar with martyred Saints by A.Allori, 1574; the predella shows the Palazzo Pitti before its enlargement **11** Polyptych by Maso di Banco **12** Behind the bronze railing is the marble sarcophagus of the Florentine politician Neridi Girno Capponi, 1388-1457, attributed to Bernardo Rosselino, 1458 **13** Copy by F.Ficherelli after the Virgin Mary appearing to St.Bernard by Perugino in the Alte Pinakothek in Munich **14** Madonna and Child and St.John as a boy, to whom the founders are being presented by St.Martin and St.Catherine; a work by Filippino Lippi, c. 1490 **15** Statue of St.Nicholas by Tolentino; it is unclear whether the statue is based on a work by Sansovino; at the side are angels by Franciabigio **16** Copy by Baggio Bacci, 1549, of Pietà by Michelangelo in St.Peter's, Rome **17** Stained-glass window of the Descent of the Holy Spirit, to a design by Perugino

Florence, Santo Spirito 1 Copy of the Risen Christ by Michelangelo (S.Maria Sopra Minerva, Rome) by T.Landini **2** Entrance to sacristy **3** Ante-room to sacristy by Cronaca, 1492-4, to plans by Giuliano da Sangallo; coffered vault with

times since then. The foundations were begun in 1436, but they were not completed until 1487. The octagonal sacristy was added by G. da Sangallo

SS.Annunziata, Pietà by B.Bandinelli

Uffizi, portrait of a man by Botticelli ▷

and Cronaca from 1489–92 and the campanile dates from 1543. The dome over the crossing was not finished until 1601–02 when the lantern was added. In the late 16C the cloisters were incorporated into the existing medieval scheme of buildings. The cloister accessible from the sacristy portico dates from *c.* 1600 and is by A.Parigi, while the other, older cloister (belonging to the area governed by the military district administration) was built by Ammannati in 1564–9. Owing to unresolved artistic problems the façade was left plain. The side walls are enlivened by windows alone. The side aisles continue around the entire building except for the façade, and each bay ends in an apsidiole vaulted with a calotte to form a chapel. The reduction of all decorative features means that the grand effect of the architectural elements is the primary and dominant feature. Of interest inside include: a *marble Pietà* by Nanni di Baccio Bigio after the Michelangelo Pietà in St.Peter's (16); a polychrome and gilded wooden statue of St.Nicholas of Tolentino after a model by J.Sansovino (15); the 'Apparition of the Madonna before St.Bernard' by Perugino (a copy of the original in the Alte Pinakothek picture gallery in Munich; 13); a polyptych by Maso di Banco (11). The structure and decoration of the Cappella Corbinelli are both by A.Sansovino (7). Opposite is a panel of the Madonna and Child with Saints and donors), an early work by Filippino Lippi (14). The sacristy is particularly fine (4).

The refectory (cenacolo), whose wall was frescoed by Orcagna in *c.* 1360, is all that survives from the former *Augustinian monastery*. Ghiberti attributed the fresco to Orcagna and this was confirmed by research following the restorations of 1941. The upper part has a dramatic Crucifixion with a crucifix projecting far into the sky, while the badly damaged lower part depicts the Last Supper. The *collection donated by Salvatore Romano*, the

Neapolitan art dealer, is housed in the refectory. Along with architectural fragments, there are sculptures from the pre-Romanesque period until the 15C, including a caryatid by Tino di Camaino, two fragments from a background relief of the Donatello altar for the basilica of St.Antony in Padua, a Virgin Mary by J. della Quercia, and another Virgin Mary from the circle of artists surrounding Donatello.

Spedale Degli Innocenti with picture gallery (Piazza della SS.Annunziata): This foundling hospital, set up by the silk-weavers' guild in 1419, was designed by Brunelleschi. He built the loggia of nine arches between 1419 and 1426 and it is the first Renaissance example with columns and engaged pilasters. The proportions are exemplary, as is the captivatingly clear scheme of the architectural articulation and rhythm. Arch spandrels have terracotta medallions (infants in swaddling clothes), ten of which are by A. della Robbia (early works from *c.* 1463; the others are imitations). The middle vault of the portico, and the lateral lunettes, have frescos by Poccetti.

Synagogue (Tempio Israelitico i Via Farini): Built by M.Treves and V.Micheli in Moorish style in 1872–4.

Theatre: Teatro Communale (Via Magenta): The classical façade is all that survives of the original theatre after devastation from fire and war. The hall with its 2000 seats is used not only for the usual concert and opera season, but also for performances of the 'Maggio Musicale Fiorentino'. **Teatro alla Pergola** (Via della Pergola): Built in wood by F.Tacca in 1656. Taken over from the Grand Ducal courtyard and altered in 1681–94. Rebuilt in stone in 1755.

Torre del Gallo with the Villa la Gallina annexe (Piazza di Volsan-

Uffizi, portrait by Francesco Francia ▷

miato): A villa with a fresco by A. del Pollaiolo (young dancing nudes) adjoins the well-restored tower which had once belonged to the Galli family and has since been in the possession of the Lamberteschi and Manfredini.

Environs: Badia di Ripoli (3.5 km SE): This abbey of Ripoli is a Benedictine foundation from 790 with an 11C abbey church (extended in 1598). Nearby is the church of **S.Pietro a Rípoli**, which was mentioned as early as the 8C. The fine interior has a nave and two aisles. Above Bagno a Ripoli and Ponte a Ema is the church of **S.Caterina dell' Antella**, built in 1387 and subsequently decorated with frescos (the legend of St.Catherine) which are some of the finest works of Spinello Aretino. **L'Antella** has the fine Romanesque church of *S.Maria*.

Galluzzo (5 km. SW): The *Certosa del Galluzzo* which was begun in 1341 has a splendid picture gallery which, in addition to the five lunette frescos by Pontormo (1522–5), has a panel ascribed to Masolino.

S.Martino a Ménsola (to the NE,

reached by the Via G. d'Annunzio, near Converciano): A 9C abbey church. Visible in the present Renaissance structure dating from 1460 are remnants of an 11C Romanesque structure. In the right aisle there is an altar triptych by T.Gaddi. Nearby stands the **Villa I Tati,** which the art historian Bernhard Berenson acquired in 1905 and equipped with his rich library and art collection. The works in the collection are mostly of the Florentine school of painters, from Giotto until the early 16C.

Settignano (7 km. E.): This is known to be the birthplace of several Renaissance artists, such as the sculptor Desiderio da Settignano, the Rossellino brothers and the architect L.Fancelli. The 15C *parish church of the Ascension* has a terracotta by the school of A. della Robbia behind the high altar. There is a small ciborium to a design by D. da Settignano. On the road towards Terenzano is the **Villa Gamberaia,** one of the finest 16C villas.

Villamagna: The beautiful Romanesque church of *S.Donnino,* dates from the 11C.

Grosseto, cathedral, façade detail

58100 Grosseto

Grosseto   p.136☐D 7

Grosseto is the centre of the Maremma, a wild, marshy area of alluvial land around the mouth of the Ombrone which used to be severely affected by malaria—indeed it was only from about 1960 onwards that the district was made fertile. The city of Grosseto was first mentioned in the 10C and became a diocesan seat in the

12C. After being conquered by Siena in 1336, it fell in 1559 to the duchy of Tuscany which ordered the fortress and the city walls to be built in 1574–93. The city was ravaged by malaria (the population of Grosseto was only 2,300 in 1835) and never gained particular importance.

Cathedral of S.Lorenzo (Piazza Dante): Work on building the cathedral began in 1294 on the remains of a Lombard Romanesque church (*c.* 1180). The red-and-white marble façade was rebuilt in 1840–5 and the pilasters with their capitals are the work of Sozzo di Rustichino, the cathedral architect. Its richly decorated portal and the bell tower with its one-, two-, three- and five-arched windows above one another both date from 1402. Some very unfortunate restoration was carried out in the 19C in the interior, which has a nave and two aisles. Its contents include the large font by A.Ghini (*c.* 1470), a 16C marble ciborium in the ante-room of the sacristy, a 15C wooden cross in the Cappella del SS.Sacramento, and the 15C altarpiece of the Assumption

Grosseto, cathedral, E. portal, tympanum

Grosseto, cathedral, façade detail ▷

by Matteo di Giovanni in the left transept.

S.Francesco (Piazza Indipendenza): Inside this simple 13C brick building is a panel crucifix by Duccio di Buoninsegna (1289). There are also remains of Sienese frescos (14&15C), and the 16C cloister known as the Pozzo della Buffa.

Museo Archeologico (Via Mazzini): This museum, which has been housed in the Palazzo del Liceo since 1975, displays some excellently arranged finds representing a large proportion of the excavation sites of the province, among them Roselle, Vetulonia, Populonia, Talamone and Poggio Buco.

Museo Diocesano di Arte Sacra (above the cathedral sacristy): Works

of art from the churches of Grosseto and paintings from the Sienese school of the 13–17C are displayed here—the 'Madonna degli Ciliegie', Sassetta's masterpiece, being the outstanding item.

City wall: Work on the hexagonal ring of walls was begun in 1574 to a plan by B.Lanci. The wall surrounds the old city in a similar manner to Lucca, a fact which earned Grosseto the nickname 'Piccolo Lucca'. In 1833–5, Leopoldo II had the glacis and bastions converted into streets and gardens.

Also worth seeing: *S.Pietro* (on the Corso Carducci), with its 11C Romanesque apse, is the oldest church in Grosseto. The *monument to Leopoldo II* (Piazza Dante Alighieri) was built by L.Magni in 1846 in memory of the

victory over malaria—a victory in large part due to Leopoldo II.

Environs: Istia d'Ombrone (7 km. NE): This town surrounded by an early-14C wall was once the feudal seat of the bishops of Roselle.

In the *Franciscan church* there is a painting of the Virgin by an anonymous Sienese artist (*c.* 1400).

Magliano in Toscana (25 km. SE): This medieval town, surrounded by a wall which survives in good condition, stands on a high hill; note the 16C *Porto Nuova* and the *Porta S.Martino*. In the 7C BC there was a prosperous Etruscan settlement engaged in farming and mining and under the Romans there was a fortress, the so-called municipium heba.

Paganico (25 km. NE): Paganico, which was founded in Etruscan times, was the seat of the Aldobrandeschi family in the Middle Ages before falling to Siena. Inside the 12C church of *S.Michele Arcangelo* there are a 'Madonna and Child with Saints' by Andrea di Niccolò and frescos painted in 1368 by the Sienese artist Bartolo di Fredi.

Roselle Scavi (12 km. N.): The *excavation sites* of Roselle Scavi, an area settled during the Villanova period, are some 4 km. to the N. of the Terme di Roselle (today the town of Bagno di Roselle) which was known in classical antiquity.

Roselle Scavi, built on a hill some 980 ft. in height, was an important member of the Etruscan confederation of twelve cities. While most of the Etruscan cities allied themselves with Rome in the early 4C BC, this one, now called Rusellae by the Romans, waged a long struggle for independence. But in 294 BC, after a long siege and heavy fighting, it had to submit to Rome. As a Roman colony, Rusellae, a rich farming area, was compelled in 205 BC to supply cereal and pine wood to the fleet which, under Scipio's command, was opposing Carthage. Although devastated by the Barbarians, it became the seat of a bishop in the 4C, and it was only in 1198 that the diocese was moved to Grosseto. Marshes encroached on the Maremma district, and the malaria which spread as a result led to the complete depopulation of Roselle

Roselle Scavi (Grosseto), Etruscan city

Scavi over the following centuries. The walls have survived almost in their entirety. They are over 3,300 yards long and have four gates that have been uncovered. Built of polygonal blocks in the 6C BC, the wall is still up to 23 ft. high in places, although the remains of the W. sections are built of square blocks and date from the 2C BC. Apart from numerous fossa tombs, chamber tombs and rock tombs outside the old walls, some Barbarian tombs have also been discovered in the centre of the town. The items uncovered within the town walls include a Roman amphitheatre, several Roman buildings (houses, stables etc.), an Etruscan house, a road, water pipes, and the Roman forum with a basilica. It has not yet been conclusively established whether the foundations of a square tower in the S. part of the town belong to the medieval castle of the Aldobrandeschi, who owned Roselle Scavi until 1243, or whether they are part of the bell tower of an 8C Christian basilica.

50023 Impruneta
Florence   p.134☐E 4

Impruneta, which in the 12&13C was held by the famous Florentine family of Buondelmonte, is 15 km. S. of Florence on the edge of the Chianti district, which is renowned for its wines. This little town is not known merely for its excellent wines, however, but also for its beautiful ceramics and straw hats. The 'Fiera di S.Luca', a fair formerly held annually on 18 October, was one of the most

Roselle Scavi (Grosseto), Etruscan city

Impruneta, S.Maria, cloister

Impruneta, S.Maria, triptych

important trade fairs in Europe and is still much visited today.

S.Maria dell'Impruneta (Piazza Vittorio Emanuele): This church was consecrated in 1054, enlarged in the 15C and finally had to be thoroughly restored after suffering severe damage in World War 2. The battlemented Romanesque bell tower dates from the 13C. The portico, to which a clock tower with baroque decorations has been added, was built in 1634 in late Renaissance style. In 1453–6, two new chapels designed by Michelozzo were constructed on either side of the choir of the single-aisled interior. A miraculous 13C Byzantine image of the Virgin Mary, and the terracotta figures of St.Luke and St.Paul by Luca della Robbia, are to be found on the altar of the left hand chapel, known as the Cappella della Madonna. The terracotta Crucifixion in the Cappella della Croce (to the right of the high altar), and all the coloured majolicas in both chapels, are also the work of della Robbia.

Also worth seeing: The *Piazza Vittorio Emanuele* is surrounded by numerous arcades. There are also several splendid *villas* (14–18C) around Impruneta. However, it is difficult to obtain access to them because they are all privately owned today.

Environs: S.Casciano in Val di Pesa (11 km. SW): There was a much-contested fortress here on the border between Florence and Siena. Some remains still survive of the surrounding wall, which was built in 1335 by the Florentines. From 1512 until his death in 1527, Niccolò Machiavelli, the Florentine politician, historian and writer, lived in a small country house known as Albergaccio (which means an inn for the rabble) in Sant' Andrea a Percussina, a little way outside the town.

57100 Livorno

Livorno   p.134☐B 4

Livorno grew up around the coastal fort of *Liberna*, which was first mentioned in 904 and was fortified by Pisa prior to 1392, being the outworks of Porto Pisano (port of Pisa) some 3 km. to the N. After being held by Genoa for a few years, Livorno was finally sold to Florence in 1421. A new harbour was built in 1540–70 by order of Cosimo I de' Medici, and major reconstruction work was carried out in the town. In the period that followed, La Città Ideale (the ideal city) was built inside a pentagonal ring of walls to a plan drawn up by Buontalenti in 1577. From 1593 onwards, outlaws (such as pirates), refugees and persecuted persons from all over the world were able to settle in Livorno by reason of the Constituzione Livornina, which was established by Ferdinand I and which gave Livorno the status of a free port. The economic importance of Livorno increased continuously over the following centuries until 1868, when the bubble burst after the abolition of the free port status. The city has now

Livorno, harbour fortress

recovered from the severe damage suffered in 1940–3 and today, with its oil refineries, metal works and shipyards, it is the most important port in Tuscany, with goods of all kinds being landed for distribution throughout the region. Livorno is now also important as a port of departure to Elba, Corsica, Sardinia and other holiday islands.

Cathedral of S.Francesco d'Assisi (Piazza Grande): Begun in 1594 to a design by Buontalenti, it was completed by A.Pieroni in 1606. The cathedral was almost entirely rebuilt in 1946–50 after being badly damaged in the war. The portico, with its three arches supported by pairs of columns, is of marble, as is the windowed façade behind it, which ends in a triangular gable.

S.Giulia (behind the cathedral): The most valuable work of art in this small church is a panel on which St.Julia and eight scenes from her life are depicted. This is attributed to the school of Giotto.

S.Ferdinando (also known as the Chiesa della Crocetta, near the Via Venezia): This church designed by G.B. Foggini was built in 1707–14. The interior impresses by its elegant stucco and fine ceiling paintings.

Fortezza Vecchia (near the Via Caprera): This massive fortress was built by A. da Sangallo il Giovane in 1534 beside the Medici port. The *Mastio di Matilde*, which is close by, is an 11C round tower which was part of the Pisan coastal castle which Countess Matilde presented to the cathedral chapter of Pisa in 1103.

Fortezza Nuova: The moated New

Fortress was built in the late 16C but has now been partly destroyed.

Monumento dei 4 Mori (Piazza Micheli): This monument in honour of Ferdinand I is the landmark of Livorno. The figure of Ferdinand on its tall pedestal is by G.Bandini (1595); and the four negro figures (quattro mori) chained to the pedestal, from whom the monument derives its name, were cast in bronze by Pietro Tacca in 1624.

Museo Civico Giovanni Fattori (in the park of the Villa Fabricotti, near the Piazza Matteotti): Apart from some classical and prehistoric finds, such as burial objects, the main items on display here are works by the so-called Macchiaioli (a group of artists in the 2nd half of the 19C who were opposed to Academism). Thus we find paintings and drawings by Lega, Nomellini, Signorini and, above all, Fattori, but also Modigliani.

Acquario Comunale (Via Italia): The town aquarium has a collection of plants, fish and other Mediterranean sea creatures, and also a museum of natural history.

Also worth seeing: The *Torre del Marzocco* is an octagonal tower built by the Florentines in 1423. The *synagogue* (Via Cairoli) built in the 16C was restored throughout after World War 2. The *Cisterino*, a water cistern built in the classical style in 1842, is on the Via Grande. The church of the *Santissima Annunziata* (Via della Madonna) has a good baroque façade. To the S. of the Acquario Comunale is the 18C baroque church of *S.Iacopo in Acquaviva*, and opposite the cathedral is the *Palazzo Grande* built in 1629 and rebuilt after World War 2. The *Viale Italia* has gardens, palazzi and villas, and there is also the *Terrazza Mascagni*, with its plants and a fine view of the island of Gorgona.

Environs: Gorgona (37 km. SW):

Livorno, S.Ferdinando, altar

This rocky island, which rises 835 ft., has been the site of a penal colony since 1869, and for this reason it can only be visited with the permission of the Italian Ministry of Justice.
Santuario di Montenero (9 km. S.): This pilgrimage church stands 635 ft up on the side of the Colle di Montenero (1,025 ft.) and was founded in 1345, although it was not completed until 1575. The interior, with its baroque elements, was rebuilt in 1771. From the church terrace there is a splendid view of Livorno, the sea, the islands of the Tuscan archipelago and, on a clear day, even as far as Corsica.

55100 Lucca

Lucca   p.134☐C 3

Within its massive 15&16C city walls,

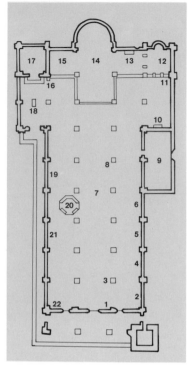

Lucca, cathedral of S.Martino 1 Marble group of 'St.Martin on horseback with the Beggar' by an unknown, probably Lombard-Luccan artist of the early 13C **2** Altarpiece by D.Passignano, 1594 ('Nativity') **3** 15C holy-water stoup **4** Altarpiece by F.Zuccaro (1595, 'Adoration of the Magi') **5** Altarpiece by Tintoretto (c. 1592, 'Last Supper') **6** Altarpiece by D.Passignano (1598, 'Crucifixion') **7** Floor of coloured marble inlay; 'Judgement of Solomon' by A.Federighi **8** Pulpit by M.Civitali (1494-8) **9** Sacristy; paintings including an altarpiece by D.Ghirlandaio (late-15C, 'Madonna and Saints'); also by Ghirlandaio: 'Entombment', 'Conversion of Paul', 'Martyrdom of St.Clement' and 'Martyrdom of St.Sebastian' **10** Monument to Pietro da Noceto by M.Civitali (1472) **11** Monument to Domenico Bertini by M.Civitali (1479) **12** Cappella del Sacramento; 2 angels by M.Civitali (1477); fresco by S.Tofanelli (c. 1800) **13** Chapel: altar of S.Regolo with statues of St.John the Baptist, St.Regulus and St.Sebastian by M.Civitali (1484) **14** Sanctuary; stained-glass window by Pandolfo di Ugolino da Pisa (1485); choir stalls by L.Marti (1452-7); marble railings by M.Civitali (c. 1475) **15** Cappella della Libertà; altar with 'Resurrection' by Giambologna (1579) **16** Sculpture of 'John the Evangelist' by J. della Quercia (c. 1410) **17** Cappella del Santuario; altarpiece by Fra Bartolom-

meo (1509, 'Madonna and Child between St.Stephen and John the Baptist') **18** Monument to Ilaria del Carretto by J. della Quercia (1408) **19** Altarpiece by J.Ligotti (1596, 'Visitation') **20** Tempietto del Volto Santo; eight-sided small marble temple, by M. Civitali, 1482-4, for the 11C crucifix known as 'Volto Santo'; small altar by F.Juvara (1725); outside the Tempietto is a 'St.Sebastian' by M.Civitali (1484) **21** Altarpiece by G.B. Paggi ('Annunciation') **22** Frescos by C.Rosselli ('Deposition' and 'Annunciation')

Lucca, situated in the fertile plain of the Serchio N. of Monte Pisano and S. of the Apuan Alps, has preserved its charming and harmonious old quarter through the centuries, with its numerous churches, palazzi and picturesque alleyways. The visitor to Lucca, which is often referred to as an 'open-air museum', will immediately be captivated by its unique, delightful atmosphere.

The city developd from a Ligurian settlement in the extensive marshy areas of the Serchio. After being subjugated by the Etruscans, this settlement finally became a colony of Rome in c. 180 BC. The Romans adopted the name *Luca* from the Ligurian-Etruscan word for marsh ('luk'). In 89 BC, Lucca, like many other cities in Italy, was granted Roman civil rights. Gaius Julius Caesar met Pompey and Crassus here in 56 BC—since 60 BC these three had formed the triumvirate—and Caesar now secured the proconsulship of Gaul (where the Gallic War had just entered upon a winter lull) for another five years by giving Spain to Pompey and Syria to Crassus. The amphitheatre outside the Roman walls survives from that period, and so do some parts of the regular Roman grid of streets.

In 568, the Lombards occupied the former region of Etruria, which was byn then called *Tuscia*. After this, it was not Florence that was chosen as the seat of the Lombard Dukes, but Lucca, owing to its excellent links with the Lombard capital of Pavia. The city was also granted this

Lucca, cathedral ▷

important status under the Carolingians (*c*. 800). In 1119, the consuls who had been elected from 1080 onwards declared Lucca to be a 'Libero Comune' (free community), and in 1162 this was confirmed by Emperor Frederick Barbarossa, probably because the city had, in exemplary fashion, acknowledged the supremacy of the Empire and had also assisted the Empire in some important affairs. After two centuries of great advancement, including the enlargement of the old ring of walls (completed in 1250), the city was taken in 1314 by the Pisan Signore (dictator) Uguccione della Faggiuola. But two years later, Castruccio Catracane degli Antelminelli, who had once been banished from Lucca and in 1314 was still one of the retinue of Uguccione della Faggiuola, seized power and rose to become Signore di Lucca. After the early death in 1328 of Castruccio, who was very successful and loyal to the Emperor, Lucca was once again conquered by Pisa before again being granted the status of a free city by Emperor Charles IV in 1369. The small aristocratic

republic of Lucca now flourished for four peaceful centuries before Napoleon presented it to his sister Elisa Baciocchi-Bonaparte in 1799 as a principality. After the defeat of Napoleon, the Duchy of Lucca was created at the Congress of Vienna in 1815 and was awarded to Marie Louise of Bourbon-Parma. In 1847, her son Carlo Lodovico bequeathed it to the Grand Duchy of Tuscany before it finally fell to the newly created Kingdom of Italy in 1860.

Lucca was the native city of the Berlingieri family of painters (13C), the sculptor and architect M.Civitali (1436–1501) and his sons, and the composers L.Boccherini (1743–1805), A.Catalani (1854–93) and G.Puccini (1858–1924).

The 'Sagra Musicale Lucchese', where the works played are mainly by composers from Lucca, is held in spring and summer of each year and attracts a large audience. On 13 September, the religious fraternities bear the Holy Cross of Volto Santo (preserved in the cathedral) through the city in a candlelit procession, known as the Luminara di S.Croce.

Lucca, cathedral portal

Lucca, cathedral, portico

Cathedral of S.Martino (Piazza S. Martino): Founded in the 6C, probably by St.Frediano, and originally dedicated to St.Regulus, this church was not made a cathedral until the 18C, from which time on it was dedicated to St.Martin of Tours. The present structure was built in 1060 by Bishop Anselmo da Baggio, who later became Pope Alexander II. Several parts were rebuilt from 1196–1204, and the interior was altered in Gothic style from 1372 onwards, mainly by M.Civitali. The asymmetric façade begun in 1204 is in white and black marble and its upper section, with its three-storeyed Pisan arcades, is by the sculptor Giudetto da Como. A noticeable feature is that the gable is incomplete.

The lower storey is a portico with three large arches. The right-hand arch is narrower than the other two in order to fit in between them and the campanile, which pre-dates the portico. This sturdy, battlemented bell tower is pierced by arches borne on columns, and the windows are wider at the top than at the bottom. To the right of the central arch in the portico there is a copy of a statue of St.Martin handing half of his coat to a beggar (the original is inside the cathedral). Niccolò Pisano's *Descent from the Cross* (1260–70) in the tympanum of the right portal is one of the outstanding reliefs in the portico. The scenes on the lintel are by the same artist (*Annunciation, Nativity* and *Adoration of the Magi*). But the bas reliefs on the left and central portals should also be noted (they include *scenes from the legend of St.Martin* and the *Months*).

The Gothic interior is subdivided into a nave with two side aisles, and a two-aisled transept. The arcades of the lofty nave are supported by pillars above which there are galleries running across the transept as far as the choir. The polychrome marble floor has various geometric designs by the school of Civitali. Thus the floor of the nave is decorated by a depiction of the *Judgement of Solomon* by A.Federighi. To the right of the main portal is the original of the abovementioned *St.Martin on horseback with the beggar*, which was carved in the early 13C by a Lombard-Luccan

Cathedral, Roman sculpture

artist and is difficult to fit into any stylistic category. In 1482–4, Matteo Civitali built an octangular tempietto, the so-called *Tempietto del Volto Santo* (in the middle of the left aisle) for the wooden crucifix which is known as the *Volto Santo*. This probably dates from the 11C, and is said to have been carved from cedar wood by St.Nicodemus and angels. The Saviour is clothed in a sumptuous garment of Gothic gold embroidery. The wooden cross, which was mentioned by Dante, is unveiled only a few times a year and is borne through the streets of Lucca every 13 September. The *Last Supper* painted by Tintoretto in 1592 is to be found at the 3rd altar of the right side aisle. Paintings by D.Ghirlandaio (e.g. *Madonna and Saints*, late-15C) and others are housed in the sacristy (entrance by the 5th altar of the right side aisle). The *monument to Ilaria del Carretto* (d. 1405) in the left transept was made by the Sienese artist J. della Quercia in 1408: the recumbente effigy of Paolo Guinini's second wife, who died young, lies above her sarcophagus; at her feet is a little dog, a symbol of her faithfulness to her husband. The statue of St.John the Evangelist (*c.* 1410) at the left pillar of the Cappella della Libertà (immediately to the left of the presbytery) is also by J. della Quercia. The chapel commemorates Lucca's liberation from Pisa. Just to the left of this chapel, the Cappella del Santuario houses the painting of the *Madonna and Child with Saints* painted by Fra Bartolommeo in 1509. The Cappella del Sacramento behind the right transept has frescos by S.Tofanelli (*c.* 1800) and two angels by M.Civitali (1477).

Other features to be noted are a monumental altar dating from 1579 with statues by Giambologna (by the choir), the *stained-glass windows* by Pandolfo di Ugolino da Pisa (1485; in the choir), altarpieces by Passignano at the 1st and 4th altars of the right side aisle (1594–8) and by F.Zuccaro at the 2nd altar of that aisle (1595),

and the choir stalls by L.Marti (1452–7).

S.Michele in Foro (Piazza S. Michele): This church was built in the city centre in the 12C on the site of the former Roman forum (hence the 'in foro' tag) in typical Pisan-Luccan style. Work on the flanks and the tall façade continued until the late 13C. The façade is similar to that of the cathedral and is probably by the same workshop (Giudetto da Como being one of the artists). It was really intended that the nave should be built considerably higher, and this can be seen from the tall free-standing colonnaded gable. Financial problems made it impossible for the nave and the left aisle to be built up any further. The lower section of the façade has seven blind arches with tall, slender, full columns above three portals. The lintel, decorated with reliefs, below the rose-window in the tympanum is a striking feature of the central portal, which is also the largest of the portals. Above this lintel, four tiers of loggias were built, of which the upper two, narrower loggias form the free-standing gable. This gable is crowned by a more recent, bronze-clad marble statue of St.Michael slaying the dragon, with two angels at the corners. The imaginatively designed little columns are formed in completely different ways (flat, coiled, chiselled, and covered with: coloured marble incrustation), while the capitals are decorated with monster and animal motifs. This arrangement continues along the flanks, although there is only one row of columns above the blind arches, a feature which may be compared with the cathedral of Pisa. Diotisalvi, the architect of the baptistery in Pisa, designed the apse in the clear Pisan style, that is to say with completely identical arches and columns. On the right side of the façade is the *Virgin with halo*, carved by M.Civitali in

S.Michele, façade ▷

S.Michele, gable

1480 after the city had recovered from the plague. The plain campanile has rows of arches, built in the 12C, which increase in number the further up the building they are; the top was not built until the 19C. The portals at the ends of the transepts are locked at present. They have 12C architraves, richly decorated in places.

Columns divide the interior into a nave and two aisles and some have antique capitals. In the 16C the Romanesque timber ceiling was replaced by vaults. In the right transept are a terracotta *Virgin and Child* by A. della Robbia, and a 13C painted wooden Cross from a Luccan workshop.

S.Frediano (Piazza S.Frediano): A low Romanesque church was built in the N. of the city in 1112–47 on the site of the Basilica S.Vincenzo, which had been founded by Bishop Fredia-

nus, who was later canonized. Excavations carried out in the interior in 1950 have revealed the design of the original building (particularly near the font). In the 13C, the walls of the nave were increased in height, and two chapels (the former baptismal chapel and the Cappella S. Croce), which today are beside the entrance, were incorporated in the church. The battlemented, six-storeyed campanile was built with arched windows whose number decreases the further down the tower they are (5th and 6th storeys: four windows, 3rd and 4th storeys: three windows, 1st and 2nd storeys: two windows). This campanile was for a long time used for defence. The gable rises above the narrow colonnaded gallery of the very plain façade, which is subdivided by pilaster strips. The gable is adorned by an Italo-Byzantine *mosaic* shimmering in gold and other colours,

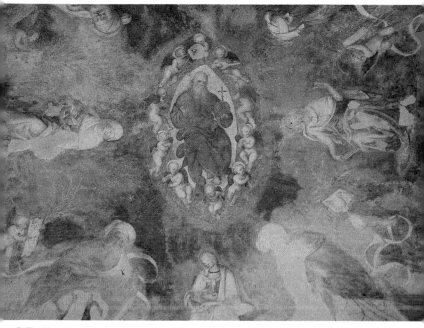

S.Frediano, ceiling fresco, 2nd chapel

with an *Ascension* which was probably painted by B. B.Berlinghieri in *c.* 1228 and was restored in 1829. The side wings with their Renaissance chapels were added later.

The interior, with its nave and two aisles, is subdivided by columns (some of these are genuine classical capitals from the Roman amphitheatre). The inside wall of the façade was frescoed by a 15C Florentine artist (*Visitation, St.Peter and St.Paul*) and by A.Aspertini (*Virgin and Saints*). Aspertini also painted the frescos in the second side chapel on the left, and the best of these is the *Transfer of the Volto Santo from Luni to Lucca*, dating from 1508–9. The altar of St.Zita, the patron saint of domestic servants, is also here. In the 1st side chapel, the baptismal chapel, there is a very delicately carved Romanesque *font*—the work of several artists in the 12C.

S.Giovanni (Piazza S.Giovanni): This church originally known as S.Reparata was the site of the cathedral of Lucca until the 8C. Only the main portal with lions and an architrave (*Virgin Mary between two angels and apostles* by Villano), and also the right side, still survive from the church which was rebuilt in the 12C. Apart from the square baptistery, which was built in the 14C and has a tall dome, the rest of the structure dates from 1622. The basilican interior has a nave and two aisles and is articulated by classical columns.

S.Francesco (Piazza D.Francesco): Work on building this single-aisled church began in 1228, the year when St.Francis died. Most of the present structure dates from the 14&17C. The early Gothic *portal* of the façade is flanked by two classical sarcophagi. Inside, apart from the intarsia choir stalls and the 14&15C frescos, there are also numerous *tombs* including that of the composer L.Boccherini (1743–1805) and Bishop Giovanni Guidiccioni (1500–41).

Chiesa del Salvatore (Piazza del Salvatore): The upper section of the façade of this 12C church was rebuilt in neo-Gothic style in the 19C. The right side portal has a portrayal of the *Baptism of the infant Nicholas* by the Pisan artist Balduino (*c.* 1180).

S.Maria della Rosa (Via della Rosa): This church, which has in the mean time been enlarged several times, was built in 1309. The Pisan Gothic arcades along the flanks, and the 15C main portal, are two charming features from the school of M.Civitali. The interior, which has a nave and two aisles and was rebuilt in 1609, contains part of the Roman city wall, on to which the church was probably built.

S.Maria Forisportam (Piazza S. Maria Forisportam): This church, also known as S.Maria Bianca, was built in the early 13C outside the then Roman city walls—hence the name 'foris portam' (outside the gate). The Luccan ornaments, which in other buildings are customary features of the columns and loggias, are absent from the 13C marble façade, which was begun in the Pisan style (the upper section is 16C, like the nave). But the three portals, whose tympana contain reliefs from the 12&13C, are more richly decorated. Works by Guercino, some classical columns and capitals, and the font made from a 3–5C sarcophagus, are features of the interior (nave and two aisles).

S.Giusto (S. continuation of the Via Fillungo): This church begun in the late 12C has a most harmonious façade. The middle portal (early-13C), with its ornaments and projecting lions (by Giudetto da Como, *c.* 1210), is built in the richly decorative Luccan style, while the two side portals were created in plain Pisan forms. The interior was altered in baroque style in the 17C.

S.Allesandro (W. of the Via Vittorio

S.Frediano, font, detail

Veneto): This 11C church is the oldest church in Lucca to have survived in its original form. The only portal of the grey-and-white striped marble façade is crowned by a triangular gable, and has a relief of Pope Alexander (13C).

S.Paolino (Via S.Paolino): This is the only Renaissance church in Lucca, and was built by Baccio da Montelupo in 1522–39 on the site of a Roman building, possibly a temple. Inside, the decorations include frescos from the life of St.Paolino (17C) in the gallery, a pre-Christian sarcophagus behind the altar, and the inlaid choir stalls (1563) by S.Magni.

S.Giulia (N. of the Via S.Croce): The upper section of the marble façade of this otherwise Romanesque chapel is Gothic, with a double window and a frieze on the arch (1334).

S.Pietro Somaldi (Via della Fratta): Work began on the present church which goes back to a foundation by Sumuald (c. 700) about 1200. In the gable of the white-and-grey striped marble façade (1248) there is a double tier of loggias consisting of columns with richly decorated capitals. The apse, and also the upper section of the massive campanile, were built in the late 14C.

S.Romano (Piazza S.Romano): This former Dominican church, built in c. 1280, contains numerous monuments to old families from the 13–15C. The area around the apse was enlarged in 1373. The baroque decorations are 17C.

S.Cristoforo (Via Fillungo): This church with its black-and-white striped façade was built in the 13C above an older structure. The three portals preceded by five arches date from this period, while the rose-window is of more recent date.

Palazzo Mazzarosa (Via S.Croce): Inside this 17C baroque palazzo there is a collection of sculptures, including a Roman sarcophagus with a depiction of Venus and Adonis. There is also a rich collection of paintings.

S.Frediano, font

S.Frediano

Palazzo Pretorio (Piazza S.Michele, corner of Via Vittorio Veneto): Matteo Civitali and his son Nicolao began the building in 1492, and it was enlarged by Vincenzo Civitali in 1588. Today this former seat of the Potestà is a law court. Other features are the open portico with its 19C statues commemorating M.Civitali amongst others, the double-arched Renaissance windows above, and the 17C clock on the façade.

Palazzo Controni-Pfanner (Via degli Asili): This palazzo was built in 1667. But the staircase with its arcades, the well-tended garden, and the statues in the garden, all date from the 18C.

Palazzo Bernardini (Via S. Croce): N.Civitali built this massive Renaissance palazzo in 1512. The portal and windows have beautiful frames, and the inner courtyard has a colonnaded portico.

Palazzo Cenami (Via Roma): This building was erected, probably in the early 16C, by N.Civitali. Roman and Florentine components were used in the structure.

Palazzo della Provincia (also known as the Palazzo della Signoria or Palazzo Ducale, Piazza Napoleone): The construction of this palazzo (today the left-hand section) with its arcaded courtyard was begun in 1578 by the Florentine architect Ammanati on the site of a small part of the enormous Fortezza Augusta which had been built in 1322–6 by order of Cartruccio Castracane degli Antelminelli. It was not until 1728 that the other wing was added by F.Pini, probably to plans by Juvarra. The interior decoration is by L.Nottolini, who carried out further alterations in 1819–47.

Palazzo Guinigi (Via S.Andrea, corner of Via Guinigi): This imposing brick building was erected for the Guinigi family and completed by 1400. There are Gothic windows with two, three and four pointed arches, and also a massive tower. Opposite there is another palazzo which dates from the 15C and belongs to the same family. It is identical to the Palazzo Guinigi apart from the tower. The two palazzi are therefore frequently known as the Case Guinigi.

Museo Nazionale di Villa Guinigi (Via della Quarquonia): This brick palace outside the then city wall (dating from 1260) was built for Paolo Guinigi, the Signore of Lucca, in 1418. The ground floor has an open portico above which there are narrow windows framed by arches. Since 1968, the clearly arranged *Museo Nazionale di Villa Guinigi* has been housed in the halls and portico of this villa, which was outstandingly well restored after World War 2. Medieval works of art and mementoes (some in memory of Puccini) are on display here, along with classical finds such as Etruscan vases (with a depiction of Theseus), mosaics, Roman marble sculptures and Etruscan burial objects.

Pinacoteca Nazionale (Palazzo Mansi, Via Galli Tassi): This palace was built for the Mansi family in the 17C. They also owned the well-known villa of Mansi near Segromigno. This building, very plain on the outside, was sumptuously decorated in the 18C (including the interior decoration and the period furniture in the halls). The State-owned collection of paintings, which was founded by Marie Louise and completed and donated by Leopold II, was recently moved into this building. The gallery includes works from the 15–19C, including some by Fra Bartolommeo (*Holy Father with Magdalene and Catherine*, 1509), Morazzone (*Annunciation*), Lorenzetti (*Madonna and*

S.Michele in Foro ▷

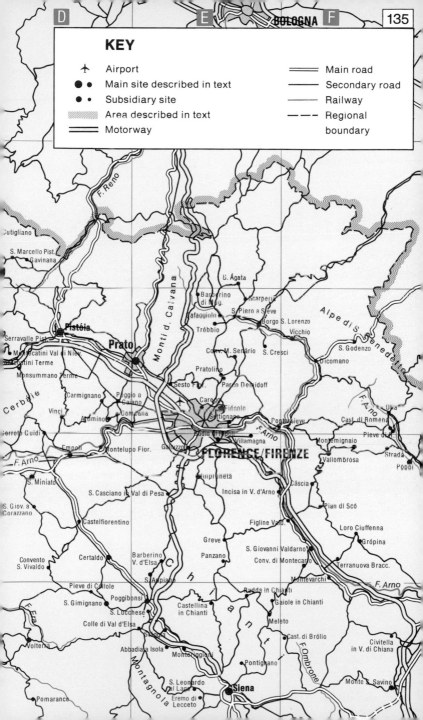

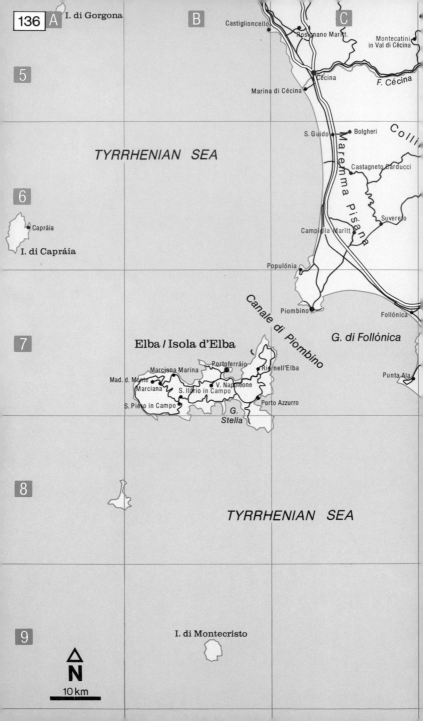

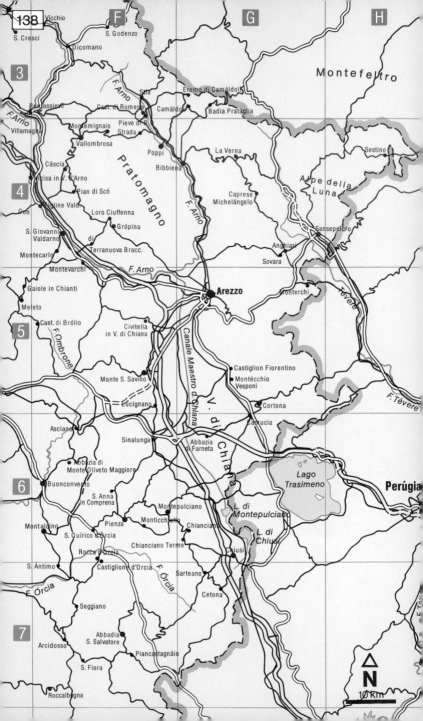

Child), Beccafumi, J. da Pontormo and A. del Sarto.

Opera del Duomo (Piazza degli Antelminelli): The most valuable item in the cathedral treasure kept here (Tesoro del Duomo) is the Cross of the Pisans. Made in 1424–39, it consists of a gilded silver tree.

Roman amphitheatre (on the Via Fillungo): This elliptical amphitheatre dates from the 2C AD but in the Middle Ages Lucca's citizens built new houses on its foundations and some of the old parts of the structure were re-used for this purpose. This can clearly be seen in two of the 54 surviving rows of arches which the visitor walking along the Via dell'Anfiteatro may observe around the former amphitheatre.

Teatro Romano: The remains of a Roman theatre have been discovered beside the houses of the Via S.Sebastiano and in the adjoining Piazza delle Grazie. The campanile of the former church of S.Agostino is on a row of arches which originally belonged to this theatre.

City walls: In Roman times, Lucca was surrounded by massive walls up to 30 ft. high. A larger ring of walls was built in the 13C, and in the 15C this was expanded once again. The present fortification was constructed by Flemish architects in 1504–1645. These walls 13,535 ft. long are 39 ft. tall on the outside and had 11 bastions defended by 124 cannons. They were also surrounded by a fosse 100 ft. wide and were regarded as impregnable. But the defences were never put to the test because the city was never besieged after the wall was built. However, in 1812, the walls protected Lucca from another great danger, that of being flooded by the wild river Serchio, which had burst its banks. From 1815 onwards, by order of Marie Louise of Bourbon-Parma, the fortifications were converted into a public park and the walls and bastions were planted with lime trees for the most part. Today the 11 bastions with their monuments (19C)

Lucca, S.Maria Forisportam, tympanum

Lucca, S.Pietro Somaldi, portal

Massa, Palazzo Cybo-Malaspina

look like lovingly tended castle gardens. Before passing in to the 'Città dall'arborato archio' (the 'city with the tree-ringed girdle'), the visitor is advised to take a walk along the fortifications surrounding Lucca, because from here there is a splendid view not only of the city, but also into the flat valley of the Serchio, stretching as far as the Apuan Alps and Monte Pisano. The rich baroque decoration of the six 17C gatehouse towers makes them look like palazzi façades. Two gates inside the present walls were both built in 1260, in addition to the ring of walls erected in the 13C.

Also worth seeing: The church of *S.Caterina* with its notable portal was built in the 18C in a side street leading off the Via Vittorio Emanuele. The church of *S.Maria Corteorlandini* (Via Tegrini) was built in the 13C,

while its baroque façade is of later date; the lion portal on the right flank is also interesting. The church of *S.Maria del Suffragio* in the Via del Suffragio has a three-arched portico built in the 17C. The church of *S.Maria dei Servi* (near the Piazza Bernardini) is 14C. The *birthplace of G.Puccini* is in the Via Poggio, opposite the church of S.Michele in Foro. The *house where the composer L.Boccherini was born* stands in the Piazza S.Michele amidst numerous medieval houses. The Palazzo Guidiccioni (Via Fillungo), built in the 16C, houses the *State archive*, where valuable documents and manuscripts associated with Lucca are preserved.

Environs: Arliano (9 km. W.): The 8C *Pieve* is probably a Lombard baptismal church.
Marlia (8 km. NE): Prince Metternich visited the *Villa Reale*, which

was built in the 18C, enlarged in 1805–14 by Elisa Baciocchi-Bonaparte, the sister of Napoleon, and surrounded by a splendid garden.

Rigoli (12 km. SW): There is an 11C font in the 12C *Pieve S.Marco*.

Segromigno (5 km. E. of Marlia): The so-called *Villa Mansi* was built in the 16C. It was the country seat of the Mansi family from Lucca, who also owned the Palazzo Mansi in Lucca.

54100 Massa
Massa-Carrara   p.134☐B 2

Massa has a charming situation on the small river Frigido and the spurs of the Apuan Alps and with Carrara it is the joint capital of the province. The earliest document to mention Massa dates from 822 and the city, which was known as *Massa Vecchia* from the 10C onwards, stood below the fortress of the Malaspina; although it was not until the 11C that it rose to any importance. The nearby marble bridge and the export harbour 4 km. to the SW (today the Marina di Massa) were the reason why, in the next century, Massa changed hands several times, passing from Lucca to Milan, Pisa and Florence. From 1442 to 1790, Massa was the Signoria of the Malaspina-Fosdivino (until 1553) and Cybo-Malaspina. Alberico the Great (1554–1623) was a member of the Cybo-Malaspina family. He ordered the New Massa (*Massa Nuova*, also known as *Massa-Cybea*), to be systematically laid out with broad streets and large squares. Today the city, which is the seat of a bishop, has several important factories.

Cathedral of S.Pietro e S.Francesco (Via Dante): The cathedral built under the Malaspina-Fondinovo in the 15C was subsequently altered in line with the prevailing style. Thus a modern façade was built of Carrara marble. There are tombs of the Cybo-Malaspina and some bishops in the baroque single-aisled interior. The baroque altar of the Cappella del SS. Sacramento has a fresco of the *Madonna* by Pinturicchio.

Palazzo Cybo-Malaspina (Piazza Aranci): This palazzo was begun in 1557 on the site of a villa. But the courtyard, with two storeys of loggias, was built in 1665 and the red-and-yellow façade dates from 1701. Today the prefecture is housed here.

Malaspina fortress: The castle, the core of which is medieval, stands on a hill above the city. In the 15&16C, the Cybo-Malaspina family built a Renaissance palace here. A colonnaded loggia connects it to the medieval buildings. The richly decorated W. *inner courtyard* is also worth seeing. The outer bastions were erected in the 16&17C.

Environs: Forte dei Marmi (11 km. S.): This town takes its name from the fortification (Piazza Garibaldi) built by P.Leopoldo in 1788 in order to protect the shipment of marble blocks. Today, Forte dei Marmi is probably the most elegant resort on the Riviera della Versilia, with splendid alleys and beautiful sandy beaches. Works, mainly by contemporary artists, are shown in

Massa, cathedral

Massa Marittima, cathedral

summer in the *Galleria Communale d'Arte Moderna* (Via Canducci).

Marina di Massa (4 km. SW): In the church of *S.Maria degli Uglivi* of this popular resort, which has a beautiful pine wood and a sandy beach, there is an interesting carved wooden St. Leonard by J. della Quercia.

58024 Massa Marittima

Grosseto   p.136☐D 6

This area on the S. slopes of the Colline Mettalifere ('metalliferous hills') between the valleys of Pecora, Zanca and Noni has been inhabited since prehistoric times. In these mountains, Etruscans and Romans extracted copper, silver (most of the deposits are still of these metals) and iron. This city, called 'Massa' ('large country estate') by the Romans, gained in importance after Populonia had been destroyed by the Saracens in the early 8C and the bishop had subsequently fled to Massa, which was further away from the sea. The resulting develop-

ment turned Massa, in the high Middle Ages (11–13C), into the most important city in the Maremma, and this was why, in the early 14C, it was given the nickname of 'Marittima', referring to the entire coastal Maremma district, not to the coast itself. In the early 13C, there were some 10,000 people living in the *Città Vecchia*, which was built mainly in the 11–13C (today it is the lower city, with mostly Romanesque buildings). Massa was a free community from 1228 onwards. The so-called 'Codice Minerario', the first mining statutes in Italy, was drawn up here, and today it is preserved in the city archive in Piazza Cavour. Massa Marittima was much contested owing to its mines. It began by being under Pisan protection until it was conquered by the Sienese in 1335. In 1365 it was annexed to the republic of Siena. The Fortezza dei Senesi, and the city wall, which is still in good condition, were built in 1337 in the upper city—the Gothic, largely 14–16C, *Città Nuova*. In 1555–9, the city, whose mines had in the mean time been closed down, was,

Massa Marittima, cathedral, detail

Massa Marittima, cathedral, bronze relief

Massa Marittima, cathedral, Roman sarcophagus, 3C, above it a 14C Madonna

along with Siena, annexed to the Duchy of Tuscany. Massa Marittima progressively declined in importance, and lost many of its inhabitants as a result of the spread of malaria. The mines were reopened again in the early 19C, and the marshy area of the Maramma has been drained. This dispelled the threat of malaria and people were able to settle here again.

Cathedral of S.Cerbone (Piazza Garibaldi): This cathedral was probably built on the remains of an 11C early Romanesque church, which is discernible on the S. side of the present building. It may have been G.Pisano who, in 1287–1304, built the Pisan Romanesque extension of the nave and erected the apse and transept. The cathedral itself dates from 1228–67 and is also Pisan Romanesque. The façade is built of warm, golden-brown stone and is decorated by tall blind arcades under whose arches there are circles and rhombi. Stories from the life of St.Cerbonius are shown in the 12C Romanesque *relief* above the main portal. In the upper section of the façade, a second, ten-arched loggia has been built above a five-arched colonnade in the triangular gable, which is crowned by three Gothic battlements. The middle columns of the loggia in the gable rest upon various figures—such as a kneeling man's back, horses, and griffins—and these are attributed to the followers of G.Pisano. The green-and-white transverse strips between the two loggias continue in the upper part of the flanks (of the nave) above the slightly Gothic arcades. The square campanile, with its arched windows that increase in size the further up the campanile they are, was built in the 13C. In 1928, the crown of this campanile was torn down and

Massa Marittima, Palazzo Comunale

Massa Marittima, gatehouse tower

rebuilt.The columns in the interior, which has a nave and two aisles and was not vaulted until the 17C (there was a timber roof until then), are of varying height and they support Corinthian and Romanesque capitals. The large *rose-window* (on the inner wall of the façade), with its scenes from the life of St.Cerbonius, is the work of Girolamo da Pietrasanta (14C). The *baptistery* in the right aisle has an octagonal *font* which was chiselled from a single block of travertine and, in 1267, was decorated by Giroldo da Como with a relief from the life of St.John the Baptist (from the annunciation to Zacharias to the beheading) and various other images (including Christ). Above this, in the middle of the font, a marble tabernacle crowned by ag figure of John the Baptist and dating from 1447 has 12 niches with patriarchs and prophets. The *Cappella della Madonna* (in the

left arm of the transept) preserves a panel painting dating from 1316 which was probably influenced by the 'Maestà' by Duccio di Buoninsegna in the cathedral museum in Siena. The gold *reliquary of St.Cerbonius*, a 16C Sienese work in the form of a Gothic temple, is among the valuable church treasures in the underground *Cappella delle Reliquie* (entrance to the left of the main altar). The visitor passes through this reliquary chapel into the crypt which is underneath the apse and contains the marble sarcophagus known as the *Arca di S.Cerbone* made by the Sienese artist Goro di Gregorio in 1324. Scenes from the life of St.Cerbonius are depicted in eight reliefs at the sides of the sarcophagus. (cf. the above-mentioned relief over the main portal.) There are ten more reliefs in medallions on the cover. 11 marble statues stand against the walls, and there are also some frescos (Crucifixion, Passion) from the school of Duccio di Buoninsegna.

S.Agostino (Corso A.Diaz): The façade of this Romanesque-Gothic church begun in 1299–1313 is built of travertine and is entirely plain, while the portal is Romanesque. The Gothic polygonal apse was built from 1348 onwards to designs mainly by Domenico di Agostino. The flanks have pointed windows. The single-aisled interior with its timber roof houses a marble ciborium (in the apsidal chapel) and a 15C terracotta of the Madonna and Child (in the chapel to the left of the choir).

S.Francesco (near the Via G. Verdi): The transept and the chapels around the sanctuary are all that survive of this 13C church.

Palazzo Pretorio (also known as Palazzo dell'Podestà, Piazza Garibaldi, opposite the front of the cathedral): From the second storey upwards, rows of fine double-arched windows give a more open appearance to the façade of this Romanesque palazzo, which was built of travertine from 1230 onwards. Coats-of-arms from Massa Marittima and also Siena, together with other features, were attached to the façade between 1426 and 1633.

Palazzo Comunale (Piazza Garibaldi, beside and to the right of the Palazzo Pretorio): The sturdy battlemented tower, the *Torre dei Conti di Biserno* (to the left of the Palazzo Comunale proper) joins this Romanesque palazzo, which was built of travertine by Sienese artists in the 13&14C, to the two-storeyed 13C house of the Counts Biserno. Three storeys with double-arched windows were built above the arcaded ground floor (13&14C). Like the tower, the Palazzo Comunale is also crowned by a battlement (19C). The Medici coat-of-arms between the first and second rows of windows dates from 1563.

Inside, the works of art include the *Madonna Enthroned* which was painted by A.Lorenzetti in 1330 and is probably one of the most famous examples of Sienese painting, *ceiling frescos* dating from *c.* 1525, and two panel paintings by Sassetta (*c.* 1450).

Fortezza dei Senesi (NW of the Piazza Matteotti, Città Nuova): This fortress built by the Sienese in 1337 was partially torn down in 1774 and 1845 owing to the construction of the hospital. However, large sections of the wall (some of them part of the hospital) still survive.

Arco dei Senesi (Piazza Matteotti): This arch was built in 1337 in order to link the square clock tower (Torre del Candeliere, 1228) to the double gate (Porta alle Silici) of the Fortezza.

Museo Archeologico (Piazza Matteotti, opposite the Torre del Candeliere): This museum, which is closed from November to March, is housed in the splendid Renaissance Palazzo delle Armi. In addition to a collection of Etruscan finds (mainly burial objects such as vases and urns) and Roman coins and vases; majolicas from Faenza and Gubbio, as well as various panels from the Sienese school (including *Gabriel* by Sassetta) and mementoes of Garibaldi are on display here.

Also worth seeing: The dilapidated *Loggia del Comune* (Piazza Garibaldi) was restored from 1872 onwards, while the upper storey was not built until later. A Roman she-wolf, the emblem of the city of Siena to which Massa Marittima belonged from 1365–1555, stands on a column at a corner of the *bishop's palace* (Piazza Garibaldi), which was restored in 1914. Massa Marittima minted its own coins (zecca) in the Romanesque-Gothic *Palazzina della Zecca* which was built in 1317 and stands to the left of the Palazzo Pretorio. Massa Marittima was still a free city at that time.

Environs: Chiusdino (26 km. NE): It was here, in the old village belonging to the bishop's castle, that Galgano Guidotti, the knight, spent the wild years of his youth. There is a Byzantine copper Cross in the church of *S.Martino*, and by the church of the *Compagnia di S.Galgano* we find a relief of St.Galgano dating from 1466.

Follonica (23 km. SW): The cast-iron portico on the *parish church* is a reminder of the fact that Follonica, in the 19C, was the administrative centre of the Colline Metallifere. Today Follonica is a popular resort with a wonderful view of the island of Elba. The 'Carnevale Maremmano' is celebrated here every year.

S.Galgano (32 km. NE): The *abbey* took its name from its founder, the knight Galgano Guidotti, who in 1180 lived here as a hermit on Monte Siepi (1,110 ft.) and built a small Romanesque church. This round chapel contains *frescos* by A.Lorenzetti. The Cistercian order settled here in the 13C and built a monastery which soon attained great importance. Thus, the monks of S.Galgano were often

appointed as arbitrators and took over the duties of notaries. After the abbey had been devastated by Hawkwood, the 14C condottiere, it was finally abandoned in the 16C and subsequently fell into decay—with the vaults collapsing in the 18C and so on. The cruciform church has a nave, two aisles and a square-ended sanctuary, and was built in 1224–88 of brick and travertine (for the supporting elements) in the purest Gothic forms. Sixteen sturdy pillars, each having four attached columns and wonderful capitals, divide the roofless structure into a nave and two aisles, while at the sides most of the vaults have survived. Apart from the abbey of Fossanova, the ruins are also probably the most characteristic example of the Cistercian Gothic style in Italy.

Scarlino (20 km. SW): There is a fine view of the island of Elba from the ruins of the 13C Pisan *castle*. The town of Scarlino was an Etruscan foundation. 13 km. E. of Scarlino is the village of **Gavorrano**. Like Scarlino, it was settled by the Etruscans. Still very medieval, it contains the remains of *walls, bulwarks* and *gates*.

Abbazia di S.Antimo (Montalcino), abbey church

Montalcino, Abbazia di S.Antimo 1 13C wooden crucifix **2** Capitals on columns and pillars with animal figures, plants and geometrical patterns (chessboard, etc.) **3** At the high altar is a 12C wooden carving (Madonna and Child) **4** Choir ambulatory separated from sanctuary by columns; 3 chapels

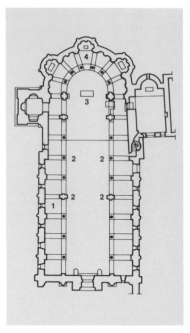

53024 Montalcino

Siena   p.136□F 6

This medieval city on a hill above the valleys of the rivers Ombrone and Asso is surrounded by a well-preserved wall. It was inhabited by the Etruscans and Romans, and was under the protection of the abbey of S.Antimo from 814 onwards. However, in the 11C it became a free community which was soon hotly contested by Florence and Siena owing to its good hillside position. After Siena had taken control of the city in 1202 in the face of considerable resistance by the inhabitants, Montalcino joined the Florentine Guelphs in 1260. After suffering a devastating defeat at Montaperti in September 1260 at the hands of the Ghibellines of Siena, Montalcino was completely destroyed. The Sienese built a new castle in 1361, and this castle, as the last stronghold of the 'Repubblica di Siena in Montalcino', resisted the attacks of Cosimo I of Tuscany for four years from 1555 onwards until, in the peace of Câteau Cambrésis (1559), Montalcino was finally incorporated into Cosimo I's Grand Duchy of Tuscany.

Cathedral (N. of the Via Ricasoli): The cathedral was built in classical style in 1818–32 on the remains of an 11C Romanesque parish church.

S.Agostino (Piazza del Popolo): This 14C Romanesque Gothic brick church was built from the remains of one destroyed by the Sienese in 1260. Features include the white Gothic marble portal, the rose-window, and, inside, various 14C frescos.

Palazzo Comunale (Piazza del Popolo): This palace was built in the 13&14C and, with its tall, slender tower, bears various coats-of-arms. The statue of Cosimo I, carved by G.Bertini in 1564, is in the loggia built in the 14&15C.

Castle and city wall: The castle (rocca) was built by Siena in 1361 and dominates the city from above. The city itself is surrounded by an old wall with six gates and defensive towers.

Museo Civico (Piazza Cavour): Paintings from the 14&15C Sienese school and various small objets d'art are on display in the town museum. Amongst other exhibits, there are a 12C Bible, a polyptych by Bartolo di

Abbazia di S.Antimo, apse

Montepulciano, cathedral, Madonna and Child

Fredi, and some terracottas by the della Robbias (13&14C).

Museo Archeologico (beside the Museo Civico): Prehistoric and Etruscan finds from the surrounding area are on display in the former pharmacy of the hospital. Some of the rooms are frescoed throughout by Sodoma and Tamagni.

Museo Diocesano (Via Ricasoli): The highlights of this diocesan museum, which is housed in the former Augustinian monastery, are an Assumption by Girolamo di Benvenuto, a Madonna and Child by Bartolo di Fredi, a Crucifixion by Sodoma, and an early-13C painted wooden crucifix.

Also worth seeing: The *church* built in 1325 has some fine Romanesque

capitals, which are probably from the building destroyed in 1260. The pilgrimage church of the *Madonna del Soccorso* was built in the 17C (near the city wall).

Environs: Abbazia di S.Antimo (9 km. S.): This Benedictine abbey in the Starcia valley, standing at the bottom of a hill, was first mentioned in 813 and, owing to large Carolingian gifts, was one of the wealthiest in Tuscany. However, an inexorable decline began in the late 13C and led to the abolition of the abbey by Pope Pius II in 1462. The abbey buildings fell down almost completely, but the *church*, built in golden-brown travertine in 1118–1260, has survived and is among the finest examples in Tuscany. Its architecture is in French Cistercian (e.g. the ambulatory) and Italian Romanesque (e.g. the free-standing campanile) styles. This fact is probably explained by the intellectual and cultural links which the Carolingians established with France. The portal of the plain façade was built by the Maître de Cambestany under a double-arched window, while the lintel is by a Pisan artist. The two side portals decorated with reliefs were built of older sections from the 9C. Three apsidioles radiate from the semicircular early Romanesque main apse. The basilican interior is divided by columns and pillars to form a nave and two aisles. The *capitals* which are decorated with animals, geometric patterns (such as chessboards) and flowers are almost all of alabaster. Galleries were built above the side aisles, and in 1462 those on the right-hand side were converted into dwellings. The choir is surrounded by an ambulatory formed by columns and having three small apsidal chapels. A Roman tombstone dating from AD 347 is used as an altar in the 11C crypt.

The decorations include a carved 13C crucifix (in the left aisle) and a 12C carved wooden Madonna and Child (on the altar). The 'Carolingian chapel' abutting to the left of the apse was probably built of rough-hewn stone prior to 813.

53045 Montepulciano
Siena   p.138☐F 6

This walled city occupies a picturesque site on the elongated ridge of *Mons Politianus* above the fertile valleys of the rivers Chiana and Orcia. Montepulciano was settled in Etruscan times, when it was the outlying fortress defending Clusium (Chiusi). It was a free community from the 13C onwards. For almost 200 years it was allied alternately to Siena and Florence before joining Florence in 1390. With one short interruption (1494–1512, during the banishment of the Medici), it stayed with Florence and, along with Florence, became part of the Grand Duchy of Tuscany. In 1561, Montepulciano was granted the bishopric of Chiusi, and was also awarded the status of a town. Christina of Lorraine ruled the town as a duchy from 1609

Montepulciano, panorama

until her death in 1636. It had been bequeathed to her by her deceased husband Grand Duke Ferdinand I. After this, Montepulciano was once again attached to the Grand Duchy, and they both became a part of the Kingdom of Italy in 1860.

Cathedral (Piazza Grande): Montepulciano supplanted Chiusi as the seat of the bishop in 1561. Some 30 years later, from 1592–1630, this late Renaissance church was built to a design by L.Scalza with a cruciform ground plan on the site of the 15C parish church of S.Maria; the still incomplete campanile survives from the previous building. The façade with its three portals and three windows is still in the rough and its articulation is difficult to make out.

The very simplicity of the interior, which has a nave and two aisles divided by pillars, makes a most harmonious impression. Its finest feature is the tomb which was made by Michelozzo in *c.* 1430 for Bartolomeo Aragazzi (the secretary of Pope Martin V).

In the Sala Capitolare there is a draw-

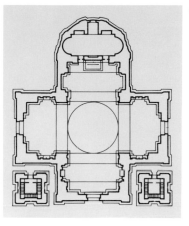

Montepulciano, Madonna di S.Biagio A building laid out in the form of a Greek cross with 2 free-standing towers and an apse added to the S.; high altar, gold stucco and frescos from the 16C

ing dating from 1885 and showing a reconstruction of the Aragazzi monument. The triptych (with the *Assumption, Annunciation, Coronation, scenes*

Montepulciano, Piazza Grande, well

Montepulciano, Madonna di S.Biagio

Montepulciano, Palazzo Comunale

Montepulciano, Palazzo Tarugi

from the Passion and *scenes from the Old Testament*) was made by Taddeo di Bartolo who completed the work not later than 1403.

S.Agostino (Via Roma): Work on the construction of this church was begun in 1427 to a design by Michelozzo, who himself built the lower section of the splendid façade in Florentine Gothic style in 1440. The portal zone is subdivided by fluted pilasters (an early Renaissance stylistic element) and by the portal itself, whose round arches are derived from Gothic forms. In the tympanum, the terracotta relief of the *Madonna and Child between John the Baptist and St.Augustine* is also by Michelozzo. There are four pointed niches for statues to the right and left of the tympanum, and in a third zone above the tympanum is a rose-window below the triangular gable.

Madonna di S.Biagio (2 km. SW, a little way outside the town): This Renaissance church was built in 1518–45 amidst open country on the ground plan of a Greek cross and has a high central dome. It is the masterpiece of A. da Sangallo the elder and its purity makes it one of the most impressive works of the late Renaissance. The semicircular apse which concludes the S. transept is closed off inside the building and is used as a sacristy. Only one of the two campaniles was completed. Although freestanding, they were built close to the façade. The tower is crowned by a pyramidal spire.

Opposite the church is the Renaissance parson's house (*Canonica*), which was built in 1595, again to a design by A. da Sangallo the elder, who was already dead at this time. Its loggia of Ionic columns stands above an arcade. Sangallo the elder also

designed the fountain outside the parson's house.

S.Maria dei Servi (Via del Poliziano): The Gothic façade of this 14C church has a fine portal with a pointed arch. A.Pozzo decorated the interior in baroque style in the late 17C. The altarpieces, which are by Sienese artists of the 14C, include the 'Madonna della Santoreggia' at the 2nd altar on the left, and the 'Madonna and Child' by the school of Duccio at the 3rd altar on the left.

S.Lucia (Via Saffi): The interior of this baroque church built by Flaminico del Turco in 1653 has been altered in the classical style and contains a 16C wooden Cross by Alessi and a Virgin by Signorelli.

Other churches: The baroque church of *Chiesa del Gesù* (Via di Vo-laia) was built in 1733. The interior decorations of this centrally planned building are by A.Pozzo and others. *S.Agnese* (outside the Porta al Prato) was built in 1311; 16&17C frescos are to be found in the cloister with its interesting colonnade. The Franciscan church of *S.Francesco* (Via Ricci) was much altered in the 18C, although a Gothic portal survives from the 13C.

Palazzo Comunale (Piazza Grande, W. side): This three-storeyed, crenellated palazzo, with its tower crowned by Guelph battlements and its tower crest, was long thought to have been built in the late 14C. It is only since 1965, when the plans were published, that it has been known that it was modelled on the Palazzo Vecchio in Florence and dates from 1440–65, having been designed by Michelozzo.

Palazzo Contucci (Piazza Grande E. side, opposite the Palazzo Comunale): Work on this palazzo was begun by A. da Sangallo the elder in 1519 by order of Cardinal Giovanni Maria del Monte (the future Pope Julius III). It was probably completed by B.Peruzzi. The upper storey was not added until the baroque and the large hall has trompe l'oeil paintings by A.Pozzo dating from the late 17C.

Palazzo Tarugi (Piazza Grande, opposite the cathedral façade): This palazzo, which has a loggia supported by pillars on the ground floor, is attributed to Vignola. It may though have been built to a design by A. da Sangallo the elder. On the second floor there is an arcade, closed today, behind a balustrade. The well in front of the palace known as the *Pozzo dei Grifi e dei Leoni* was erected in front of the palace in 1520.

Palazzo Cocconi (Via Gracciano nel Corso): This palazzo, probably built by A. da Sangallo the elder in 1518–34, was for a long time owned by the del Pecora family, who gained the Signoria of Montepulciano in the late 14C.

Palazzo Bucelli (Via Gracciano nel Corso): Pietro Bucelli, the owner, ordered Etruscan urns and Etruscan and Roman inscriptions to be embedded in three rows, one above the other, in the base of this 17C palazzo.

Palazzo Cervini (Via di Voltaia nel Corso): A building with projecting wings (1518–34), erected for Cardinal Marcello Cervini to a design by A. da Sangallo the elder.

Other palaces: The *Palazzo Avignonesi* (Via Gracciano nel Corso) was built in the 16C, probably by Vignola. Today the 14C Gothic *Palazzo del Capitano del Popolo* (Via Ricci) houses the law court. The *Palazzo Ricci* (Via Ricci, opposite the Palazzo del Capitano del Popolo) was built in the early 16C. The *Palazzo Gagnoni-Grugni* (Via di Voltaia nel Corso), begun by Vignola in the 16C, was not completed. The *Palazzo Benincasa* (Via Piana/Via Mazzini) is built of

Montepulciano, Museo Civico

brick and travertine and has a fine baroque portal.

Fortezza Medicea (Strada della Fortezza): This fortress was freely rebuilt in 1885, although still in medieval form. The Porta di Lagnano (Via del Poliziano, behind the Casa del Poliziano) was built in the 14C as part of the old medieval wall.

Museo Civico (Palazzo Neri-Orselli, Via Ricci): This brick building with its portal and double-arched windows was built in Sienese Gothic style in the 14C. Terracottas by the della Robbia family (including *St.John* and an *Annunciation*) and sacred items such as choir books are on display here along with paintings, mainly by Sienese, Aretine and Florentine artists of the 13–18C. Exhibits include a *Coronation of the Virgin* attributed to A.Puccinelli and a *Madonna and Child* by the followers of Duccio.

Also worth seeing: The *Logge del Mercato* (Piazza delle Erbe) was built by I.Scalza as a market hall in the 2nd half of the 16C. Agnolo Ambrogini was born in the *Casa del Poliziano* in 1454. This house was built in the 14C and has been altered several times since. The *Teatro Poliziano* (Piazza deglio Intrigati) was built by G. and S.Barchi in 1793–5.

Environs: Chianciano Terme (8 km. SE): Set amidst wooded hills, this is one Italy's premier spas, with sanatoria surrounded by beautiful parks and linked by avenues. 2 km. to the N. of Chianchiano Terme is **Chianciano.** Inside its town wall, some of which survives, is the 13C *Palazzo del Podestà*, decorated with coats-of-arms. The Palazzo dell'Arcipretura houses a *museum* with religious works of art from the 14–16C.

52048 Monte San Savino
Arezzo   p.138☐F 5

Monte San Savino, located on the ridge of a hill to the W. of the Valdi-

Montepulciano, Museo Civico, heraldic beast

Monte San Savino, S.Chiara, terracotta

chiana, was a border fortress between Arezzo and Florence and it was a place of exile for Guelphs and Ghibellines who had been banished. A.Sansovino, the architect and sculptor, is the town's most famous son. Today it is known for the manufacture of fine majolicas.

S.Agostino (Piazza di Monte): This 14C church was rebuilt by A.Sansovino in the early 16C and later enlarged.

S.Chiara: This church was built in the 17C above a bridge leading to a Sienese castle which dates from 1383 and still stands today.

Palazzo Ciocchi di Monte (also known as the Palazzo Comunale, Corso Sangallo): This powerful edifice was built by A. da Sangallo the elder and A.Sansovino in typical Florentine Renaissance style.

Loggia dei Mercanti (Corso Sangallo): This five-arched loggia with Corinthian columns is another product of the co-operation between Sansovino and A. da Sangallo the elder.

Also worth seeing: Two 13&14C *gates*, the *Porta Fiorentina* and the *Porta Romana*, and also large sections of the *town wall*, still survive from the old fortifications.

Environs: Civitella in Val di Chiana (20 km. N.): This town at a height of 1,715 ft. was used as a refuge by the Ghibelline bishops of Arezzo. The *castle* survives in very good condition.

Lucignano (8 km. S.): This hill town is laid out in an elliptical shape. It still retains much of medieval appearance and the surviving features include the 14C *castle*—the so-called Cassero, which survives along with some of its towers—and considerable sections of wall, with gates and the remains of a Medici fortress built in the 16C. 13&14C frescos, some of them probably painted by Bartolo di Fredi, are to be found in the church of *S.Francesco*, built in 1248, with a fine Gothic portal (14C). 15C frescos are to be found in some of the rooms of the 14C *town hall*, which houses the *Museo Civico* on its upper storey.

Sinalunga (8 km. S. of Lucignano): First mentioned under the name of *Asinalunga* in 1197, in the Middle Ages Sinalunga belonged alternately to Siena and Florence. Garibaldi was held prisoner here in 1867. The *Collegiata S.Martino* was built from the ruins of the devastated castle; a panel of the 'Madonna and Saints' by Sodoma is to be found in the single-aisled interior (with side chapels). There are also some Renaissance and baroque *buildings*.

58015 Orbetello

Grosseto   p.136□E 9

This town lies on an isthmus in the middle of the Laguna di Orbetello. a salt lagoon, known for its large fish stocks, which is enclosed by two artificial strips of land (Tombolo in Italian)—the Tombolo di Giannella to the N., and the Tombolo di Reniglia to the S. Orbetello was settled by the Etruscans in the 8C BC. Its salt production and fishing led to Roman and later Sienese interest. The

Orbetello, view

Spanish, led by Philip II, occupied the town in 1555. From 1557 onwards they built fortresses and harbours and developed it into their Italian naval base.

Cathedral: This was built in 1376 on the remains of an older church. It was then rebuilt in the 17C, but the travertine Gothic façade was spared.

Antiquarium Civico (Via Ricasoli): This Etruscan-Roman museum has been housed in the Palazzo Pretorio since 1923. The exhibits include burial objects from Etruscan and Roman tombs in Orbetello (to the E. of Orbetello, near the link with the Via Aurelia), and some finds from the islands of Giannutri and Giglio.

Etruscan walls: The remains of the walls, which were built of polygonal stones in the 4&3C BC and were intended to protect the area from the sea, are to be found by the bank of the canal to the W. of Orbetello.

Town walls: The walls were begun by Philip II of Spain in 1557, but were not completed until 1620. Parts of this *ring of walls*, which is strengthened by bastions, survive in very good condition, and there are also the three *gatehouses*, which were probably built in the early 17C.

Environs: Ansedonia (Cosa): This town 11 km. to the SE stands on a rocky hill above the sea (by the E. end of the Tombolo di Feniglia). It was founded by the Romans in 273 BC and was known as *Cosa*. After being converted to Catholicism in the 4C, the town, now known as Ansedonia, was a refuge for the Arians in the 7C. After the Saracen invasions beginning in the 9C AD and the onset of malaria, many of the inhabitants left Ansedonia, which was finally completely destroyed by the Sienese in 1330. The settlement was reconstructed as a result of excavation work carried out here by the Accademia Americana from 1948 onwards. The best-preserved item is the *ring of walls*. This was built of polygonal blocks in the 3C BC, was defended by 18 towers and had three gates (of which the *Porta Romana* still survives). Other surviving features are parts of the *forum* with a Roman basilica (hall of justice) and two temples, the remains of Roman dwellings buildings, and the walled *acropolis* which occupies a somewhat higher site. At the summit, which offers a wonderful view of the lagoon, there are the remains of the *arx* (castle) and the capitol, Orbetello and the island of Giannutri. A pillar from the former harbour gate has survived from the ancient port, which was at the foot of the hill. To the W. of this a great rock projects from the sea. A canal, the so-called *Tagliata Etrusca*, was cut into this rock. It is divided into the outer Tagliata, which does not have a roof, and the inner

Tagliata which joins the outer Tagliata at an obtuse angle and forms a tunnel 50 ft. long. This technical tour de force by Roman engineers (who had learned their engineering skills from the Etruscans) was intended to control the water level of the lagoon of Burano and to prevent the harbour from silting up.

15 km. to the NE of Ansedonia is **Capalbio.** This town, which is still surrounded by a medieval wall, was also founded in classical antiquity. 14 km. to the NW of Capalbio at **Marsiliana** there was an enormous necropolis, the so-called Banditella, at the foot of a wooded hill above which there projects the spire of a tower. The numerous magnificent finds which were discovered here in 1908–16 and from 1919 onwards by Count Tommaso Corsini, the owner of the land, along with the archaeologist A.-Minto, are all in the Archaeological Museum in Florence. The finds include: a hollowed-out block of stone with a basin; lances; shields; gold and ivory items of jewellery; the well-known brooch named after Count Corsini with its arc in the form of a

Orbetello, cathedral

Orbetello, cathedral tower

snake; and numerous bronze objects.

Isola del Giglio (an island 30 km. W.): Ships ply twice a day between Porto S.Stefano and this island, which is part of the Tuscan Archipelago and was inhabited by the Etruscans. The island belonged to the Roman patrician family of Domitii Ahenobarbi, and in the early Middle Ages it was owned byz a series of noble families and abbeys. From the 12–14C it belonged to Pisa, and in the 15C to the Piccolomini. Chaireddin Barbarossa laid the island waste in 1544 and sold all the surviving inhabitants into slavery, leaving the island completely uninhabited. Along with Siena, it fell to Tuscany in 1555 and was populated again over the following centuries. This 'island of lilies' is partly covered by sloping vineyards and covers an area of 8.16 square miles. Today, with its rocky coast and its crystal clear sea, it is an attractive holiday resort. From the harbour of *Giglio Porto* (E. coast) with its Roman ruins, a road leads 9 km. up to *Giglio Castello* (1,330 ft.). A picturesque wall with towers surrounds this village, which was built in the 15C and contains the 14C *castle* with its gate and lighthouse. A road leads from here to the extensive bay of Campese on the W. coast.

Isola di Giannutri (27 km. S.): This small, crescent-shaped island can be reached only by motor boat. The Isola di Giannutri, girt by tall cliffs, was for many years privately owned by a man who lived all alone on it for almost 40 years (until 1921). Thus the island is still fairly unspoilt even today.

Port'Ercole (7 km. S.): This harbour town stands at the E. edge of Monte Argentario. Its enormous *castle* with its bastions dates from the period of Spanish occupation, as in the case of Orbetello. There are *villas* and *Spanish palaces* at the foot of the castle, which stands on a hill. Some 2 km. W. is Monte Telegrafo (2,085 ft.)—the highest of the peninsula's mountains—which offers a splendid view across the islands of the Tuscan Archipelago.

Porto S.Stefano (9 km. W.). This picturesque, much-frequented holiday resort with its natural, now modern, harbour is on the N. coast of the peninsula of Monte Argentario

Orbetello, cathedral, portal

Orbetello, cathedral, portal detail

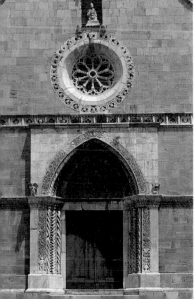

and the bay is overlooked by a Spanish *fortress*. The 'Palio Marinaro', a naval tournament performed in historical costume, is held each 15 August to commemorate a Saracen raid on Porto S.Stefano.

Talamone (23 km. N.): Legend has it that this town, which stands on a rocky cape and is dominated by a sturdy fortress built by the Spaniards on an existing structure, was founded by Telamon, who took part in the expedition of the Argonauts. In 225 BC, the Gauls who had invaded Italy suffered an annihilating defeat near this town, which the Etruscans called6 *Tlamu*. The town, and also the harbour, important in classical times, were destroyed in 82 BC by Sulla. The Sienese planned a harbour of their own here in the Middle Ages, but this project was doomed to failure, owing to the encroachment of swamps and the danger of malaria. Some foundations, Etruscan terracottas from the 6&5C BC, and various grave goods such as vases, have recently been excavated.

Pescia, cathedral portal

51017 Pescia

Pistoia   p.134☐C 3

Originally Luccan, the city of Pescia, which stretches along both banks of the river of the same name, was sold to Florence in 1329. The river divides the city into a religious half (left bank) containing the cathedral and churches, and a secular one (right bank) where the Palazzo dei Vicari stands. Today Pescia is known for its flowers, the central market, held daily, even being visited by foreign buyers.

Cathedral: This was built in 1693 on the remains of an older Romanesque church. The campanile built in 1306, with its arched windows which increase in size the lower down the building they are, is probably a remnant of the Romanesque structure.

S.Francesco (Via Battisti): This church was built in 1298 above a chapel erected in 1211; its façade has subsequently been altered several times. The finest work of art inside is the famous panel painted by Bonaventura Berlinghieri of *Six stories from the life*

Pescia, S.Francesco

Pescia, Porta Fiorentina

of *St.Francis* which dates from 1235 and is on the 3rd altar to the right.

S.Antonio Abbate (Via C.Battisti): Inside this 14C oratory there is a late-13C sculpture of the Deposition and 15C frescos.

SS.Pietro e Paolo (Piazza Mazzini, right bank): This Renaissance church of 1447 is also by Buggiano (see the Cappella Orlandini-Cardini in S.Francesco). Once again, it is in the style of Brunelleschi, his father by adoption.

Palazzo dei Vicari (Piazza Mazzini): Today the town hall is housed in this Romanesque palace built in the 13C, with a tower and a façade decorated with coats-of-arms.

Museo Civico (in the Palazzo Galeotti, Piazza Mazzini): The main exhibits here, apart from various sculptures and illuminated books, are paintings by Tuscan artists and engravings by Dürer and Ribera.

Diocesan museum (in the bishop's palace near the cathedral): The museum houses sculptures and paintings from the 13–15C (including some altarpieces on gold grounds). Other features are a *chapel* decorated with della Robbia terracottas, and the 15C *cloister*.

Also worth seeing: An 18C city gate, the *Porta Fiorentina*, leads to the cathedral. There are several *baroque and Renaissance buildings* on the Piazza Mazzini.

Environs: Buggiano (5 km. S.): The Romanesque *parish church* contains some 15&16C paintings, and in the baptismal chapel there are some fine 13C marble carvings. The *Palazzo del Podestà*, built in the 12C and decorated with numerous coats-of-arms, is one of the features of the main square.

Castelvecchio (12 km. N.): There is a richly decorated arcaded frieze on the façade and apse of the 11C *Pieve S.Ansano*. The crypt and the fine capitals are features of the interior.

Collodi (6 km. W.): This is the birthplace of Carlo Lorenzini (1826–90) who, under the pseudonym Collodi, wrote 'Pinocchio'. The *Parco Monumentale di Pinocchio*, with a Pinocchio monument by E.Greco (1954) and recreations of scenes from the book, is laid out to the right of the stream. A flight of steps leads to the *Villa Garzoni*, built in 1633–62 on the remains of a medieval castle. The garden was laid out on a series of terraces below the villa and contains baths, statues and fountains. The summer pavilion, with its original two-storeyed façade, was added in *c*. 1750. 5 km. N. of Collodi is **Villa Basilica.** The Romanesque *church* built on a Pisan model in the late 13C contains a 13C Cross by Bonaventura Berlinghieri.

Montecatini Terme (9 km. SE): The great healing power of the springs here, which contain sulphur and soda, was known to the Romans. They are especially effective for metabolic disturbances and diseases of the stomach and intestines. The first thermal baths and spa buildings were constructed by order of Grand Duke Leopoldo in *c*. 1780. Today, this town, with its modern sanitoria, extensive parks, and recreation facilities, is among the best-known health resorts in Europe. 5 km. to the NE of Montecatini Terme is **Montecatini-Val di Nievole** (or Montecatini Alto). This town high above Montecatini Terme can also be reached by cable railway from Viale Diaz. Montecatini-Valdinievole is crowned by the *castle*, which is visible from afar. Its walls were razed after 1554. 7 km. to the NE of Montecatini Terme is **Serravalle.** Its Romanesque *church of S.Michele* has a loggia built in 1616. The parish church's 12C tower is known as the *Torre Barbarossa*, and there are the ruins of the 12–14C *castle*. 4 km. to the E. of Montecatini Terme is **Monsummano**

Pienza, view

Terme. Occupying the N. spurs of Monte Albano, it is also a thermal spa. Sweating-cures, and cures in which the waters are taken, may be undergone in the Grotta Giusti.

Uzzano (3 km. E.): This picturesque mountain town features the *Palazzo del Capitano del Popolo*, built in the 14C or 15C.

52017 Pienza
Siena   p.138☐F 6

Originally known as *Corsignano*, Pienza is picturesquely situated, surrounded by cypresses, on a hill above the valley of the river Orcia. Enea Silvio Piccolomini, the humanist, poet and much-travelled diplomat of the Papal Court, was born on 14 October 1405 in the insignificant town of Corsignano, which was the country estate of the Sienese Piccolomini family. He became Pope on 19 August 1458 and took the name of Pius II. In 1459, Pope Pius II commissioned the Florentine architect B.Rossellino to build a model town combining the Gothic and the Renaissance in Corsignano. This was to be the new summer residence of the Pope and the Papal Court. The buildings around the trapezoidal main square were completed as early as 1462 and the importance attached to the individual buildings is reflected in differences in size, building materials and decorations. By using buildings of different sizes and by his manner of arranging them around the trapezoidal square (thus, the Palazzo Piccolomini and the Palazzo Vescovile are diagonally opposite one another to the right and left of the cathedral), Rossellino succeeded in achieving a peculiar and very impressive perspective effect. In the same year of 1462, the locality, which was now called *Pienza* after Pope Pius, was granted the status of a town, and the diocese was also founded. Pope Pius II intended to have more palazzi built by wealthy cardinals around the existing core, and in this way to expand Pienza into the summer residence of the Papal Court. This plan was not pursued any further after his death on 15 August 1464. By that time, only Cardinal

Pienza, cathedral, ceiling detail

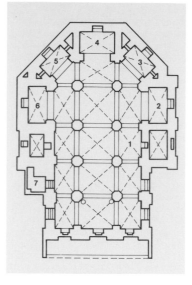

Rodrigo Borgia (the future Pope Alexander VI) and Cardinal Giacomo Ammannati had either built or begun their palazzi, and so it was that this probably unique project for a model town designed as a single entity did not come to fruition.

Cathedral of S.Maria Assunta (in the main square, known as Piazza Pio II): The cathedral was built in 1459–62 to a design by B.Rossellino. The unorthodox Renaissance façade built of travertine is articulated by pilasters standing on tall pedestals, with columns to the sides. On the ground floor, the columns with their Corinthian capitals merely frame the three portals, which are set within arches, but in the upper storey the columns themselves are linked by arches and frame the two side niches and the central round window. At the top, the large, round coat-of-arms of Pope Pius II occupies the space below the triangular gable. The choir, on the

Pienza, Palazzo Massaini

hillside above the valley of the river Orcia, is in late Gothic style, and so is the tracery of the transept windows. The interior, which is full of light and has a nave and two aisles, is a hall church (i.e. the nave and aisles are all of the same height) and it was probably at the behest of Pius II that the church was built in this form. During his journeys north of the Alps he was very impressed by this type of church, which is common in Germany. Further elements of Northern Gothic can be seen in the choir chapels and in the responds.

S.Francesco (beside and to the right of the Palazzo Piccolomini): This Gothic church was built in the 13C, long before the 'model town' was laid out. The single-aisled interior with its flat roof contains frescos with scenes from the life of St.Francis (14&15C), a panel Cross by a pupil of Duccio di Buoninsegna (13C), and a Virgin in imitation of the style of L. Signorelli.

Pieve di S.Vito (about 1 km. W.): Enea Silvio Piccolomini, the future Pope Pius II, was baptized in this church—the parish church of the old town of Corsignano. Although a church was mentioned as early as the 8C, the present building dates from the late 12C, while the cylindrical body of the campanile is 11C.

Palazzo Piccolomini (beside the cathedral and to the right of it): This two-storeyed palazzo, built in 1460–2 on an almost square ground plan, is Rossellino's masterpiece and was probably modelled on the Palazzo Rucellai in Florence, which had been designed by Alberti, Rossellino's teacher. The façade is articulated horizontally by projecting cornices, and vertically by pilasters between which there are double windows beneath decorated round arches. The inner courtyard is surrounded by beautiful arcades with Corinthian capitals.

Palazzo Vescovile (to the left of the cathedral, opposite the Palazzo Piccolomini): The bishop's palace was built by order of Rodrigo Borgia, the future Pope Alexander VI and the father of Cesare and Lucrezia Borgia. Its features include the portal, the

San Quirico d'Orcia (Pienza), portals of the Collegiata

Pietrasanta, cathedral, pulpit

windows which were probably based on Roman models, and the Borgia coat-of-arms at the corner.

Palazzo Comunale (opposite the cathedral): This palazzo (built of travertine in 1463) has an open colonnaded loggia on the ground floor, and above this there are double windows with round arches and a tower crowned with double battlements. The building was restored in *c.* 1900.

Museo Diocesano (Casa dei Canonici, behind the Palazzo Vescovile, on the left side of the cathedral): The diocesan museum founded in 1901 is in this house belonging to the cathedral chapter. Paintings of the Sienese school (including 14C altarpieces by Bartolo di Fredi) and 16C Flemish tapestries are on display here, along with Etruscan and Romans finds from the immediate vicinity.

Also worth seeing: The *Palazzo Ammanati* (beside and to the left of the Palazzo Comunale) was built by order of Cardinal Giacomo Ammannati, a friend of Pius II. However, the palazzo was never completed, as can be seen from the top of the tower and other features. There is another small cardinal's *palazzo* further to the W., towards the Pieve di S.Vito. Beside and to the right of the Palazzo Comunale there is a 15C *brick house*. The *Palazzo Massaini* is 4 km. NE.

Environs: Monticchiello (7 km. SE): The 13C *parish church* has a Gothic portal and rose-window. Inside there is a painting by P.Lorenzetti and the remains of a 14C fresco.
S.Anna in Comprena (7 km. N.): The parish church and part of a former monastery founded by Bernardo Tolomei in 1324. B.Tolomei also founded the well-known Olivetan abbey, Monte Oliveto Maggiore, some 20 km. N. of S.Anna in Comprena.
San Quirico d'Orcia (10 km. SW): A walled town on the hill above the valley of the Orcia and the Asso. Originally settled by the Etruscans, it later developed from a village which the Romans called *Vicus alecinus*. The building which since 1648 has been known as the **Collegiata** was mentioned in 712 under the name of Pieve di Orsenna (SS.Quirico e Giulitta). The present structure was built in travertine in the late 12C. The transept was enlarged in 1298 and the bell tower was completed by 1806. The church is impressive mainly for its *portals*. The colonnaded portal in the simple façade, which dates from *c.* 1080, has a relief depicting a battle of monsters on the architrave. The narrow side portico is supported by Atlantes standing on lions and is thought to be a 13C work by G.Pisano. A third portal (right transept) with a decorative gable in the Gothic style dates from 1298. The single-aisled interior has a triptych by Sano di Pietro dating from the 2nd half of

Pietrasanta, cathedral, pulpit stairs

Seravezza (Pietrasanta), cathedral

the 15C, inlaid choir stalls by A. Barili (1482–1502), and the tombstone of Henry of Nassau, who died in S.Quirico d'Orcia on his way back from Rome. Behind the church is the baroque *Palazzo Chigi,* built by C.Fontana in 1679 on the orders of Cardinal F. Chigi (much damaged in World War 2). 7 km. to the S. of San Quirico d'Orcia is **Castiglione d'Orcia,** a high-lying town whose *fortifications* have survived in excellent condition. A chapel in the *parish church* has a Madonna and Child by P.Lorenzetti. 6 km. to the S. of San Quirico d'Orcia is **Rocca d'Orcia,** a picturesque medieval village with a ruined tower.

55045 Pietrasanta

Lucca   p.134☐B 3

This, the main town of the district of

Versilia on the W. spurs of the Apuan Alps, was founded by Guiscardo Pietrasanta in 1242–55 below the castle of Sala which has stood here since the 12C. The town, which was named after its founder, changed hands frequently over the following centuries, flourishing briefly under Castruccio Castracane, who made it his military base in the Versilia. However, a rapid decline then followed, mainly because of the spread of malaria, a problem not overcome until 1820 when Grand Duke Leopold II of Tuscany liberated the entire Tyrrhenian coast from the curse of this disease. Today Pietrasanta is among the most important centres for onyx- and, in particular, marble-working.

Cathedral of S.Martino (Piazza del Duomo): Begun in 1330 and last restored in 1821. The free-standing campanile built in red brick was begun in the 15&16C but never completed. The façade has round-arched portals with reliefs which may be from the Pisano workshop (14C), a rose-window and a frieze of arches in Luccan style. The interior, divided by columns into a nave and two aisles, was altered in the 17C. 16C holy-water stoup carved by S.Stagi from Pietrasanta; 17C marble pulpit designed by the Pisan artist Bitozzi. 17C altarpieces and sculptures; at the high altar there is an Annunciation by an unknown 14C artist. Marble choir stalls date from 1502–06. The *baptistery* to the right of the cathedral dates from 1608 and has a font of 1509 by D.Benti.

S.Agostino (beside the cathedral): 14C Gothic church with a marble façade. The campanile dates from 1780. The cloister has a 16C fresco cycle of scenes from the life of St.Augustine.

Also worth seeing: Passing through the Porta Pisana, part of the former fortifications, the visitor comes to the *Piazza del Duomo*, still the centre of modern Pietrasanta. The cathedral square has a *clock tower* (1530–4), a *marble fountain* dating from 1545, the *Palazzo Pretorio* (with a portal of 1515), and a *memorial column* with a Florentine lion in honour of Leopold II. Some remains of the 13C castle (Rocca Sala) and the crenellated walls have survived.

Environs: Camaiore (9 km. SE): This town developed around a Benedictine abbey mentioned as early as the 8C. The *abbey church of S.Pietro*, (rebuilt in the 11C and redesigned several times) has a 15C altarpiece of the 'Virgin Mary with Saints' by A.Anguilla. The late Romanesque *Chiesa della Collegiata* (in the Piazza S.Bernardino) was built in 1278, while its tower, which is crowned with Ghibelline battlements, dates from 1350.
Marina de Pietrasanta (4 km. SW): A seaside resort on the Riviera della Versilia, it has long beaches of fine sand and is composed of four villages: Fiumetto (adjoining Forte dei Marmi), Tonfano, Motrone, and Le Focette.

Populonia (Piombino), Etruscan tomb

Seravezza (7.5 km. N.): Some of the marble Michelangelo used came from quarries around here e.g. that used for sculptures intended for the tomb of Julius II. The *Renaissance cathedral* with crenellated tower and dome was built in the 16C. Inside there is an interesting font. The *Palazzo Mediceo* (today the town hall), which has a fountain and fine arcaded courtyard, was built in 1555 for Cosimo I to a design by B.Ammannati. 4 km. to the N. of Seravezza is **Azzano**, a high-lying town surrounded by chestnut forests. The Romanesque *Pieve della Cappella* is 14C and has a fortified tower.

Valdicastello Carducci (3.5 km. E.): The birthplace of Giosuè Carducci (1835–1907), the famous lyricist who won the Nobel Prize.

57026 Piombino

Livorno   p.136☐C 7

Built by the Romans on the SW tip of the headland known as Piombino the secondary port of *Porto Falesia* was intended to relieve the more northerly one of Populonium which had become overburdened by the iron-working trade. However, it was only after the Pisans had built a watchtower here in 1115 that the settlement really developed. After Pisa lost its power, Piombino fell to the Appiani family from Pisa (1399–1603), and then to the Roman families of Ludovisi (1634–1706) and Buoncompagni (1706–1805), before Napoleon presented it to his sister Elisa Bacciocchi-Bonaparte in 1805. At the Congress of Vienna, held after the defeat of Napoleon, Piombino was incorporated into the Grand Duchy of Tuscany, becoming part of the Kingdom of Italy in 1860.

SS.Antimo e Lorenzo: Built in 1374 on the orders of Pietro Giambacorta, the Signore of Pisa. The building has been restored several times and all that now survives of the original structure is the pointed arch in the façade. The interior is divided into two aisles of unequal sizes. The late Gothic *font* was carved by A. Guardi in 1470.

Populonia (Piombino), Etruscan tomb

Populonia (Piombino), Etruscan tomb

Palazzo Comunale (Piazza Verdi): Built by the Pisans in the 13C and restored several times. The clock tower was added by the Count of Appiani in 1598. The *Porta S.Antonio* outside the palazzo is probably a remnant of the Roman town wall.

Also worth seeing: The *marble fountain*, built in 1468 and decorated with coats-of-arms and portraits of the Appiani family, stands in the Piazza Cittadella opposite the chapel built by A.Guardi in *c.* 1470 and next to the ruins of the Pisan fort. Another *fountain* dating from 1247 can be seen near the old canal harbour. The *hospital* was built using remains of the early Gothic church of S.Anastasia.

Environs: Campiglia Marittima (18 km. NE): In the graveyard there is a *church* with a 12C portal decorated with reliefs and a façade of coloured marble (1163). The *Palazzo Pretorio* (15&16C) is decorated with coats-of-arms.

Populonia (14 km. N.): This town high up above the sea was known as early as the 9C BC when it was a centre for the processing of copper from Monti Metalliferi and Campiglia Marittima. *Pupluna*, the only Etruscan city actually on the sea, developed an important industry, which resulted in the construction of a lower city around the workshops by the harbour. Remains of a wall built around both cities in the 4–3C BC have survived. The city reached its heyday in the 7&6C BC, when Velathri (today's Volterra), and also Vetulonia and the more remote Chiusi, were supplied with iron. From the 3C BC onwards it became the most important iron forge used by the Romans, employing raw materials mainly supplied from Elba. Thus, in

Populonia (Piombino), Rocca

205 BC, Populonia provided the navy with large quantities of processed iron when Scipio sent his navy into action against Carthage. Populonia declined in importance after 79 BC, when it was destroyed by Sulla in the civil war. The town became even less important with the construction of a larger port and workshops in Pozzuoli (Naples) in c. 40 BC. Populonia became the seat of a bishop in the 4C but, owing to the spread of malaria and the danger posed by the Saracens, the bishop fled to the safe town of Massa Marittima in 835.

The *tombs* dating from the 9–3C BC (most of them are tumuli with pseudo-domes) are to be found by the Gulf of Baratti and all survive in very good condition. In the *San Cerbone burial ground* there are several box tombs over which mounds of earth were heaped.

The main feature of the *Porcareccia*

burial ground is the 'dei Flabelli' tomb (near the chapel of S.Cerbone), where bronze fans, bronze helmets, gold jewellery and other items were found. Near the 'delle Oreficerie' tomb (only discovered in 1940; valuable burial objects), there is a smelting furnace with the remains of a chimney from the 3C BC.

The former upper city, which is now the town of Populonia, is surrounded by the remains of the *walls* built by Pisa in the 14C and the medieval *Rocca* with a crenellated cylindrical tower and a square tower.

56100 Pisa
Pisa   p.134☐B/C 4

Pisa was probably founded by Greeks in the 7C BC. After the Ligurians and Etruscans, it was taken over in c. 180

BC by the Romans who established the colony of *Julia Pisana* . The settlement was to the N. of a lagoon in the area around the mouth of the river Arno (which flowed into this lagoon) and around that of the river Serchio (which flowed into the Arno). Pisa, the Etruscan word for 'mouth', refers to the double river mouth, and was adopted by the Romans who altered it into *Pisae*. After the lagoon (known to the Romans as Sinus Pisanus) silted up in the 6C AD, the Arno burrowed its way onwards for another 10 km. as far as the Mediterranean, and the Serchio now also no longer flows into the Arno, but into the Mediterranean at a point 15 km. away. Pisa was directly linked to the sea by this lagoon, which was made bigger by order of Augustus, who built the port of Portus Pisanus (today's Livorno) at the S. tip of the lagoon. In the 9C, to protect itself from Saracen invasions in the Mediterranean area, Pisa built up a navy which soon gave the city considerable economic impetus and a great reputation. Pisa drove the Saracens out of Palermo in 1063, and over the following decades it also seized Sardinia, Corsica and the Balearic Islands from the Saracens (1114). In 1135 the maritime republic of Amalfi was completely destroyed by Pisan warships, and from that time on Pisa was the absolute ruling power in the W. Mediterranean and maintained close trading relations with places as far away as Tunis, Constantinople and the Holy Land.

Apart from the economic impetus, the city also experienced its great artistic and intellectual heyday in the 11–13C. Thus work on the cathedral began in 1063, and in 1193 a law school known as *Universitas* was founded. From the 10C onwards, two consuls and a council of twelve wereu elected in Pisa. The council was intended to assist the consuls, but also to examine their activities. When these 'Pisan customs' were confirmed by Emperor

Pisa, cathedral façade ▷

Cathedral, bronze door

Henry IV in 1081, the city was thereby granted a degree of autonomy while at the same time acknowledging the supremacy of the Empire. In 1162, Emperor Barbarossa secured for Pisa not only autonomy, but also a large possession stretching from Portavenere to Civitavecchia. Pisa was Ghibelline at this time, and extremely loyal to the Emperor. After the end of the Hohenstaufen period, Pisan supremacy was threatened more than ever before by the land power of Florence and, in particular, by the maritime power of Genoa which, like Florence, was Guelph. In 1284, the Pisan navy was completely destroyed at Meloria (off Livorno) by a powerful navy belonging to the Genoese. At this time, Pisa was governed by a Podestà elected for one year. After the defeat at Meloria, Admiral Ugolino della Gherardesca, who was already 80 years old had himself elected

Podestà. He concluded peace with Lucca and Florence in order to place himself in a better bargaining position vis-à-vis Genoa regarding the release of the prisoners. But this tactical move was not understood by the Pisans, and after Ugolino had created a Signoria, that is to say after he had made himself dictator, Ugolino and his relatives were thrown into the Gualandi tower. The old Count died here two years later, although not of hunger as Dante's 'Inferno' claims.

Over the following decades, Pisa lost all its possessions except for Elba, some smaller islands in the Tuscan Archipelago, and a coastal tower in Piombino. Until 1399, Pisa was a free city ruled by a Signore, but after the death of Signore Pietro Gambacorta the Appiani sold the city to the Milanese family of Visconti, who in turn ceded it to Florence for a large sum in 1406. But the Pisans defended their

Cathedral, bronze door, detail

city with great fortitude and it was only on 9 October 1406, after Pisa had been starved for a long time, that Florence was able to take over the city.

Pisa declined even more under Florentine rule, and the population was reduced to 8500 inhabitants as a result of malaria which spread unchecked. Only under Cosimo I de' Medici, after the foundation of the Grand Duchy of Tuscany, did mattters improve for the city and the alluvial land of the Arno and the Serchio was cleaned up and bridges were built. In 1543, the Tuscan University was founded and the seat of the military order of St.Stephen, founded in 1563, was moved to Pisa.

The city occupies both banks of the Arno to the S. of Monte Pisano some 10 km. from the sea. Having recovered from the damage caused by an air raid in 1944, today it is visited by art lovers from all over the world. The artistic centre is the cathedral square which is known as the 'Piazza dei Miracoli', square of miracles.

Pisan architecture and sculpture exemplifies an artistic style all of its own, the so-called Pisan Romanesque (later Pisan Gothic). This style influenced the buildings of Lucca, Pistoia and Prato, and even reached as far as Sardinia and Corsica.

Cathedral square (Piazza dei Miracoli): Work on building the cathedral began in 1063 outside the then city wall. At the time it was thought that the subsoil was firm. However, today the campanile stands at an angle, as do the cathedral itself and many other buildings. Although building in the square did not finish until over 200 years later (construction work on the camposanto began in 1278), cathedral, baptistery, campa-

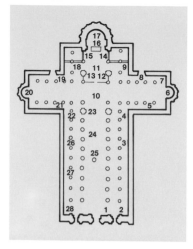

Pisa, cathedral 1 Monument to Matteo Rinuccini; bronze crucifix by P.Tacca (1582); 17C bronze statues above the holy-water stoups **2** Frescos by the 15C Pisan school **3** Marble altar by Stagio Stagi; 'Madonna delle Grazie' by A. del Sarto and G.A. Sogliani **4** Marble altar by S.Stagi; marble urn and sculptures (God the Father) in the lunette by B.Ammanati **5** Painting of 'Virgin Mary among Saints' by G.A. Sogliani and P. del Vaga **6** Cappella di S.Ranieri; sarcophagus of G.B. Foggini; sculptures by B.Lorenzi and others **7** Monument to Emperor Henry VII by Tino di Camaino (1315) **8** Porta di S.Ranieri; bronze door, decorated with reliefs, by Bonanno Pisano (1186); to its left is a marble altar with St.Blasius by S.Stagi and Fancinelli **9** Sacristy and treasure chamber; Virgin Mary by G.Pisano (1299) **10** Dome with frescos by O. and G.Riminaldi (1631, 'Assumption'); 12C floor **11** Sanctuary; bronze candlestick by Giambologna (1620); carved choir stalls with inlay (late-16C, rebuilt in 1616) **12** 'St.Agnes' by A. del Sarto **13** 'Madonna and Child' by Sogliani **14** 'St.Catherine and St.Margaret' **15** 'St.Peter and John the Baptist' by A. del Sarto **16** High altar (1733) with bronze crucifix by Giambologna and 6 angels by Pogliaghi **17** Apse; 'Angels making music' by Ghirlandaio; 'Deposition' by Sodoma (1540); panel showing scenes from the Old Testament by Beccafumi; in the apse dome is a mosaic by various artists including Cimabue (1302): 'Christ Enthroned with the Virgin Mary and John the Evangelist' **18** 13C Byzantine panel **19** Monument to Archbishop d'Elci by G.B. Vacca **20** Cappella del Sacramento; architecture by B.Lorenzi, sculpture by F.Mosca (1563); statues by C.Fancelli; altar by G.B. Foggini (1685); 14C mosaic ('Annunciation') **21** Marble altar by St. Stagi **22** Altar by B.Lorenzi (1592) **23** Expressive pulpit by G.Pisano (1302-11); a bishop's chair in front of the pulpit **24** Gilded Renaissance cofferwork ceiling in the nave **25** Bronze lamp by Lorenzi (1587); Galileo Galilei is said to have discovered the law governing a pendulum's

Cathedral, ceiling

movement by means of this lamp **26** Altar by V.Salimeni **27** Altar by Passignano **28** Altar by G.B. Paggi

nile and camposanto make a homogenous impression, owing to the uniform building material (white Carrara marble) and the oft-repeated architectural features such as the arcaded ground floor and colonnaded loggias in the upper storeys (this does not apply to the camposanto).

Cathedral: Shortly after the Saracens had been defeated by the Pisans at Palermo in 1063, the treasure captured in the battle was loaded on to six cargo boats and brought to Pisa where it was used for the cathedral. The resulting building, the first and at the same time classic example of the Pisan Romanesque, is among the most important work of Italian architec-

Cathedral

ture. Building was begun by Buscheto who, according to Vasari, was of Greek extraction. Reinaldo lengthened the nave in 1100–30 and added a new façade, the upper storeys of which were completed by 1160.

The *façade* is 115 ft. wide and has four dwarf galleries above a row of tall blind arcades. It was often imitated, particularly in the neighbouring cities of Pistoia and Lucca. Three portals flanked by columns open out under the seven arches on the ground floor. While the portals' arches are decorated with various reliefs, lozenge shapes and glass and marble inlay were inserted under those of the arches which have no doors. Buscheto's sarcophagus can be seen under the first arch on the left. The *bronze doors* were cast by Bonanno Pisano in 1186 and recast by Giambologna in 1595 after a fire. The next horizontal level of the façade consists of two rows of columns, the upper of which peter out on either side to accommodate the sides of the downward-sloping roofs of the side aisles. Two further rows of columns above forming the top section of the façade are as wide as the nave. The upper row occupies the triangular gable which is crowned by a Virgin Mary by N.Pisano; there are also two angels. The strikingly regular arrangement of the columns lends great charm to the façade, whose scheme of blind arcades and two rows of columns, appears again on the apse. The row of arcades running through two storeys continues around the entire ground floor of the building. The bronze doors of the Porta di S.Ranieri (on the side leading to the campanile) were made in 1180 by Bonanno Pisano, who looked to Hellenistic and Roman, but also Byzantine models. The

Cathedral, detail of column

reliefs depict stories from the life of Christ and the Virgin.

For the first time in Italy, the *interior* is laid out in the shape of a cross. Nave and four aisles continue in the choir and underneath the dome they cross the three aisles of the transept which, like the nave, ends in an apse. The nave is separated from the aisles by round arches standing on 68 supporting columns with capitals, most of which are Corinthian. The aisles have arcades of pointed arches on columns with capitals based on Islamic models. Above the aisles there are galleries. The latter, which may be copied from Hagia Sophia in Constantinople, continue into the choir. The transept also has galleries. In 1595, the aisles were vaulted and the nave's richly carved and gilded coffered ceiling was built. The breadth of the light, airy interior points to the influence of early Christian Rome,

but its black-and-white marble strips also show Oriental characteristics. The *pulpit* (near the crossing on the left), the work of G.Pisano (1302–11), is one of the finest masterpieces of Italian sculpture. Dismantled in 1599 because it was unfashionable, the surviving sections were re-assembled in 1926. Lost fragments were reconstructed. The hexagonal pulpit is supported? by ten columns and statues rising up from a round pedestal. Two of the outer columns are supported by lions in the process of slaying a horse. Four more columns are in the form of figures: the heathen Hercules, Michael the Christian fighter, Christ borne by the four Evangelists, and Ecclesia above the four cardinal Virtues. The central supporting column has three figures representing Faith, Hope and Charity. Magnificent relief panels show scenes from the New Testament (birth of John the Baptist, scenes from the life of Christ, Last Judgement). The *monument to Emperor Henry VII of Luxembourg* (right transept), who died in Buonconvento in 1313, was carved by Tino di Camaino in 1315. The Cappella di S.Ranieri, decorated with sculptures by B.Lorenzi and others, is also in the right transept. The large choir apse has a mosaic of *Christ Enthroned with the Virgin Mary and St.John the Evangelist* by Cimabue (1302). Other things of interest in the apse include scenes from the Old Testament painted by Beccafumi, and a *Deposition* by Sodoma.

Other features include a 14C *mosaic* of the Annunciation in the apse in the left transept, a 16C *St.Agnes* by A.del Sarto (right dome pillar), *Madonna and Child* by Sogliani (left dome pillar), and the numerous *altars* by Stagio Stagi, Salimbeni and others.

The *cathedral treasure*, which includes an ivory statuette of the Virgin by G.Pisano (1299), is on display in the sacristy (to the right of the sanctuary).

Leaning Tower of Pisa ▷

Campanile: In 1173, Bonanno Pisano, who was responsible for the bronze doors of the cathedral, and a certain Guglielmo, began building the free-standing campanile, which was designed to harmonize with the cathedral and has a tall blind arcade on the ground floor and rings of columns on the upper storeys. However, after the completion of the third storey of columns the tower began to lean, probably because of the sandy nature of the alluvial ground of the Pisan area. Hence this world-famous campanile became known, and not only to the Italians, as *Torre Pendente*, (leaning tower). Numerous other buildings in Pisa also stand at an angle (for example, the cathedral façade inclines some 8.5 inches). About 100 years later in 1275, Giovanni di Simone added three more rows of columns, inclined slightly in the opposite direction in the hope that they would stabilize the tower. However, the tower continued to lean over more and more until, in 1350–73 Tommaso da Pontedera pulled it down and rebuilt it, adding the round belfry. Today the height of the tower is 181.16 ft. in the N. and 178.87 ft. in the S., with a deviation from the vertical of 14 ft. Despite being supported by injections of cement, the tower still leans another 0.03 inches annually; provided there is no further damage this unique tower should stand for some centuries to come.

Baptistery: In Pisa, as in many Italian towns, a baptismal church was built opposite the cathedral. Diotisalvi began construction in 1153. The Romanesque lower storey of this circular building has vertical black marble strips and tall blind arcades on the ground floor above which there is a gallery. This part is similar in style to the cathedral façade and is clearly distinguishable from the Gothic upper storeys, which are the work of

Camposanto, 'Triumph of Death' fresco ▷

N.Pisano and date from 1260. Gothic gables and finnials crown the gallery and above these there are 20 round-arched windows with pointed gables, in the middle of each of which there is a small rose windows.

The *interior*: The central section is divided from the ambulatory by eight columns (richly decorated with figures) and four pillars. Above the ambulatory there are galleries. In the middle stands the octagonal *font*, three steps up, carved by G.Bigarelli in 1246. A statue of John the Baptist dating from 1520 stands on a column rising from the middle of the font. The six-sided, free-standing *pulpit* is the work of N.Pisano and dates from 1260. It rests on seven columns, three of which stand on lions. The figures on the columns represent the Virtues (e.g. Hercules for strength) and John the Baptist. The central column is embellished with animals and human figures. Sculptures of Prophets and the Evangelists appear in the three-lobed arch spandrels (above the columns and below the body of the pulpitx proper). The five *relief panels* on the pulpit are modelled on Roman sarcophagi and depict scenes from the life of Christ as well as the Last Judgement.

Camposanto (the graveyard, to the left of the cathedral): It is said that in 1203 when Archbishop Ubaldo de Lanfranchi returned to Pisa from the First Crusade, he brought with him earth from Mount Golgotha in Palestine, in order to bury Pisans in holy soil. From 1278 onwards, Giovanni di Simone built around this holy field (Italian: Camposanto) a rectangular roofed ambulatory like a cloister. At this time Di Simone was at work on the campanile. The cloister has an arcaded wall facing the meadow. The outer wall has tall round arches and was designed to resemble the façades of the other buildings in the cathedral square. It has two portals, above one of which there is a Virgin Mary and Saints by the school of G.Pisano.

One of the finest frescos is the monumental wall painting of the Triumph of Death (beside and to the left of the entrance in the S.section). The most

Cathedral, monument to Henry VII by Camaino *Baptistery* ▷

View of cathedral and baptistery from the campanile

recent research ascribes it to F. Traini, who is thought to have painted it in *c.* 1340–5. The best-known section shows living men coming before the corpses of three kings lying in open coffins in varying stages of decomposition. In the N. part there is the *Creation* (1390) by Piero di Puccio. 23 *scenes from the Old Testament* (dating from 1468 onwards) and the *Adoration of the Magi* (above the entrance to the Cappella Ammanati) are both by B. Gozzoli.

Museo dell'Opera del Duomo (Palazzo della Primiziale, opposite the left transept of the cathedral): Apart from Pisan sculptures from the 12–17C by N. Pisano, G. Pisano, Tino di Camaino, and B. Gozzoli (David and Goliath), the exhibits here include inscriptions, Roman milestones and documents concerning the history of Pisa.

S. Caterina (Piazza S. Caterina): The lower Romanesque section of the façade, with its tall blind arches and portals, dates back to the Dominicans, who built this church in 1251. The façade acquired its characteristic Pisan features with the addition of two graceful rows of loggias and the rose window. The campanile, with its two- and three-arched windows, was gutted by fire in 1651. The single-aisled interior, which has a timber ceiling, houses the *monumental tomb* of Bishop Saltarelli by N. Pisano (1342), an *Annunciation group* by the same artist (beside the high altar), 14C *frescos*, and sculptures and altarpieces by F. Traini, Fra Bartolommeo, T. Gaddi and others. *S. Francesco* (Piazza S. Francesco): Founded by the Franciscans in 1211. In its present form—attached campanile and six transept chapels—it dates back to Giovanni di Simone (1265–70). The upper section of the façade was redesigned in 1603. The marble *Madonna and Saints* on the high altar was carved by T.Pisano in the 14C; the vault frescos are by T.Gaddi (1342). Count Ugolino della Gherardesca, who died in the Gualandi tower in 1291, is buried in the 2nd chapel to the right of the choir.

S.Michele in Borgo (Via Borgo Stretto): Work on the church began in 990 above the remains of a temple of Mars. The *façade*, which was completed by Fra G.Agnelli in the 14C, clearly shows the transition from Romanesque to Gothic style. Three rows of columns decorated with marble inlay were added above the Romanesque ground floor which has three portals beneath tall blind arcades. Columns and pillars subdivide the interior into a nave and two aisles.

S.Stefano dei Cavalieri (Piazza dei Cavalieri): The church and campanile were built in 1565–72 to a design by G.Vasari. The marble façade goes back to Giovanni di Medici (1606). The single-aisled interior with its fine wooden ceiling contains trophies (figureheads, etc.) from the sea battle of Lepanto in 1571, a gilded bronze reliquary of St.Roch by Donatello (1472), a marble, bronze and porphyry altar, a holy-water stoup designed by Vasari, an altarpiece depicting the Stoning of St.Stephen by Vasari (1571), and a large organ.

S.Maria della Spina (Lungarno Gambacorti): Extended in 1323, the church is rich in marble decoration (canopies, tabernacles, crockets, niches, baldachins etc.) and is one of the finest examples of Pisan Gothic. Beneath the round arches in the façade—which is threaded with strips of black marble— and the right flank, there are portals and rows of three and four windows. The rich Gothic decorations above are from the workshop of N.Pisano.

Pisa, Camposanto, detail of altar

S.Paolo a Ripa (Piazza S.Paolo a Ripa): There was a church on the site in 805 but the present structure was built on the remains of this in the 11&12C. The five arches of the lower section of the façade are conspicuous for their individuality; three Romanesque portals were inserted under the first, third and fifth arches. The upper storey consists of three rows of columns one above the other, the topmost row being accommodated in the triangular gable. The façade is in imitation of the cathedral, as are the left side and the transept. The interior (badly damaged in 1943) has nave, two aisles, transept, and a pendentive dome over the crossing. 14C *frescos and altarpieces* have survived in part, as has a Roman *sarcophagus*.

S.Pierino (also known as S.Pietro in Vinculis, Piazza Cairoli): Built in 1074–1119 (consecrated in 1119) possibly on the site of a Roman temple. The façade is articulated by blind arcades and two-arched windows. The campanile on the left side is probably older than the church. The elevated interior is divided into nave and two aisles by ancient columns; frescos (restored) and 13C floor mosaics. Groin vaults in the large, four-aisled crypt are supported by columns and pillars.

S.Sepolcro (Piazza S.Sepolcro, on the Lungarno Galilei): An octagonal building with a dome with a pointed top and a square campanile (incomplete), it was begun in 1153 by Diotisalvi, who also worked on the baptistery.

S.Nicola (Piazza Carrara): Built in the 12C, the church was much altered during the following centuries; the only things to have retained their original appearance are the Pisan Romanesque arches on the lower part of the façade. The octagonal campanile, with tall arches and rows of columns, stands at a slight angle like the leaning tower.

S.Frediano (Via S.Frediano): Built in the 11&12C, the church has a Pisan-Romanesque façade with inlaid decoration beneath blind arches. After a fire, the interior was redesigned in 1675 in baroque style with Romanesque capitals on classical columns.

Other churches: *S.Matteo* (Lungarno Mediceo), built in the 11–13C and altered in the 17C, houses a 13C Pisan wooden cross. The octagonal Romanesque chapel of *S.Agatha* (Lungarno Sonino) dates from the 12C. The church of *S.Martino* (Via S.Martino), was built in 1332. The façade has five round arches; the single-aisled interior has 14C frescos and a 'Virgin Mary and Child' by Passignano.

Palazzo dei Cavalieri (also known as Palazzo della Caranova, Piazza dei Cavalieri): Cosimo I founded the Order of the Knights of St.Stephen in 1548, and in 1562 he commissioned Vasari to rebuild the ruined medieval Palazzo del Populo as the mother house of the Order. The *façade* of the

S.Caterina

three-storeyed palazzo was completely covered with graffito by Vasari. On the third storey there are six niches with busts of the Grand Dukes of Tuscany. The fountain and the marble statue of Cosimo I outside the 19C open-air staircase are by Francavilla and date from 1596.

Palazzo Gambacorti (Lungarno Gambacorti, near the Ponte di Mezzo): 14C palazzo in Gothic-Pisan style with two rows of Gothic double windows. Today it is the town hall.

Palazzo Medici (Piazza Mazzini): 13C palazzo altered in the 14C and today the residence of the prefects. It belonged to the Appiani family 1392–9 and fell to the Medici in the 15C. Lorenzo il Magnifico was among those to reside in the building, which has tall arches supported by pillars.

Palazzo dell'Orologio (Piazza dei Cavalieri): Also used by the Order of St.Stephen which, in 1607, added a gate arch to connect two tower buildings—the Pisan State prison and the Palazzo Gualandi. Count Ugolino della Gherardesca, the self-appointed Signore di Pisa, was thrown into the Gualandi tower in 1289. According to the description given by Dante, he died here two years later. For this reason this palazzo is often also often known as the 'Palazzo della Gherardesca'.

Other palaces: Lord Byron lived in the 16C *Palazzo Toscanelli* in 1821–2; today the State archive, with documents dating from 1091, is housed here. The *Palazzo Upezzinghi* in the Lungarno Pacinotti dates from the 17C. The tower behind the palazzo is 13C. In the Piazza dei Cavalieri are the Renaissance palaces, *Palazzo del Collegio Puteano* (1605) and the *Palazzo del Consiglio* built by Francavilla in 1603.

Domus Galilaeana (Via S.Maria): Apart from memorabilia of Galileo Galilei, (born in Pisa in 1564), the Galileo museum also houses a library with old editions of his works.

Logge di Banchi (Piazza XX. Settembre): An elegant building with a

S. Stefano dei Cavalieri

colonnaded hall on the lower floor built by C.Pugliani in 1603–05 to a design by B.Buontalenti.

Università degli Studi (Via XXIX. Maggio): The university dates back to 1193 when a law school called 'Studio' was founded here in Pisa. In 1543, Cosimo I re-opened it as a university, since when it has become known the world over, especially for science. Galileo worked here as a professor of mathematics from 1610 onwards. Parts dating from the 15C were rebuilt under Cosimo I in the mid-16C (the Renaissance courtyard is of interest); the façade was last restored in 1907–11. *Library* with valuable manuscripts, *museums*, and *collections*.

Museo Nazionale di S.Matteo (Lungarno Mediceo): Since 1948 the halls and part of the cloister of the former Benedictine monastery of S.Matteo have housed the National Museum, which has a valuable collection of Tuscan (mainly Pisan) paintings and sculpture dating from the 12–16C. Ancient sarcophagi and sculpture, as well as works by Flemish, Catalan and German artists, are also on display here. The ground floor has a sibyl and a female dancer by G.Pisano, numerous architectural fragments and sculptures from the baptistery, 'Christ blessing' (13C Pisan), 'Annunciation' by A.Pisano, and works by A. del Verocchio, Donatello and others. On the upper storey there are several 13C Crucifixion scenes painted on crosses, an altarpiece of the Virgin Mary from S.Martino, a polyptych by S.Martini dating from 1319, St.Paul by Masaccio (1426), a Virgin suckling the infant Christ by N. and (or) A.Pisano, a Crucifixion by Cecco di Pietro, a Resurrection of Lazarus by Paolo Schiavo, and Virgin Mary by Gentile da Fabriano (*c*. 1415).

Also worth seeing: Of the five bridges in the city centre, the oldest is the *Ponte Mezzo*, rebuilt after the war. In the Lungarno Simonelli, there are six *brick halls* which date from 1388 and were originally storehouses for the galleys belonging to the Order of St.Stephen. The *citadel*, rebuilt by the Florentines in 1406, is also on the Lungarno Simonelli.

Environs: Calci (12 km. E.): A town on the S. slopes of Monte Pisano. The Pisan-Romanesque *Pieve* was built in the 11C and has double arcades on the façade and an incomplete campanile. Basilican interior with ancient columns.

Certosa di Pisa (1 km. E. of Calci): A fine monastery with church, residential buildings, hostel, monks' cells, and large courtyard, dating from the 2nd half of the 14C; largely rebuilt in the 17C. A staircase with two flights leads into the monastery church, which was rebuilt in the 18C, when it received a fine baroque façade. The interior has 18C *frescos*, 15C inlaid choir stalls, and a marble wall with a portal which separates the church into two main areas.

S.Piero a Grado (5 km. SW): This Romanesque structure was built in the mid-11C above a 6C basilica. The first church was built on the supposed site of St.Peter's landing on his arrival from Sardinia, a spot known as 'Sinus Pisanus', where the Arno formerly flowed into the lagoon. (see introduction to Pisa).

After Peter had built a church on the site of a stone altar, he travelled via Pisa to Rome where he was martyred. The outer walls of the basilica, which has a nave and two aisles, are built of white and black tufa stone and are decorated with pilaster strips and a Romanesque frieze of small arches running round the entire building. In addition to the three apses in the E., there is a further apse in the W. The campanile was destroyed in 1944 but its lower storey has been rebuilt. 24 columns with classical capitals and

S.Maria della Spina ▷

Palazzo dei Cavalieri

Pisa, Roman baths

two pillars divide the interior into a tall nave and two aisles. In the late 13C D.Orlandi painted *frescos* on the walls above the arcades in the nave.

Vicopisano (16 km. E.): Town picturesquely built on a ridge below Monte Pisano. Pisan Romanesque church. The old *castle* is surrounded by walls and has towers built by Brunelleschi.

51100 Pistoia

Pistoia   p.134□D 3

This city in the S. of the Apennines developed from an oppidum (fortress) known as *Pistoriae* which was built by the Romans at the point where the Via Cassia divided into two. Pistoia was governed by imperial deputies until 1115, when it declared itself a free community with consuls and city

councillors elected by the city itself. In 1177 a constitution was drawn up and today this is one of the oldest city constitutions in Italy. The city experienced a heyday in the 12C and its financial institutions enjoyed a good reputation throughout Europe. Numerous buildings were erected in Pisan Romanesque style and the city was surrounded by a new wall with 60 towers. However, this golden age of the Ghibelline city (loyal to the Emperor) came to an abrupt end in 1254 at the hand of Guelph Florence. During the following years Pistoia suffered greatly from the battles between 'black' and 'white' Guelphs and in 1306 this resulted in another siege of the city by Luccan and Florentine troops. The massive city walls were torn down, Castruccio Castracani (the Signore di Lucca) seized the city in 1315, and in 1329 it came under Florentine protectorship.

Although the city had now lost its political independence, it retained a degree of economic independence and erected a surrounding wall—most of which is still visible today—as well as also several buildings of obvious Florentine influence, like the church of S.Maria delle Grazie. In 1550 as part of the Florentine city state, Pistoia fell to the Grand Duchy of Tuscany, which had been established by Cosimo I. Along with the Grand Duchy, Pistoia became part of the Kingdom of Italy in 1861.

S.Zeno (Piazza del Duomo): The cathedral was built in the 12&13C in Pisan-Romanesque style on the site of the old cathedral (5C) which had burned down shortly before. The three tiers of the upper section of the façade are unusual. The first tier takes the form of arcading over the nave but columns alone over the sloping side

S.Piero a Grado, to the W. of Pisa

Pistoia, cathedral

Pistoia, cathedral portal

aisles. The second row has arcading the width of the nave but the third row, beneath the triangular gable, consists of columns. In 1311 the ground floor was given a portico with horseshoe and semicircular arches and green-and-white marble decorative facings in strips (as in the upper storeys) and rectangles. The terracottas in the coffered tunnel vault under the central, highest arch and the terracotta *Madonna and Child* in the lunette, were both carved by A.della Robbia in *c.* 1500. It is thought that the lower part of the 220 ft. *campanile* was originally a Lombard watchtower. However, work on the campanile probably did not begin until 1199. Its three storeys of arcades with green-and-white marble strips visually linking them to the cathedral façade are said by Vasari to have been built by G.Pisano and Fra Guglielmo.

The tower's spire, which rises above crenellations, was added in the 16C.
The *interior* is divided (by columns and a pair of pillars with decorated capitals) into a flat-roofed nave and groin-vaulted side aisles; the sanctuary is raised. The *silver altar of St.Jacob* in the Cappella di S.Jacopo (by the right aisle) dating from 1287–1456 is attributed to various silversmiths and is among the best of Italian silverwork. The silver altar is decorated with 628 figures (singly and in groups) and clearly shows the stylistic developments of Florentine Gothic. 15 scenes from the New Testament, 9 from the Old Testament, and 9 scenes from the life of St.Jacob were carved by Andrea di Jacopo d'Ognabene (New Testament scenes), Leonardo di Giovanni (St.Jacob scenes), Brunelleschi (2 half-figures of prophets), and other artists. The left choir chapel has

Cathedral, monument to Cardinal Forteguerri

Pistoia, cathedral, terracotta by A. della Robbia

the tombstone of Bishop Donato de'-Medici, carved by A.Rossellino in *c.* 1475, and the *Enthroned Madonna and Child between John the Baptist and St.Zeno* (the so-called *Madonna di Piazza*) which was designed and begun by A. del Verrocchio and completed by his pupil L. di Credi in 1485. The monumental *tomb of Cardinal Niccolò Forteguerri* (1419–73) in the left aisle is also by A. del Verrocchio and pupils (including L. di Credi). Opposite, in the right aisle, lies the tomb of the poet Cino da Pistoia, which was carved by an unknown sculptor from Siena in 1337. The sacristy leads into the *Museo Capitolare*, where the *church treasure* (statue of a kneeling man dating from *c.* 1440, silver cross dating from 1330, liturgical vestments, missals, etc.) is kept. To the left of the high altar is the *font* carved

by Ferrucci da Fiesole in *c.* 1490 to a design by B. da Maiano. A painted Cross by Coppo di Marcovaldo in the right aisle dates from 1275, and in the choir there is a *bronze candelabrum*, dating from *c.* 1440 which is probably the work of Maso di Bartolommeo.

Baptistery (opposite the cathedral façade): A tall, octagonal building in green-and-white striped marble with Gothic decorations and a row of columns running round the building below the steep roof crowned by a turret. Built by Cellino di Nese in 1338–59 to a design by A.Pisano, its octagonal shape and roof are strongly reminiscent of the baptistery in Florence, although the latter's roof is much less steep.

S.Andrea (Via S.Andrea): One of the most striking churches in Pistoia. The

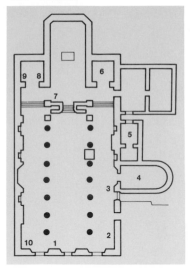

Pistoia, cathedral of S.Zeno 1 Font by Andrea Ferucci to a design by B. da Maino (2nd half of 15C) **2** Monument to Cino da Pistoia (1337) **3** Painted crucifix by Coppo di Marcovaldo and his son Salerno (1275) **4** Cappella di S.Jacopo; silver altar of St.James by artists from Florence, Pistoia and Siena (1287-1456); front side by Andrea di Jacopo di Ognabene (1361-4), left side by Leonardo di Giovanni (1367-71) **5** Museo Capitolare (church treasure); items include silver cross (1330), Romanesque alabaster sculptures, statue of a kneeling man (c. 1440) **6** Monument to St.Alto (d. 1153) **7** Bronze candelabra by Maso di Bartolomeo (1440) **8** 'Madonna Enthroned with Child between John the Baptist and St.Zeno' (known as 'Madonna di Piazza'), begun by Verocchio, completed by L. di Credi by 1485 **9** Tombstone, decorated with reliefs, of Bishop Donato de' Medici by A.Rossellino (c. 1485) **10** Monument to Cardinal Niccolò Forteguerri (d. 1473) by Verrocchio and his assistants (including L. di Credi)

12C Pisan-Romanesque façade has green-and-white marble strips (the upper section is incomplete) and five blind arches with columns beneath which there are 3 portals and lozenge-shaped decoration. Reliefs on the architrave *(Journey of the Magi, Meeting with Herod, Adoration of the Christ child)* above the main portal were carved by Gruamonte and his brother Adeodato in 1166, while the fine capitals on the columns are by Enricus, their contemporary. Columns, some of them classical, articulate the tall interior (timber ceiling) into a nave and two aisles. The best of the decoration is the hexagonal *marble pulpit*, supported by seven red porphyry columns, some of which rest on lions, by G.Pisano (1298–1301). It was probably modelled on the famous pulpit by his father, Nicola, in Pisa's baptistery and as with the latter it depicts, in relief, scenes from the New Testament—although more dramatically.

S.Giovanni Fuorcivitas (Via Cavour): Construction of the present structure began in the 12C on the site of an 8C church, which as its name suggests was 'outside the town'. It was not until the 14C that the building was completed by a craftsman from Como. The main façade remained incomplete, while the N. side wall, with its white and green marble strips, tall blind arches, and two further rows of blind arades above, was built in Pisan Romanesque style. Pistoian elements were also employed in the extensive marble striping, in the richly decorated capitals and especially in the rows of arches, whose size decreases (while their number increases) the further up they are. In 1162, Gruamonte carved a relief of the *Last Supper* on the architrave of the portal. The single-aisled interior contains some fine art.

S.Maria delle Grazie (Piazza S.Lorenzo): Church with a simple façade and fine portal built in 1452–69 to a design by Michelozzo. The single-aisled interior, with its hemispherical dome supported by four columns, has 14–16C painting.

S.Bartolomeo in Pantano (Piazza S.Bartolomeo in Pantano): This, the oldest Romanesque church in Pistoia, was built in the 8C 'in the marsh' (in Pantano), that is to say outside the

Pistoia, cathedral, silver altar of St.James ▷

city walls. Most of the present building dates from 1159. The lower section of the façade, with five blind arches around lozenge-shaped recesses, is characteristically Pisan Romanesque. The upper part is 17C (unfinished). In 1167, with ancient models (sarcophagus figures) in mind, Gruamonte carved the relief of *Christ and the Apostles* on the architrave. The interior is subdivided by columns with fine capitals to form a nave and two aisles, and the best of the decorations here is the rectangular *pulpit*, carved by Guido da Como in 1250, with reliefs of the life of Christ.

S.Pietro Maggiore (Piazza S.Pietro Maggiore): 13C church founded by the Lombards as early as 748. The lower section of the façade is faced with green-and-white marble strips and displays Pisan Romanesque elements (blind arches around lozenge-shaped recesses).

Madonna dell'Umiltà (Via della Madonna): In 1494 on the site of the church of S.Mari Forisportae, Ventura Vitoni began building this church in the style of Brunelleschi. By 1568 it had been completed by Vasari. The church consists of the vestibule of 1494 and an adjoining three-storeyed octagonal structure, to which Vasari added a dome in 1561.

S.Francesco (Piazza S.Francesco d'Assisi): This broad, single-aisled church with five choir chapels was begun in 1294, but not completed until somewhat more than 100 years later (around 1400). The plain, green-and-white striped façade actually dates from as late as 1717. Inside the church there are numerous 13&14C *frescos*.

S.Domenico (Corso Umberto): Work on this T-shaped church belonging to the Mendicant order was begun in the late 13C. It was extended in *c*. 1380 and, after suffering severe war damage, rebuilt from 1970 onwards. Inside there are remains of *14C frescos*, (e.g. in the square-ended Gothic chapel in the choir) and several 15&16C *tombs*, including the monument to Filippo Lazzari carved by B. and A.Rossellino in 1467–8.

Pistoia, S.Andrea

Pistoia, Palazzo del Podestà

S.Paolo (corner of Corso S.Fredi/Via Canal Bianco): Built in 1291–1302. Its façade was restored in the 14C and shows not only Pisan-Romanesque structural elements (blind arches, etc.), but also Gothic features (rose window in the roof gable, canopy, etc.). There is a row of Pisan columns above the tall blind arches which surround the richly decorated portal and the pointed-arched tomb niches. The single-aisled interior contains a wooden crucifix dating from 1399 and several 16C altarpieces.

S.Antonio del Frati T (Corso Umberto): This single-aisled chapel, built in the 14C and deconsecrated in 1774, derives its name from the Greek letter tau, which the followers of St.Antony marked on their cloaks. Inside the church there are numerous 13&14C frescos, including some by Niccolò di Tomaso.

Palazzo del Podestà (or Palazzo Pretorio, Piazza Duomo): Built for the Podestà in 1367 and decorated with coats-of-arms and paired Gothic windows. In 1836–46 an extra storey

and a wing were added. Beneath the portico (broad arches on heavy pilasters) in the *courtyard*, which is also decorated with coats-of-arms, there are stone benches for the accused, court desks, and a judge's seat rebuilt in 1507 with an interesting Latin inscription (Hic locus odit, amat, punit, conservat, honorat—Nequitiam, Leges, Crimina, Jura, Probos = This place hates wickedness, loves laws, punishes crimes, maintains the right, and honours the honest).

Palazzo del Comune (Piazza Duomo): Begun in 1294 on the orders of the Florentine Podestà Gino della Bella (owner of the Palazzo Vecchio in Florence); work was temporarily halted in 1385. A roofed bridge joining the palazzo to the cathedral was added in 1637. The upper storeys have two-arched and three-arched windows with slightly pointed arches. A black *marble head*, set in the wall just to the left of the central window on the 1st storey, is possibly the portrait of the dreaded Moorish king Mugahid, defeated by the Pisans in 1113 or that of Fliippo Tedici, who

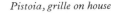

Pistoia, Palazzo del Comune, stall *Pistoia, grille on house*

betrayed the city in 1315 during an occupation. The Medici coat-of-arms with the Papal keys of Leo X, is seen above this window. Some rooms are decorated with 15&16C *frescos*. The council hall has a 15C timber ceiling and beautiful 15C seats. To the right of the portal there are some standard measuring rods made of iron. The courtyard dates from 1353. The main items on display in the *Museo Civico*, which occupies on the top storey, are Florentine and Sienese paintings (L. di Credi and others) and ceramics from the 13–18C.

Ospedale del Ceppo (Via F.Pacini): Founded in the 13C, the hospital derives its name from a hollow tree trunk (Ceppo) in which donations were collected for the public care of the sick. The *portico* with slender columns was added in 1514 and is modelled on that of the foundling-hospital built by Brunelleschi in Florence. G. della Robbia and his workshop decorated it with *brightly glazed terracottas*. Coats-of-arms of the Medici, the hospital and Pistoian families, as well as depictions of the Virgin Mary, appear in *medallions* in the spandrels between arches.

Also worth seeing: The *Palazzo Vescovile* (Piazza del Duomo) built in the 14C. The 18C *Palazzo Fabroni* and the *Palazzo Sozzifranti* built in 1588, both of which are in the Via S.Andrea. The *Palazzo Panciatichi* in the Piazzetta del Soli dating from as early as 1313. Behind the baptistery are the *Palazzo del Capitano del Popolo* (built in 1292 on the remains of an older tower), a 13C family house known as '*Palagetto*', and the *rag market*.

58017 Pitigliano

Grosseto   p.136☐F 8

This little town occupies a picturesque site on a steep rocky spur overlooking deep gorges, which two rivers cut out of the volcanic tufa-rock plateau in prehistoric times. The Etruscans settled on this easily defended spur, which needed to be safeguarded by a wall on one side only and there are numerous Etruscan tombs carved out of the tufa which date from this time. These so-called 'dovecotes' were used by the Romans as wine cellars and as stables or barns today. Above these caves the houses are built in yellowish-red tufa and appear to grow out of the rock itself. An Aldobrandeschi castle was built here in the Middle Ages. In 1293 the settlement which developed around the castle came under the influence of the powerful Roman Guelph family of Orsini, and they raised Pitigliano to the status of a town. A protectorate under Cosimo, it became part of the Grand Duchy of Tuscany in 1608. It was not until 1660 that Pitigliano, where the Bishop of Sorano had resided since the time of the Orsini officially became a see.

Cathedral SS.Pietro e Paolo (Via Roma): 13C or 14C like its massive campanile which originally served as the castle tower. In the 18C the façade was rebuilt in baroque style.

Palazzo Orsini (Piazza Repubblica, town centre): A battlemented palazzo with a beautiful courtyard built in *c.* 1330. G. da Sangallo added the richly decorated portal and portico with Ionic columns in the 15&16C.

Also worth seeing: The Orsini *Citadella* (fortress) and the *aqueduct* with 15 elegant arches which was also built under their rule, both date from 1545. A *column* dating from 1490 with the Orsini bear stands in the main square. The *synagogue*, for the Jewish community resident in Pitigliano from the 15C, was built by V.Manin. Important finds from nearby including pottery, are preserved in the *Museo Civico* (in the former Hebrew school). The façade of the *church of*

S.Maria is Renaissance. Some sections of the old *Etruscan walls* are to be found by the Porta Capo di sotto.

Environs: Poggio Buco (9 km. W.): Lying high up, Poggio Buco is inaccessible by car. The ancient town of *Statonia* is said to have originally stood here, as reliefs slabs from a temple which no longer survives show. On the W. of the plateau a *necropolis* has tombs of very simple design.

Sorano (9 km. NE): Like Poggio Buco, this town is also picturesquely sited on a tufa rock above a steep gorge. The Orsini built another *castle* here in the 15C overlooking the still-medieval village. Here too there are numerous *dovecote tombs* cut into the rock. Single *Etruscan tombs* have been discovered in the vicinity.

Sovana (8 km. NW): On a plateau above deep gorges, Sovana was settled by Etruscans in the 7C BC and flourished until the 6C BC. The Roman town experienced a new impetus in the 3C BC and this continued until the then diocesan seat was devastated by the Lombards. After affluent times in the 10–13C, when it was held in fee by the Aldobrandeschi, the following centuries saw a decline in importance.

Sovana is overlooked by the splendid *ruined castle* of the Aldobrandeschi (at the entrance to the town), which was built in the 13C and razed in the 17C. The main square (Piazza del Pretorio) is surrounded by medieval houses, including the 13C *Palazzo Pretorio* , (with coats-of-arms and 16C frescos in the conference room), the *16C Palazzo Bourbon del Monte*, a *loggia* with Medici coats-of-arms, the ruined *church of S.Mamiliano*, and the 12Ci Romanesque *church of S.Maria*, inside which there are 16C frescos and a pre-Romanesque marble ciborium unique in Tuscany. Pope Gregory VII was born in No. 29 Strada di Mezzo. The *cathedral* (at the end of the town) was built in the 12–13C from the remains of a 9–11C structure. Although the façade and vault have been rebuilt in Gothic style, the cathedral is basically Romanesque, with an apse, fine portal reliefs and a crypt with columns dividing the nave

Pitigliano, panorama

Pitigliano, Palazzo Orsini

and four aisles. The interior of the church has a nave and two aisles, capitals decorated with figures, on the semi-columns of the pillars (for example the last pillar but one has a scene from the Old Testament), and the monument to St.Mamilianus, bishop of Palermo. The remains of a small *Etruscan temple* from the 3C BC were discovered to the N. of the cathedral in 1905 (today they are in the Archaeological Museum in Florence). Around Sovana there are several *Etruscan burial grounds*, most of whose tombs date from the 4–3C BC, although there are also some from the 7C BC. The most famous tomb is the *Tomba della Sirena* (3C BC) which lies on a densely wooded slope. This aedicule tomb is built in tufa and has an interesting but unfortunately much weather-worn relief above the niche. The *Grotta Pola*, which was hewn from the tufa rock and originally had eight columns, is a temple tomb. The most important tomb is the monumental *Tomba Ildebranda* (late-2C BC), also a temple tomb. It had a total of twelve columns along three sides, the capitals of which were decorated with carved heads and leaves (only one complete column stands today). Two external staircases lead up to the building which stands on a podium. A narrow passage leads underneath the podium into the burial chamber which has a Greek cross ground plan. The scanty finds from the tombs around Sovana include Greek terracottas, vases, buccheri and a few bronze objects from the 7C BC (today housed in the Archaeological Museum in Florence). 14 km. to the W. of Sovana is **Saturnia**, formerly part of the city state of the Vulci, and one of the oldest settlements in the region. The *Porta Romana* was inserted into the *Etruscan wall* by the

Sorano (Pitigliano), view

Romans. Composed of large polygonal blocks this ancient wall has only partially survived.

53036 Poggibonsi
Siena   p 134☐E 5

A town in the valley of the Elsa on the road from Siena to Florence. In the Middle Ages Poggibonsi had one of the strongest castles *(Podium Boniti)* in Tuscany. In 1270, Guido di Monforte, the Podestà from Florence, destroyed this castle and the entire village. In 1478 Lorenzo il Magnifico ordered a powerful new castle to be built as a border fortress to confront Siena. However, Cosimo I became Grand Duke in 1569 and building stopped. After suffering severe damage in World War 2, Poggibonsi has rapidly developed into a thriving little town, producing wine and furniture.

Rocca di Poggio Imperiale (2 km. above the town): Built in 1478 on the orders Lorenzo il Magnifico to the plans of G. da Sangallo; unfinished because of the formation of the Grand Duchy.

Also worth seeing: The church of *S.Lorenzo*, built in the 14C and rebuilt after World War 2; 14C crucifix. The Gothic *Palazzo Pretorio* has a medieval crenellated tower and a coat-of-arms on an outside wall.

Environs: Barberino Val d'Elsa (9 km. N.): The hill above the valley of the Elsa and Pesa rivers was occupied by Etruscan peasant farmers. 13C walls; 15C Palazzo Pretorio and medieval houses. Some 5 km. to the NW of Barberino Val d'Elsa is the *ruined castle*, Semifonte, loyal to the Emperor and destroyed by Florence in 1202. 5 km. SW of Barberino Val d'Elsa is the *Pieve S. Appiano*, a 13C Romanesque *country church* with apse and tower and a relief of St.Michael within.

Castellina in Chianti (13.5 km. E.): A typical Chianti village and an important wine centre amid fine Tuscan countryside. Since the 19C red wine grown over an area which ranges N–S from Florence to Siena and E–W from Pisa to Arezzo has been marketed as Chianti, the wine towns of the Chianti mountains (Castellina, Gaiole, Greve, Radda and others) having given their wine the designation Chianti Classico in an attempt to prevent its name being abused. Sights include the *15C fortress* and, in particular, the enormous *Etruscan tumulus tomb* (165 ft. in diameter) known as 'Monte Calvario'. Four burial chambers were built at the end of corridors in the low burial mound. Each chamber is different in design. The S. tomb is most impressive, having a corridor, cells at the sides, an anteroom and burial chamber. 18 km. N. of Castellina in Chianti lies **Greve**, which became a small market town some time after 1555 and is situated in the border area studded with castles between Siena and Florence. The irregularly-shaped **market place** is of interest as each house owner built his part of the encircling arcade. The *monument* (1913) to Giovanni di Verrazzano (1485–1528) commemorates the seafarer who was born in nearby Verrazzano and who explored the coast of North America for Francis I of France. 11 km. to the N. of Castellina in Chianti is **Panzano**, also a Chianti producer and a former Florentine border fortress destroyed in 1260 after the defeat at Montaperti. About 1 km. to the S. of the centre of the village is the 10C *Pieve S.Leonino* with three apses, colonnaded hall and 14C cloister. 13 km. E. of Castellina in Chianti is **Radda in Chianti**, a Chianti village on a mountainous spur, with the church of S.Maria and also a *castle* formerly belonging to the Guidi counts. 9 km. S. of Radda in Chianti is **Meleto**,

Poggibonsi, Rocca

Radda in Chianti (Poggibonsi), S.Maria

which has a fine small *castle*, whose interior has survived in good condition. 11C round corner towers; 18C rebuilding. 8 km. SE of Meleto is **Castello di Brolio**, a well-preserved 9C *castle* with surrounding wall and massive towers. Owned by the Ricasoli counts since 1147, they last rebuilt it in the original style in the 19C. The chapel dates from 1343 and the crypt has monuments to the Ricasoli family. Fine weapon collection in Gothic residence. The well-known 'Chianti – Brolio' wine is stored in the Ricasoli wine cellar. 5 km. to the NE of Meleto is **Gaiole in Chianti**, another town known far and wide for its wine. The *Pieve di S.Maria e Spaltenna* is early 14C.

Colle di Val d'Elsa (10 km. SW). In the possession of the bishops of Volterra until the 12C. Thereafter it was a free community with Guelph affiliations and as such a much-used refuge for Guelphs banished from Siena. The town finally came under Florentine rule in 1333. Since 1592, Colle di Val d'Elsa has been a diocesan seat and been raised to the status of a town. It consists of the very well-preserved upper town (Colle Alta) and the lower town (Colle Bassa), now an industrial area. The lower town includes the 13C church of *S.Agostino* with paintings by Taddeo di Bartolo, Ghirlandaio and others. Colle Alta, which still has a medieval appearance, is surrounded by the remains of the old town wall and has a number of interesting buildings. The *Museo d'Arte Sacra* with artistic objects of a religious nature (including a 14C Sienese triptych) is housed in the old priest's house beside the late-Renaissance *cathedral*. 15–17C works by R.Manetti, S.Conca and others are on display in the *Museo Civico* in the Palazzo dei Priori. The Palazzo Campana, begun by Baccio d'Agnolo in 1539, has remained incomplete. The 14C *Palazzo Pretorio* is decorated with coats-of-arms and houses an aquarium. In 1240 the Florentine architect Arnolfo di Cambio is said to have been born in the 12C residential tower, the *Casa di Arnolfo* which was later named after him. The *Via della Volte* is interesting. Houses with

Radda in Chianti (Poggibonsi), fountain

coats-of-arms. **Monteriggioni** (12 km. SE): In 1203 Siena began building a *castle* to defend herself against Florence. Standing on a low hill it can, nevertheless, be seen from afar and has a ring of fortifications 1870 ft. long which have survived in their entirety. Its 14 square and very well-fortified towers were compared to giants by Dante. Even today the walls surround the entire town. Around about Monteriggioni there are numerous, mainly circular, Etruscan chamber tombs dating from the 6–4C BC. Most of the burial objects and urns are today housed in the National Museum of East Berlin. 3 km. to the W. of Monteriggioni is **Abbadia a Isola,** a Cistercian monastery founded in 1101 and originally built on an island (Isola) within a marshy area. The 12C Romanesque *church* is all that survives of the abbey. The interior has nave and two aisles, an Etruscan-Roman urn, a 15C font, and frescos by Taddeo di Bartolo.
S.Lucchese (2 km. S.): A Gothic *church* on a hill built by the Franciscan order in the 13C on the remains of a previous Romanesque structure.

Portico and cloister. Inside there are fine 14C *frescos* and a terracotta altar probably carved by the della Robbia workshop in the 16C. The frescos in the sacristy were painted by Gerino da Pistoia (1513).
Staggia (7 km. S.): A medieval village in the mountains with the remains of the 14C wall. The castle, with one square and two round towers, dates from the 15C.

54027 Pontremoli

Massa-Carrara   p.134☐A 1

This town, surrounded by hills covered with sweet chestnut trees, occupies the valley of the Magra in the northernmost part of Tuscany. Pontremoli was mentioned in *c.* 990 as a stopping post on the Via Francigena and over the following centuries Pontremo's strategically important location has led to much fighting for control of the town between Genoese and Florentine aristocratic families. Today Pontremo is one of the centres of the Alta Lunigiana.

Colle di Val d'Elsa (Poggibonsi), Colle Alta

Fortress of Cacciaguerra: High-lying castle built by Castruccio Castracani in 1322. Today it houses a *museum*, the Museo Lunigiana, in which statues and archaeological finds from the Lunigiana district, including the unusual pictorial columns, are on display.

Also worth seeing: The church of *S.Francesco* has a Romanesque campanile and a 15C polychrome relief of the Madonna and Child. A small 15C octagonal marble temple, decorated in the style of Sansovino, can be seen in the 15–16C *church of Santissima Annunziata* (to the S., a little way outside the town). Other features include the baroque *cathedral* with its classical façade, and the 18C *church of the Madonna del Ponte*.

Environs: Fivizzano (21 km. SE): Some 1225 ft. above sea level, the town is the birthplace of the poet Giovanni Fantoni (1755–1808). Places of interest include the *Palazzo del Governatore* (today the town hall), the *Porta Sarzanese*, and the church of *SS.Jacopo e Antonio* with an altar-piece by P.Sorri. 3 km. outside the town is the Romanesque *Pieve di S.Maria Assunta*, built in the 12C. Columns with capitals with figures divide the interior into a nave and two aisles. **Villafranca in Lunigiana** (10 km. S.): This town is overlooked by a ruined castle of the Malaspina. The *church of S.Francesco* was built in 1525–50, and rebuilt after suffering severe damage in World War 2.5 km. to the NE of Villafranca de Lunigiana is **Bagnone**, with a *castle* with a cylindrical tower dating from the 16C. 3 km. to the S., in Castiglione, there is a 13C *castle*. 11 km. to the S. of Bagnone is **Licciana Nardi**. Here there is another Malaspina *castle*. The Piazza del Municipio has a *monument*, obviously inspired by ancient sarcophagi.

52014 Poppi

Arezzo   p.138☐F 4

Poppi, standing on a hill and still partly surrounded by walls, is the most important town in Casentino

Colle di Val d'Elsa, S.Agostino

Pontremoli, S.Francesco

Pontremoli, view of city with cathedral and fortress

along with Bibbiena. On the upper Arno, it is bounded by Pratomagno in the W., and extends from Monte Falterone in the N. (where the Arno rises) to Arezzo in the S. Idyllic Casentino with the fertile valley of the Arno is covered with meadows, vineyards, olive groves, and forests. During the last few years Casentino has developed into a leisure centre used mainly by Italians. In the Middle Ages, the secluded Casentino district was studded with monasteries and castles belonging to the landed gentry. The aristocratic Guidi family resided here from the 11C onwards and at Poppi they built a massive castle which dominates the valley and became one of the most important of the Ghibellines' strongholds in Tuscany. Mino da Fiesole, the famous sculptor (1430–84), was born here.

Castello: This imposing castle,

which is still in splendid condition, was built in the 13C by order of the Guidi counts. The Guelph city of Florence was recognized by the originally Ghibelline Guidi from 1440 onwards, and after this the main building (with Gothic two-arched windows beneath round arches) and the massive tower were both crowned with Guelph crenellations. The *gatehouse*, decorated with coats-of-arms, leads to the splendid *courtyard* which has escutcheons and an external staircase.

Also worth seeing: The so-called *devil's tower*, the first castle built by the Guidi, stands opposite the Castello. On the arcaded Via Cavour 12C *S.Fedele* has a crypt and some paintings.

Environs: Camaldoli (16 km. NE): The former *monastery* of the Camal-

Pontremoli, cathedral, section of portal

dolensians, which was founded by St.Romuald in 1012 and named after this town, is in a picturesque mountain gorge 2675 ft. above sea level in the middle of a thick forest. The extensive complex consists of various buildings, some of which are used today for study courses and congresses. The colonnaded hall of the *hospice* dates from the late 11C, and a small *cloister* was added in the 15C. The 11C *church* was rebuilt in baroque style in the 18C and houses a Virgin Mary by Mino da Fiesole and a painting by Vasari. The *refectory*, with a painting by Pomarancio, was constructed in the early 17C, as was the *pharmacy*, which is decorated with original furniture and vessels. The monastery's own liqueur is still sold in the pharmacy. The *library* was dates from the 13–15C. Above the abbey, some 3680 ft. above sea level in an isolated situation under dark pine

trees stands the *hermitage (Eremo di Camaldoli)*. The monk Romuald from Ravenna retreated here to live in complete seclusion according to strict rules. Romuald, one of the most important advocates of ecclesiastical reforms in the 11C, was an adviser to Emperor Otto III and the founder of the Camaldolensian order. Three of the 20 cells (little houses with small gardens separated by walls) date from 1012, when the hermitage was built, while others were added up until the 17C. The *church*, whose façade is flanked by two towers, was redesigned in baroque style in the 17C. Inside there are a 16C marble tabernacle, rich stucco decorations and a 17C wooden lectern. The hermitage also includes the *chapel of St.Anthony* which has various terracottas. 9 km. E. of Camaldoli is **Badia Prataglia**, which stands at some 2740 ft. above sea level, is becoming increasingly

Poppi, view of town

popular as a holiday resort. The Romanesque *parish church*, built in 1005 with a raised choir and a wooden roof, has been restored in the original style.

Castello di Romena (12 km. NW, district of Pratovecchio): A massive *ruined castle* (2000 ft. above sea level) with three ruined towers and the remains of walls, it was probably the strongest of the castles built by the Guidi counts. Mentioned by Dante in his 'Inferno', the castle is likely to have been his first refuge during his exile from Florence. Some 5 km. W., on the SS 70 to Florence, at the turn (the SS 310) for Stia, there is a *memorial column* commemorating the Battaglia di Campaldino, fought here in 1289. One of the bloodiest battles between Guelphs and Ghibellines, it resulted in a victory for the Florentine Guelphs over Ghibelline Arezzo. 2

km. to the S. of Castello di Romena is **Pieve S.Pietro di Romena** on a hill 1560 ft. above sea level. Work on this basilica, which has a nave and two aisles, began in 1152. The church was built on the site of an older church, as is confirmed by remains discovered in the sacristy. An inscription on a capital states that the owner was a priest called Albericus. The architects may have been a group of Lombard stonemasons who worked on other churches in Casentino (such as those in Montemignaio and Stia). There is a double row of blind arcades on the front of the transepts and on the apse. Inside there are two rows of blind arcades on the apse, while the side aisles end in small rooms. The capitals of the columns (probably ancient) are Romanesque and have animals, plants, human figures and grotesques. 13C panel painting; other paintings are 13–14C. 4 km. to the N. of Pieve

Castello di Romena near Poppi

S.Pietro di Romena is **Stia**, a town at the foot of Monte Falterona and a popular base from which to climb the mountain (5425 ft. high). The *Pieve di S.Maria Assunta* was built in *c.* 1160. After the side aisles had been vaulted in the 1st half of the 17C, the façade was redesigned in classical style in the 18C.

Strada (8 km. NW): The *Pieve di S.Martino a Vado* was built in *c.* 1175 and redesigned in baroque style in 1745. However, its original appearance was restored some years ago.

50047 Prato

Florence   p.134☐D/E 3

This city on the little river of Bisenzio is often referred to as 'Italy's Manchester', owing to the textile industry for which it is widely known. The city centre, which is still partly surrounded by a wall, has some impressive art, much of which is early Renaissance. The area of the city was probably settled by the Etruscans. The Romans founded a settlement of traders and craftsmen here and called it *Pagus Cornius* (Pagus = a settlement of a certain size, to be compared to the smaller vicus). Under the Lombards this developed into the *Borgo al Cornio* on higher ground. The inhabitants took refuge here in time of war. Below the Borgo was the *Prato* (meadow), where a market was later held. In the 11C, the settlement—now known as Prato—came into the possession of the powerful feudal counts of Alberti, along with the castle (of which the bases of two towers still survive in the Castello dell'Imperatore). After an unsuccessful attempt by the powerful Guelph countess Mathilda of Canossa to cap-

Poppi, Castello

Prato, cathedral, side portal

ture the castle in 1107, Prato elected its own consuls in 1147 and, in 1187, Emperor Barbarossa confirmed the freedom of Prato, which was loyal to the Emperor. The unique castle (Castello dell'Imperatore) was built by Emperor Frederick II in 1237–48 in the style of Hohenstaufen castles in Sicily. Violent disputes arose in Prato in the 13&14C between the Ghibellines (the Dagomari family) and the Guelphs (the Guazzalotri family). The latter were finally victorious. When the freedom of the inhabitants of Prato was threatened by the nearby cities of Florence and Lucca, Prato placed itself under the protection of the Anjou from Naples. However, in 1351 the city was sold for 17,500 guilders to the Florentines. Prato was not granted municipal rights or a see (which it shared with Pistoia until 1954) until sometime after 1653, and for this reason there was no cathedral

before that time. In the 13–15C, Prato was known all over Europe for its wool and silk processing. Francesco Datini (1330–1410), the wholesaler and banker who invented bills of exchange, was one of the most successful and probably also the most famous of the numerous wealthy merchants of that period. Prato declined in importance from the 16C onwards and many inhabitants left the city. From the late 19C onwards the city's fortunes improved and the population rapidly increased, multiplying tenfold between 1920 and 1960.

Cathedral of S.Stefano (Piazza del Comune): The Pieve di S.Stefano, which was mentioned as early as the 10C, has only been used as an episcopal church since 1653. The present structure dates mainly from the 13&14C. The façade and right nave wall were built by Guidetto da Como

Prato, cathedral, section of portal

in 1211 in Pisan-Luccan style. The façade was redesigned with late Gothic stylistic elements in 1385–1457 to plans by G. Pisano. The right wall of the nave, however, remained in its original form with blind arcades, even though it was faced with green and white marble and additional decorations. Like the right side, the façade was faced with green-and-white marble strips. The Gothic portal is flanked by pointed pillars; the terracotta, glazed in white and showing the Madonna and Child with Saints, was carved by A. della Robbia in 1489. At the right corner of the façade is the famous *external pulpit of Pergamo del Sacro Cingolo*, which dates from 1434–8 and is one of the finest works of the Renaissance. From the pulpit the relic of the Sacro Cingolo (Holy Girdle) is displayed to the people on certain holidays. Legend has it that the Virgin Mary gave her girdle to a priest who handed it over to Dagomari, a tradesman from Prato. Before his death, Dagomari bequeathed the Sacro Cingolo to the provost of the cathedral and prominent citizens. Today the girdle is preserved in the cathedral in the locked Cappella del Sacro Cingolo. One key to the chapel is in the possession of the bishop and the only other in the keeping of the municipality.

1313–68, the church was expanded by the addition of a transept with five chapels. The crypt, however, was destroyed in the process. 1340–56 the campanile was altered and two upper storeys with Gothic three-arched windows above a storey with two-arched windows were built above the three lower storeys which have Romanesque two-arched windows.

Heavy, dark green marble columns supporting wide arches (a Lombard feature) divide the Romanesque inter-

Prato, Cathedral of S.Stefano 1 Outside pulpit 'Pergamo del Sacro Cingolo' (1434-8); by Michelozzo, 7 reliefs with copies of the originals by Donatello **2** Wooden crucifix by G.Pisano or his pupils (c. 1320) **3** Tabernacle with 'Madonna del Olivo' by G. and B. da Maiano (1480) **4** Panel painting by Fra Filippo Lippi (1452, 'Death of St.Jerome') **5** Cappella del Crocifisso; frescos by A.Franchi (1873-6); 12C wooden crucifix **6** Cappella dell'Assunta; frescos by P.Uccello or the so-called Maestro di Prato (c. 1445, 'Nativity of the Virgin Mary', 'Presentation in the Temple' and others) and Andrea di Giusto (c. 1455, 'Stoning and Preservation of St.Stephen', 'Betrothal of the Virgin Mary') **7** Main choir chapel; fresco cycle by Fra Filippo Lippi and Fra Diamante (1452-68, left wall: 'Story of St.Stephen', right wall: 'Story of John the Baptist'); bronze crucifix by F.Tacca (1653) on the high altar; stained-glass window by L. da Pèlago (1459) **8** Chapel; frescos attributed to A.Gaddi (early 15C, 'Legend of St.James the Great and of Margaret of Cortona') **9** Chapel; monument to Filippo Inghirami (1480), Simone di Niccolò da Bardi; detached 14C fresco **10** Sacristy with remains of 14C decorations **11** Cappella del Sacramento; panel by Z.Poggini (1549) **12** Bronze candlestick by Maso di Bartolomeo **13** Chalice-shaped marble pulpit, reliefs by Mino da Fiesole ('Banquet of Herod', 'Beheading of John the Baptist') and A.Rossellino (1473, 'Assumption', 'Stoning and Burial of St.Stephen'); sphinxes by Matteo da Montepulciano at the base **14** Cappella del Sacro Cingolo (1385-95); bronze railing, begun by Maso di Barrtolomeo, completed by P. di Matteo da Montepulciano (1438-67); on the altar is a 'Madonna and Child' by G.Pisano (c. 1317); frescos by A.Gaddi and assistants (1392-5 'Legend of the Holy Girdle' and 'Life of the Virgin Mary') **15** Museo dell'Opera del Duomo (cathedral building museum) with originals of the reliefs by Donatello on the outside pulpit, detached frescos by Fra Filippo Lippi, P.Uccello and others; remains of the Romanesque cloister (12C)

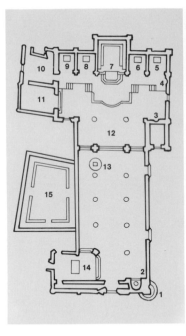

ior into nave (only vaulted in 1676) and two aisles. The green-and-white striped marble facing of the nave continues in the pilasters and embedded shafts of the transept, which is six steps higher than the body of the church. The transept has rib vaults and choir chapels. The church's finest work of art is the *fresco cycle* (1452-68) by Fra Filippo Lippi (assisted by Fra Diamante) in the choir chapel. This beautiful cycle is one of the finest Florentine works of the early Renaissance. The four Evangelists are depicted on the ceiling of the choir, while the frescos on the left wall of the choir have stories from the life of St.Stephen in 3 zones and those on the right wall have scenes from the life of John the Baptist, also in three zones.

1443-55, Andrea di Giusto and the so-called master of Prato painted the *frescos*—Nativity of the Virgin, Presentation of the Virgin, etc.—in the Cappella dell'Angelo Custode (beside and to the right of the choir). This important, unknown master of Prato has not yet finally been identified but according to recent research, it could have been P.Uccello or D.Veneziano. The *monument* to Filippo Inghirami (d. 1480) in the chapel on the extreme right is probably by Simone di Niccolò da Bardi. The frescos of the legend of St.James the Great and Margherita of Cortona in the chapel to the left of the choir are attributed to A.Gaddi and his workshop. In the right transept there is a panel, painted by Fra Filippo Lippi in 1452, of the *Death of St.Jerome*, and also a tabernacle, the

Prato, cathedral, outside pulpit

Madonna dell'Olivo, by B. da Maiano (1480). Reliefs on the chalice-shaped marble pulpit in the nave were carved in 1473; Mino da Fiesole sculpted 'Banquet of Herod' and 'Beheading of John the Baptist' and A.Rossellino did the 'Assumption' and 'Stoning of St.Stephen'. The pedestal's shaft and sphinxes are probably by Matteo da Montepulciano. In the Cappella del Sacro Cingolo (to the left of the main entrance), the *frescos* of the life of the Virgin Mary and the legend of the Holy Girdle were painted by A.Gaddi in 1392–5. This chapel also contains a Madonna and Child by G.Pisano (1317) and a bronze railing (1483) by Maso di Bartolomeo. Other objects of interest include a wooden cross by G.Pisano (to the right of the main entrance), a wrought-iron railing dating from 1348 beside the main portal and a bronze candlestick by Maso di Bartolomeo in the sanctuary.

Museo dell'Opera del Duomo: (Adjoining the left side wall of the cathedral.) Remains of a 12C Romanesque *cloister* with marble inlay, survive in the courtyard. Exhibits include the original reliefs carved by Donatello on the cathedral's external pulpit, altarpieces, gold items, missals, miniatures and detached frescos. There is also the painting of St.Lucy by Fra Filippo Lippi, a casket for the Holy Girdle by Maso di Bartolomeo, several works by Lorenzo Monaco and Botticelli and some paintings attributed to P.Uccello.

S.Maria delle Carceri (Piazza S.Maria delle Carceri): This freestanding church with a Greek cross ground plan and central dome was built by G. da Sangallo in 1484–95 on a site originally occupied by a prison (carceri). The building was to influence the design of other churches, including the pilgrimage church of the Madonna di S.Biagio in Montepulciano. The outer walls are decorated by simple geometrical shapes like rectangles (in green marble on a background of light-coloured marble), while the facing of the upper storeys was only added in 1885. The interior, which makes a very harmonious and uplifting impression, is one of the finest of Renaissance interiors. The blue and white *terracotta decorations* on the frieze and the ceiling of the dome above the four wide arches, are by A. della Robbia and date from 1492. The aedicule, in antique style, at the high altar was built in 1514 to a design by G. da Sangallo.

S.Francesco (Piazza S.Francesco): A brick building with a green-and-white striped marble façade, tall round-arched portal, rose window and blind arcades on the apse and sides. It was probably begun in the late 13C; the gable was only added in *c.* 1500. The single-aised interior houses the *monument to Gimignano Inghirami* by B.Rossellino (*c.* 1460), and also the tomb slab of Francesco Datini by N.Lamberti (*c.* 1411; Francesco Datini was a merchant and the inventor of the bill of exchange). 15C wooden cross at the high altar. Passing through the cloister, which was designed in the 15C, probably by B.Rossellino, the visitor reaches the monastery *chapterhouse*, which N. di Gerini decorated with frescos in 1395 (scenes from the lives of St.Anthony and St.Matthew the Apostle).

S.Domenico (Piazza S.Domenico): Begun in 1283 under the supervision of Fra Mazetto and completed by 1322 after certain modifications, some by G.Pisano. There is a continuous row of peak-arched tomb niches on the left side wall and around the Gothic marble portal in the incomplete façade. The 13C brick campanile is decorated throughout with Gothic two- and three-arched windows. The single-aisled interior,

redesigned in baroque style after a fire in the 17C, houses a *Croce dipinta* by N. di P.Gerini (14C). 15C cloister with portico and loggia. Today there is a *museum* (Museo di pittura murale) in the adjoining monastery.

Palazzo Pretorio (now known as **Galleria Comunale**, Piazza del Comune): This massive palace consists of two buildings obviously built at different times. The residential tower on the right was built in brick in the early 13C. Sometime after 1333 an ashlar building with Gothic two-arched windows beneath pointed arches and an 'orator's balcony' was added. Until 1799, there was a statue of Charles I of Anjou-Naples in the niche above the portal. The external staircase, tower and crenellations all date from the 16C.

The *Galleria Comunale* is housed inside the palazzo. Paintings and other objects on display here are mostly by Florentine and Tuscan artists of the 14–18C, but there are also some works from Dutch and Neapolitan schools. Notable exhibits include: the 'Legend of the Holy Girdle' by B.Daddi dating from 1328 and once part of the predella of the cathedral's former high altar; the 'Madonna del Ceppo' by Fra Filippo Lippi; a frescoed tabernacle depicting the Madonna and saints (1498) by Lippi's son Filippino; the original figure of Bacchus and other bronze sections of a fountain by F.Tacca dating from 1665 (copy on the fountain outside the palace); there are also works by Fra Bartolommeo, L.Signorelli, L.Monaco, K. van Wittel, G.B. Caracciolo and the della Robbia family.

Palazzo Datini (Via Rinaldesca): Francesco Datini, the wealthy merchant and banker (1330–1410), lived here. He bequeathed all his possessions to the poor and founded the Ceppo charity organization. In 1411 the outer walls of the palace were painted throughout with stories from the life of Datini, but of these only remnants, mostly preliminary drawings, survive today. The loggia and windows on the ground floor were added in the 16&17C. N.Gerini painted frescos in some of the rooms. Exhibits include business correspondence and textile samples dating from 1380 until Datini's death.

Castello dell'Imperatore (Piazza S.Maria delle Carceri): This Hohenstaufen castle, unique in central and northern Italy, has an almost square ground plan and was built by Apulian architects from 1237–48 for Emperor Frederick II as a stronghold on the imperial road from Germany to Sicily. Bases of two towers from the 10C fortress were taken over and used as watchtowers. Pentagonal towers were added between the square towers at the corners. A Ghibelline crenellation surrounds the wall and the top of the tower. The framework of the main portal, which is crowned by a triangular gable with two stone lions, is faced with green-and-white striped marble inlay.

Also worth seeing: The *Oratorium Madonna del Buonconsiglio* (Via Garibaldi) built in the 15C with fine terracottas by A.della Robbia on the portal and altar. Other buildings in the Piazza del Comune include the *Palazzo Comune* (14C, altered in classical style in *c.* 1800), a monument dating from 1896 dedicated to Francesco Datini the merchant and a copy of the Bacchus fountain built by F.Tacca in 1659. The elegant and popular *Teatro Metastasia* (Via dei Tintori) dates from 1838.

Environs: Poggio a Caiano (8 km. S.): A splendid Medici villa built to plans by G.da Sangallo in 1480–5. The ground floor of the building is entirely surrounded by arcades which at the same time form a terrace accessible from four rooms of the first floor. A double staircase, built in the 18C, leads from an arcade, which is crowned with a classical temple gable, to the extensive early Renaissance park. *Frescos* of scenes from ancient history and the history of the Medici were painted for Lorenzo's son Gio-

S.Francesco, monument to Franceco Datini

Prato, Palazzo Pretorio, façade

vanni de'Medici (later Pope Leo X), by A. del Sarto, Franciabigio and A.Allori on the ceiling of the large, two-storeyed banqueting hall. *Apple Harvest*, a famous fresco by J. da Pontormo, can be seen above the french window in this central hall. The apartments modernized by Vittorio Emanuele II of Savoy are on the first floor. A certain notoriety attaches to the villa as Francesco I and his wife Bianca Cappello died in the villa within a few hours of one another in 1587 under highly mysterious circumstances (according to official statements, the cause of their death was malaria). 3 km. to the S. of Poggio a Caiano is **Comeana**. Near this town, which was settled by Etruscans at an early date, there are several *burial mounds* dating from the 7C BC and these are still being examined. The monumental *Tomba Etrusca di Montefertini* is also interesting. 4 km. to the S. of Comeana is **Artimino**. The free-standing *Villa Artimino*, which has two corner towers and a colonnaded loggia at the top of the monumental external staircase, was built by B.Buontalenti in 1594 for Grand Duke Ferdinando I. The rooms, which are decorated in a 19C style, are not open to visitor because the villa is privately owned. There is a beautiful *garden*. The early Romanesque *church of S.Leonardo* (a little way outside the town) was built in the 11C and has survived in very good condition. Several *Etruscan tombs* were recently discovered in the area around the town. 5 km. to the W. of Poggio a Caiano is **Carmignano**. The parish church has a painting of the Visitation by J. da Pontormo (1530).

Sesto Fiorentino (10 km. SE): This town is known for its porcelain manufacture and the *Museo della Porcellane di Doccia* documents the development of the Doccia porcelain factory, which was founded in 1735. 14 km. NE of Sesto Fiorentino is **Pratolino**. The former *Medici villa* sits in the middle of an enormous park which covers an

Poggio a Caiano, Villa Medici

area of 104 acres and is surrounded by high walls. Count Demidoff lived in the house of the Medici pages and hence the ruins are known today as the Villa Pratolino-Demidoff. A colossal statue crouching by a pond personifies the Apennines. 8 km. to the S. of Pratolino is **Careggi**. A medieval country seat acquired by the Medici in 1417, it was converted by Michelozzo into a *villa* for Cosimo the elder after 1435. There is a tower, loggia and courtyard. Cosimo Medici died here in 1464, and Lorenzo il Magnifico, who entertained the great poets, philosophers and artists of his day in the villa, also died here (1492). The villa has survived in its original form and today it is part of a large clinical complex belonging to Careggi. Inside there are 16C frescos by A.Bronzino and J. da Pontormo.

53037 San Gimignano

Siena   p.134☐D 5

San Gimignano stands on a ridge above the Elsa valley. The Italians often refer to it as the 'town of beautiful towers' for it has a distinctive

medieval appearance with 15 fine *towers* belonging to various noble palazzi. There were originally 72, and an old regulation stipulated that none of these should be higher than that of the Palazzo del Podestà. Incidentally, when the new Palazzo del Podestà was built in *c.* 1300, the *Torre Grossa* was built some 10 ft. higher than the *Rognosa* which was part of the first palace. Another regulation stated that an inhabitant had to prove he possessed a certain sum of money in order to obtain permission to build such a tower. The tombs and burial objects discovered near San Gimignano show that the town was inhabited by Etruscans. For a long period after the Etruscans, the town was of little significance. A new town developed in the 9C around the early medieval castle and this was given a surrounding wall in the early 11C. The town was named after Bishop Gimignano who died in Modena in 347 and was later canonized. In the 12C San Gimignano—which until then had been ruled by the bishops from Volterra even though it possessed elected consuls—declared itself a free community and it opposed both Siena and Volterra until the 14C. San Gimignano was not a diocesan seat and was thus not granted the status of a town. Nevertheless, the same political development can be observed here as in the other towns of Tuscany. Hence a Podestà controlled by counsellors replaced the former consuls in San Gimignano too. In the 13C, bloody internal battles arose between the Ghibellines (especially the Salucci family) were loyal to the Emperor, and the Guelphs of the Ardinghelli family loyal to the Pope. In 1300 Dante advocated San Gimignano's entry into the Tuscan Guelph league headed by Florence, but Dante's proposal was unceremoniously rejected. 25 years later, however, San Gimignano assisted Florence in the battle against Ghibelline Lucca and in 1352 the town voluntarily came under Florentine protection. Very few of the buildings are baroque or Renaissance but Gothic-Romanesque appears in many different variations—Pisan, Luccan, Sienese and Florentine.

Cathedral or **Collegiata S.Maria Assunta** (Piazza del Duomo): This church, dedicated to the assumption of the Virgin, is also known as a cathedral, even though San Gimignano was never a diocesan seat. Originally Romanesque with a plain façade (1239) rising above a tall external staircase, it stands in the cathedral square along with several palazzi and towers. The basilica originally had a nave and two aisles but was extended in the 15C. Some time after 1456 G. da Maiano added a transept with six chapels and lengthened the choir, thereby creating the new ground plan in the shape of a Latin cross. Romanesque columns divide the interior into a nave and two aisles, the vaults

and walls of which are decorated with fine 14–15C *frescos*. Frescos of *Paradise* the *Last Judgement* and *Hell* (from left to right) on the interior wall of the façade are by Taddeo di Bartolo (1393), while the fresco of the *Martyrdom of St.Sebastian* below the Last Judgement is by B.Gozzoli (1465). Paintings of saints Augustine, Bernard and Jerome on the pillars are also by Gozzoli. Wooden *Annunciation figures* by J. della Quercia (*c*. 1421) are also on this wall. The very detailed *fresco cycle* of Scenes from the New Testament in the right aisle was painted by Barna da Siena up to the Crucifixion scene, at which point he fell off the scaffolding and died (1381). His pupil Giovanni d'Asciano completed the work. The *Scenes from the Old Testament* in the left aisle were painted by the Sienese artist Bartolo di Fredi in *c*. 1360. The Cappella di S.Fina at the end of the right aisle was built by G. da Maiano (1468–75) in purest Renaissance style. St.Fina, the patron saint of San Gimignano, performed miracles and died in 1253 at the age of fifteen.

Museo d'Arte Sacra dell'Opera della Collegiata (Piazza Pecori, to the left of the cathedral): This museum of religious art is housed in the 13C *Palazzo della Prepositura*. The main exhibits include sculptures, carvings and various other works of art from the Romanesque 'cathedral'. There are also works from other churches in San Gimignano, and Etruscan finds from nearby. A 12C painted cross is of especial interest.

S.Agostino (Piazza S.Agostino): This single-aisled church of the Augustinian canons has a plain façade, slender campanile, three apses, and an open roof truss. Built in Romanesque-early Gothic style, it dates from 1280–98. The Cappella di Beato Bartolo (to the right of the main

Pinacoteca Civica, Taddeo di Bartolo ▷

portal inside the building) has the *saint's tomb* (Bartolo) and a *marble altar* with figures and reliefs by B. da Maiano. 1464–6, B.Gozzoli, painted the 17 famous *scenes from the life of St.Augustine* on the walls of the main choir chapel. The fresco of *St.Sebastian* (2nd altar on the left) is also by B.Gozzoli.

S.Jacopo (Via Folgore da San Gimignano): 13C church built in brick and travertine with a fine portal in the Pisan style and a rose window. The raised sanctuary at the end of the single aisle has 14C *frescos* by Memmo di Filippuccio ('Crucifixion' and 'Virgin Mary with Saints') and by P.F. Fiorentino ('St. Jerome').

S.Pietro (Piazza S.Agostino): Built in the 11–12C, the rather plain interior has frescos by Sienese artists.

Palazzo del Popolo or **Palazzo Nuovo del Podestà** (Piazza del Duomo, S. side): Decorated with coats-of-arms, the palazzo was begun in 1288 to a design by Arnolfo di Cambio. The *Torre Grossa*, some 175 ft. high and the tallest tower in San Gimignano, was built in 1310; the picturesque *courtyard* was added in 1323. Judgements were read out from the palazzo's loggia. The well in the courtyard dates from 1361. 18C battlements. On 7 May 1300, in the Sala del Consiglio (also known as Sala di Dante) on the 1st floor, Dante, acting on the orders of Florence, tried to persuade San Gimignano's Podestà and the Consiglio Generale (council) to join the Tuscan Guelph league. The famous *Maestà* (Madonna Enthroned with Child, Saints and the Podestà Mino da Tolomei) on the right wall is by L.Memmi (1317). Memmi modelled his work on the 'Maestà' by S. Martini in the Palazzo Pubblico in Siena. The other frescos in this hall are by Anzo da Siena (1292).

The *Pinacoteca Civica*, with works by artists active in San Gimignano in the 13–15C, is housed on the upper storeys of the palazzo. Exhibits include: an 'Annunciation' by Fra Filippo Lippi (1483); two altar panels by B.Gozzoli; 'Virgin Mary with Saints'

San Gimignano, panorama

by Taddeo di Bartolo; a painted Cross by Coppo di Marcovaldo (later than 1260); and a 'Virgin Mary with Angels' by Guido da Siena.

Palazzo del Podestà (Piazza del Duomo, opposite the cathedral): This palazzo, known as *Rognosa* (scabby), was built in 1239 and extended in 1337. The tower is 165 ft. high. An open loggia, with beautiful stone seats for the town council, occupies the ground floor. On the left the Palazzo is adjoined by the Torre Chigi (1280), which was originally owned by the Useppi family.

Palazzo Pratellesi (Via S.Giovanni): Today the town's *library* and *archive* are housed on the 1st floor of this 14C palazzo which has fine mullioned windows and Sienese arches. To the left of the palazzo is the former *convent of S.Caterina*, (house No.16) built in 1353. Diagonally opposite the palazzo and to the right of it is the *Torre dei Canpatelli*.

Piazza della Cisterna (adjoining the Piazza del Duomo in the S.) Sur-

rounded by palazzi, towers and family houses (13–14C), it is named after the well with a hexagonal base which dates from 1346. Paving stones are laid out in a fishbone pattern, as in the cathedral square. Buildings include: the 13C *twin towers of the Ardinghelli* (one of the most important families in San Gimignano); the *base of the tower of the Palazzo del Capitano del Popolo* (early 13C); the 14C *Torre del Diavolo*; the *Casa Razzi* (today the Banca Toscana); and the 14C *Palazzo Tortoli*, where the lower storey is of travertine while the upper is in bricks laid in red-and-yellow stripes.

Via S.Matteo: This picturesque street with its medieval buildings and towers adjoins the cathedral square in the N. and runs as far as the *Porta S.Matteo*, a gate built in Sienese style in the 13C. Along the street there are the *twin towers of the Salvucci* (13C) and the *Arco della Cancelleria* (the gate in the town's first wall). Opposite the Arco stand the *Palazzo della Cancelleria* (Palazzo Marsili) built in the 13&14C, the 12C *church of S.Bartolo*, the *Pesciolini tower* (c. 1200) with two-

San Gimignano, cathedral square

San Gimignano, Porta S.Giovanni

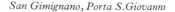

Madonna by F.Lippi in the Museo

arched windows, and the 13C *Palazzo Tinacci* which really consists of 2 residences and has fine windows in Florentine, Luccan and Sienese styles.

Fonti (a little outside the Porta delle Fonti): Originally a place for washing, this large well house has ten arches on columns and pillars. The round arches are 12C; the tall pointed arches are 14C.

Rocca: Remains of a *fortress* built in 1353 at the highest point of the town (above and to the W. of the cathedral) and razed in 1558 on the orders of Cosimo I. The central *tower* and parts of the *walls*, have survived. From the tower there is a marvellous view of the town and the Elsa valley.

Also worth seeing: The 12C *church of S.Francesco* (Via S.Giovanni) with a sturdy tower and Pisan elements in

San Gimignano, Arco dei Becci town gate

the façade. The Via del Castello with the *church of S.Lorenzo* in Ponte (1240), opposite which the Dominicans founded a 14C monastery (today a prison) on the site of the early medieval castle. The *Palazzo* and *Torre Cugnanesi* (Piazzetta dei Cugnanesi) are 13C. The *Arco dei Becci town gate* (in the Via degli Innocenti) goes back to the town's first wall.

Environs: Pieve di Cellole (4.5 km. NW): A 13C church framed by cypresses. The portal is Romanesque and the apse is decorated by columns and a frieze of arches (features of the exterior of the apse reappear inside).

52027 San Giovanni Valdarno
Arezzo   p.134□F 4

This town lies in the upper Arno valley, where the W. slopes of the Monti del Chianti are clad in vines and olive groves. The high mountain chains of the Pratomagno bound the valley in the E. The town was founded by Florence in 1296 as a border fortress to oppose the Ghibelline family of Ubertini from Arezzo. Small industrial towns developed in this valley from the late 19C onwards and one of the most important of these was San Giovanni Valdarno which, as a result of deposits of lignite, became a centre for steel production. Masaccio, the famous painter, was born in San Giovanni Valdarno on 21 December 1401.

S.Maria delle Grazie (Piazza Masaccio): The façade of this 15C church was altered in the 18C. The glazed terracotta relief under the portico is by G. della Robbia. The interior, redesigned in the baroque style,

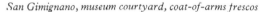

San Gimignano, museum courtyard, coat-of-arms frescos

San Giovanni Valdarno, Palazzo Pretorio

Montevarchi (San Giovanni Valdarno), church of S.Lorenzo

has paintings by Tuscan artists. Various works (mostly paintings) from the Florentine school of the 14–18C are on display in the *picture gallery* beside the church.

S.Lorenzo (Piazza Masaccio): The frescos in this 14C oratory are attributed to the young Masaccio.

Palazzo Pretorio (town centre): Early-14C palazzo with a battlemented tower built to a design of Arnolfo di Cambio, who was probably also responsible for the castle which dates from 1292.

Also worth seeing: Terracottas from the della Robbia workshop on the façade of the 15C *church of S.Giovanni* (altered in the 18C).

Environs: Figline Valdarno (8 km.

N.): The town is documented from the 12C and was rebuilt by Florence in the 14C after being destroyed. Frescos, mostly by Florentine artists, cover the walls, cloister and chapterhouse of the 14C Gothic *church of S.Francesco*. An *Assumption* is attributed to the Botticelli workshop. 12C *parish church*. The *Palazzo Pretorio* has a 14C tower. The 15C *house of the Serristori family* has a beautiful courtyard, remains of the surrounding wall and houses a picture collection. 3.5 km. to the N. of Figline Valdarno is **Incisa in Val d'Arno**. The *chiesa del Vivaio*, built in 1538–92, was decorated in late baroque style in the 18C and has a wide colonnaded hall. A palazzetto, and also the house where Petrarch's father lived, survive from the *castle* built in 1223 and rebuilt in c. 1370.

Montecarlo, Convento di (2.5 km.

S.); A church on a hill with a superb Annunciation by Fra Angelico and a painting by Neri di Bicci. Renaissance cloister.

Montevarchi (5 km SE): 12C town built below the castle of Monte Guarchi. Today it is an agricultural and industrial centre. The 14C *church of* S.Lorenzo was altered in late baroque style. The town library now occupies the *former monastery of S.Ludovico*, which also houses the Accademia Valdarno, founded by P.Bracciolini, with its collection of fossils from the upper Arno valley. Next to the 18C collegiate church there is a small *museum* with a collection of works by the della Robbia family, sculptures and items in gold. The *monastery cloister* dates from 1476. The 14C *Palazzo Pretorio* has been repeatedly altered. 3.5 km. to the NE of Montevarchi lies **Terranuova Bracciolini**,

named after its most famous son, Poggio Bracciolini, the humanist. There are also some large *ancestral houses*. 8 km. to the NE of Terranuova Bracciolini **Loro Ciuffenna** stands on a mountain spur 1085 ft. above sea level at the foot of the Pratomagno. It was settled by the Etruscans, from whom its unusual name probably derives. A painting of the Virgin Mary by Lorenzo di Bicci is housed in the 14C *parish church*. 2 km. S. of Loro Ciuffenna lies **Gropina**. The *Pieve di S.Pietro*, in the middle of chestnut woods on a spur in the Pratomagno, was given to the Nonantola monastery near Modena by Charlemagna in 780. The present building was begun in the late 12C; the sturdy campanile was completed in 1233. Remains of two earlier buildings have recently been discovered. Among the finds are a Roman marble head on the simple façade, a frieze of arches and a small row of columns on the outside of the apse. The inner wall of the apse has a double frieze of arches on columns. Monolithic columns and a pair of pillars irregularly spaced divide the basilica into nave and two aisles.

56027 San Miniato

Pisa   p.134☐D 4

A picturesque little hill town dominating the lower Arno valley. Under Augustus the Romans built their military station, *Quarto*, on one of the hill's three ridges. A Lombard settlement developed here from the 6C on. In 962, the year he was crowned Emperor, Otto I had a castle built on theô ridge above the Via Francigenia, appointing the margraves of Tuscia (Tuscany) as locum tenentes with supreme jurisdiction over the whole of Tuscany. In 1115, Countess Mathilda bequeathed Tuscany to the Pope, whereupon the dispute arose between the Ghibellines (loyal to the Emperor) and the Guelphs (on the Pope's side). In 1162, Rainald von Dassel transferred financial and fiscal administration of the Italian imperial provinces of Tuscia and Spoleto to San Miniato. In 1218 Frederick II built an imperial castle at the highest point of the town. All that survives of this castle is a single tower and this had to be restored after coming under fire from German troops in 1944. The imperial advisor Pier della Vigna, who was accused of attempting to take the Emperor's life, was thrown into this tower in 1249. Della Vigna was blinded and when he no longer saw a way of proving his innocence, he committed suicide, a tragic tale retold by Dante in the 'Inferno'. San Miniato joined the Tuscan Guelph league in 1294 and came under Florentine rule in 1369, thereby losing its independence.

Cathedral (Piazza del Duomo): Dedicated to St.Genesius, the cathedral was begun in the 12C and rebuilt or extended several times in the course of the following centuries. 13C

Figline Valdarno (San Giovanni Valdarno), S.Francesco

San Miniato, seminary building, section of portal

brick façade with three Renaissance portals, above each of which there is a rose window. The massive campanile was originally part of the old margraves' rocca.
The interior, which is divided into nave and two aisles by rows of columns, was redesigned in baroque style in the 18C.

Museo Diocesano d'Arte Sacra (near the cathedral): The chief exhibits are 16–19C paintings and sculptures by A. del Verrocchio, Neri di Bicci, Fra Filippo Lippi, Fra Bartolommeo and others.

S.Domenico (also known as S.Jacopo de Foris/Portam, Piazza del Popolo): Built in 1330, the façade is still in the rough state. The church was altered in the 17–18C. Decorations inside include 14–18C frescos by artists from Florentine, Pisan and Sienese schools, and also the *Chellini marble tomb* which has a figure by Donatello (1461).

S.Francesco (E. of the cathedral square): This romantic red brick building stands on the site of the church founded by the Lombards in 783 and dedicated to St.Miniato. The building was altered by the Franciscans in 1276 and extended in the 15C. The apses are in the pure Gothic style, but Romanesque traces can be seen in the façade beside the Gothic portal.

Santuario del Crocifisso (to the left of and behind the cathedral): A baroque church built in 1705–18, with a Greek cross ground plan. Frescos of scenes from the life of Christ; 12C wooden crucifix.

Bishop's palace (Piazza della Repubblica): Tuscan counts originally occupied the palace (Mathilda of Canossa was born here in 1046).

Seminary (opposite the bishop's palace): This elongated, curving 17C building has a fine staircase and frescos between the windows.

Palazzo del Comune (near the San-

tuario del Crocifisso): 14C town hall with a modern façade. 14C frescos in the Sala del Consiglio (council hall) include the Virgin Mary Enthroned (1410) by Cenni di Francesco.

Palazzo Grifoni (Piazza Grifoni): 16C brick palace, with Renaissance windows and a loggia in the upper storey, built by G. d'Agnolo for Alessandro de' Medici, the Duke's steward.

Bonaparte House (P. Maioli): Home of Filippo the priest, the last Bonaparte from San Miniato. Napoleon Bonaparte visited his relative here on 29 and 30 June 1796.

Tower of Frederick II (above the cathedral): The brick tower dating from 1236 and the last remnant of Frederick II's imperial castle. Destroyed in World War 2, it has now been rebuilt to its former massive appearance. From the top of the tower the view extends as far as the sea, the Apuan Alps andá Volterra.

Also worth seeing: The *monument to*

San Miniato, cathedral, ceiling section

Grand Duke Leopold II which was erected in the Piazza Buonaparte. There are several small 14&15C *palazzi* between the Piazza del Popolo and the Piazza Grifoni. Numerous other interesting churches include the 14C *monastery church of S.Chiara* which has a small *museum* (16C altarpieces), the 13C *church of SS.Michele e Stefano* (enlarged in the 14C and redesigned in the baroque style), the 14C *Chiesa del Loretino* with a fine 14C wrought-iron railing and frescos from the Giotto school, and the 16C *Chiesa della Misericordia* with a beautiful 15C painting of the Coronation of the Virgin.

Environs: S.Giovanni a Corazzano (9 km. S.): 11C *church* overlooking the valley of the Egola. Inside there is a fine 15C fresco of the Virgin Mary.

52037 Sansepolcro
Arezzo   p.138□G 4

Sansepolcro lies in the upper Tiber valley to the S. of the Alpe della Luna and on the border with Umbria. The town is still surrounded by the old wall. Tradition has it that in 934 pilgrims from the Holy Land brought with them part of the Holy Sepulchre of Christ and built an oratory for these relics which they called *San Sepolcro* (Holy Sepulchre). In c. 1020, monks from Camaldoli built a monastery here for their order. The medieval borgo then developed around this abbey which was independent of the Empire and it declared itself a Comune Libero (free community). Sansepolcro was in the possession of Ghibelline families, della Faggiuolo and Tarlati, in the 14C before voluntarily joining the pope's state. However, in 1441 Pope Eugene IV sold the city to Florence for 25,000 guilders.

Cathedral (Via Matteotti): Built by

the Camaldolensians in 1012–49, extended in the 13&14C, and altered several times since. A splendid *rose-window* was been inserted above the three portals in the plain late-Romanesque façade. Columns divide the interior into nave and two aisles. The glazed terracotta figures of *St.Romuald* (the 'wild monk' and founder of the Camaldolensian order) and *St.Benedict* in the sanctuary are from the della Robbia workshop, as is the small tabernacle in the sanctuary.

S.Francesco (Piazza S.Francesco): Begun in 1258, the church has a Gothic portal with a rose window above. The interior, which was later redesigned in late baroque style, has a Gothic altar and a painting by Rossignano. There is a Gothic cloister and a chapterhouse.

Palazzo del Landi (Via Matteotti): Renaissance palazzo dating from 1591–1602 with a fine portico.

Palazzo Pretorio (Via Matteotti): 14C palazzo, altered in *c.* 1840. The façade is decorated with terracotta coats-of-arms from the della Robbia workshop.

Palazzo Comunale (Via Matteotti 6): Originally 14C, the building has been frequently restored since then and today it houses a *picture gallery* (*Pinacoteca Comunale*). The finest exhibit is the 'Resurrection' fresco by Piero della Francesca (1463), which is now detached. The 2nd figure from the left leaning on the Holy Sepulchre is said to be a self portrait. The polyptych of 'Madonna and Saints', 'Annunciation', 'Crucifixion', and 'Five scenes from the story of the Passion', is also by Piero della Francesca (begun in 1445). Further exhibits include a 'Crucifixion' by L.Signorelli, and works by Matteo di Giovanni, Raffaellino del Colle, J. da Pontormo, S. di Tito and the della Robbia family.

Fortezza Medicea: Built in the early 16C and possibly designed by G. da Sangallo, above the remains of a 14C fortress. The 14&15C *city walls*, and the 16C *bulwarks* at the corners, have survived in good condition.

Sansepolcro, cathedral, Madonna

Sansepolcro, cathedral

Also worth seeing: The *church of the Madonna delle Grazie* (Piazza S.Francesco) with a painting by Raffaellino del Colle. The *bases of two towers* and several 15C *residences* stand in the Via Matteotti. Running parallel to the *city wall* there are *palatial houses* from the 16–18C.

Environs: Anghiari (8 km. SW): This very charming town, first mentioned as *Castrum Angulare* in 1048, stands on a hill 1405 ft. high overlooking the Tiber; still surrounded by 14C walls. Anghiari castle belonged to Florence from 1440, after the Florentines had defeated the Milanese Duke Filippo Maria Visconti in the battle of Anghiari. A charming della Robbia terracotta can be seen in the 18C *church of S.Maria delle Grazie*. The marble altar in the *Chiesa di Badia* (dating back to c. 1000 and altered several times) is attributed to D. da Settignano. The *Palazzo Pretorio's façade* is decorated with coats-of-arms; today the Renaissance *Palazzo Taglieschi* is a local museum. About 1 km. to the S. of Anghiari lies **Sovara**, with a fine 10C Romanesque *church* in

which there are good carved decorations. 8 km. SE of Anghiari is **Monterchi**: Lying some 1150 ft. above sea level, it is still partly surrounded by medieval walls. The *graveyard chapel* has a fresco of the 'Madonna del Prato' by Piero della Francesca (1460), showing the pregnant Madonna with two angels.
Sestino (40 km. NE, above Badia Tedalda): The antiquarium beside the parish church has finds from the former Roman municipium (fortress) of *Sestinus*.

53100 Siena
Siena   p.134☐E 5

Siena is built above the Arbia on three hills linked together in a Y-shape. The city, which has a university and the seat of a bishop,has preserved its medieval appearance almost unchanged, with old squares and narrow, steep alleyways. Because of its unusual site the city is divided into three sections with a total of 17 contrade (small districts). The main

Sansepolcro, cathedral, tabernacle

Anghiari (Sansepolcro), view

streets between the 'Terzo di Città' (in the SW), the 'Terzo di Camollia' (in the N., at the foot of the Y), and the 'Terzo di S.Martino' (in the SE), converge behind the Palazzo Pubblico to form the city centre. Siena is mainly a Gothic city, although there are some Renaissance palazzi and Romanesque features; as such it contrasts with the mainly Renaissance Florence. The most distinguishing architectural feature is the so-called 'Sienese arch' (arco senese), a projecting pointed arch above a compressed, almost Romanesque arch.

According to two different legends, the city was either founded by the Senones during the Gallic invasion in the 5C BC, or by Senius, the son of Remus (the she-wolf Senius is said to have brought with him has been the city's emblem since the 13C). However, all that is known for certain is that Siena was in an area settled by Etruscans and that the military *Colonia Sena Juli* was built under Augustus. The city was first documented in 751. During the following years Carolingians settled here and built castles nearby. In the 11C government of the city passed to Count-Bishops whose power, nevertheless, was restricted by the aspiring middle classes. Consuls were elected by the 'Free Commune' in the early 12C, and in 1147 the bishop was actually expelled from the city. At the same time, textile trading and banking flourished (the Holy See was among those who arranged their financial transactions through Sienese bankers), although this inevitably stirred up conflict with other city states.

The conflicts which began between Ghibellines and Guelphs in the 13C intensified the opposition between the Ghibelline city of Siena, loyal to the Emperor and the Guelph city of Florence on the Pope's side. On 4 September 1260, at Montaperti Florentine Guelphs were annihilated by Sienese troops reinforced by 800 German knights belonging to King Manfred along with banished Florentines led by Farinata degli Uberti. 10,000 Florentines died on the battlefield and 20,000 more were taken prisoner. However, only nine years later—after King Manfred had fallen in 1266 and his successor Konrad had

Siena, cathedral

Siena, cathedral

been beheaded in 1268—Siena fell to Florence between Colle di Val d'Elsa and Monterrigioni and shortly after joined the Guelph league headed by Charles of Anjou. The Guelphs originally banished from Siena now returned to their home city, deposed the 'Council of the Twenty-Four', and created new forms of government, of which the well-known 'Council of the Nine' lasted the longest (1280–1355).

During this long period of peace the roots of Sienese art, which was at its zenith in the 13&14C, were established. N.Pisano and his son G.Pisano, who were commissioned to carve sculptures for the cathedral, gave a new direction to Sienese sculpture which flourished under Tino di Camaino and J. della Quercia (1374–1438). Sienese painting, characterized by its colourful and expressiveness, came alive under Duccio di Buoninsegna (*c.* 1250–1319) and later S.Martini (1284–1344), his brother-in-law L.Memmi (d. 1357) and the two brothers A. and P.Lorenzetti (both d. 1348). G.A.Bazzi, known as Sodoma (1477–1549), who came from Vercelli,

introduced an entirely new element into Sienese painting, having been taught by Leonardo da Vinci. Beccafumi, influenced by Michelangelo, painted in early Mannerist style. Most of the Gothic buildings, such as the town hall (Palazzo Pubblico), date from the turn of the 14C.

As a visible manifestation of Siena's importance, an enormous cathedral was begun in 1339 using only the transept from the former building. Work on this colossal building ceased in 1355, however, owing not only to the plague of 1348 which killed over two thirds of the city's inhabitants, but also to errors in the calculation of loads. In 1399, Giangalozzo Visconti from Milan obtained the Signoria of Siena and, in 1487, Pandolfo Petrucci il Magnifico—described by Machiavelli as a 'typical tyrant'—established a second Signoria which lasted until his death in 1512 and which helped the city to flourish once more. After Siena allied itself with France, Emperor Charles V ordered the siege of the city. When the city walls proved unbreachable, he later gave orders that supplies should be cut off.

Cathedral, detail

Cathedral, mosaic

Eventually, most of the population surrendered, although 600 families withdrew to Montalcino along with Piero Strozzi, who had organized the city's defence. Defending themselves most bravely, they kept the 'New Republic of Siena' formally alive in Montalcino for another four years. In 1559, the city was handed over to Cosimo I, who built the huge Fortezza and absorbed Siena into his newly created Grand Duchy of Tuscany.

St.Catherine (1347–80), the patron saint of Italy, was born and worked here and St.Bernardine (1380–1444), who came from Massa Marittima, also worked here.

Cathedral of S.Maria (Piazza del Duomo): Probably begun in the early 13C, the cathedral, one of the most brilliant works of Italian art, stands at the highest point in the city. Work on the building continued over the following decades. Nave and the crossing survive from the original structure, the dome itself was added in 1259–64; the original apse was completed by 1267. G.Pisano's figures on the façade (some of which are today in the Museo dell'Opera) date from 1284–99. The choir was extended E. in 1316, and the baptistery was built as a support because of the sloping land.

When the new, colossal cathedral, some 359.4 ft. long, was begun in 1339, work on the old cathedral ceased. However, this project was abandoned for reasons mentioned in the introduction above. (Remains on the E. side of the cathedral show the intended size of the new cathedral.) The old cathedral was finally completed in 1382. In imitation of Orvieto cathedral G. di Cecco finished the upper section of the façade and increased the height of the nave, with the result that part of the external dome can actually be seen inside the building. The façade, in red, green and white marble, is decorated with rich carving (columns, statues, turrets, battlements etc.). The lower section has three late Romanesque round-arched portals crowned by pointed Gothic gables, while the façade's Gothic upper section has a rose-window (in a square panel)

Cathedral, stained-glass window, Last Supper

Siena, cathedral of S.Maria 1 Holy-water stoup by A.Federighi (1463) **2** Marble floor (1372-1562) by Matteo di Giovanni, Domenico di Niccolò, Pinturicchio, D.Beccafumi and others **3**Above the portal leading to the campanile is the monument to Bishop Tomaso Piccolomini del Testa by Neroccio (1485) **4** Cappella della Madonna del Voto or Chigi by B.Giovanelli (1661); altar, tabernacle, bronze angel by G.L. Bernini (c. 1660); altar panel 'Madonna del Voto', attributed to Guido da Siena (c. 1260) **5** Monument to Bishop Carlo Bartoli (d. 1444) by Federighi and da Como **6** Statues of Siena's four patron saints, St.Catherine and St.Bernard by di Francesco and Turapilli **7** Marble high altar by B.Peruzzi (1532); bronze ciborium by Vecchietta (1467); bronze brackets by Cozzarelli with eight angels by Beccafumi (1550); stained-glass windows after Duccio (1288, 'Life of the Virgin Mary', Saints and Evangelists); frescos by Beccafumi (c. 1550, 'Paradise'); choir stalls, side section by F. and G. di Francesco del Tonghio and others (1362-97), additions by Fra Giovanni da Verona (1503), middle section by T. di Bartolino and B. di Giovanni after Riccio (1567-70) **8** Holy-water stoup by Giovanni di Torino (1437) **9** Sacristy and access to chapterhouse (with paintings by Sano di Pietro and others) **10** Pulpit by N. and G. Pisano, A. di Cambio, Donato and Lapo di Ricevuto (1266-8); staircase rebuilt by Riccio in 1570 **11** Cappella di S.Asano; monument to Cardinal Riccardo Petroni by T. di Camaino (1318) above the altar; bronze of Bishop Giovanni Pecci by Donatello (1426) in the floor; painting by F.Vanni (1596, 'S.Asano baptizing the Sienese') **12** Cappella di S.Giovanni Battista by Giovanni di Stefano, 1482; frescos by Pinturicchio (1505, 'Scenes from the Life of John the Baptist', two portraits of Alberto Aringhieri); bronze statue of John the Baptist by Donatello (1457); statue of St.Catherine of Alexandria by Neroccio (1487); arm reliquary of John the Baptist **13** Libreria Piccolomini; outside: fresco by Pinturicchio (1503, in the lunette: 'Coronation of Pius III'); bronze railing by A.Ormani (1497); inside: frescos by Pinturicchio and pupils (1502-09, 'Scenes from the life of Pope Pius II'); desks by Barili (1496) **14** Piccolomini altar, begun by A.Bregno in 1481; statues of St.Peter, St.Paul and St.Pius by Michelangelo (1501-04); Virgin Mary in middle niche is attributed to J. della Quercia (c. 1400)

flanked by two pinnacles. The large central triangular gable above the rose window and the low gables at the sides, are filled with Venetian mosaics dating from 1878. The angel on the central gable is by Redi (1633). The white marble on the side walls has black transverse strips. The left wall adjoins the Archepiscopal Palace, while the right wall and transept are articulated by pilasters and tall Gothic double windows. The six-storeyed Romanesque *campanile* (1313) has a green-and-white striped marble facing and window openings which increase in number the further up the building they are (ranging from single-arched windows to a row of six arched windows separated by columns). The campanile is crowned

Cathedral, frescos

by an octagonal pyramid with four corner turrets at the pyramid's base. The dome is made up of six segments which are supported on a drum with two rows of columns.

Tall pillars with embedded columns divide the basilican *interior* into nave and two aisles. Both walls and pillars are banded with white and dark green marble strips, while the vaults have gold stars on a blue ground. There is a row of 208 terracotta busts of Popes and other important people (15–16C) between the cornice and arcade of the nave. The *marble floor* dates from 1369–1547, and is the work of over 40 different artists, including Beccafumi. A.Federighi, Matteo di Giovanni and Pinturicchio. Of the 56 splendid panels some are sgraffito, others are inlay; some of the floor is covered and only shown at certain times, whilst other parts have been restored or have had to be replaced by copies (originals in the nearby Museo dell'Opera). The white marble octagonal *pulpit* (left transept, by one of the pillars supporting the dome) was carved in 1266–8 by N.Pisano with his son Giovanni, Arnolfo di Cambio and other assistants. The main body of the pulpit rests on nine columns of green marble, porphyry and granite; four of the columns stand on lions. Eight figures personifying medieval arts (e.g. astronomy and music) surround the central column. Relief panels on the pulpit show the life of Christ and the Last Judgement.

In 1495, Cardinal Francesco T.Piccolomini (later Pope Pius III) had the *Libreria Piccolomini* (cathedral library) built to accommodate the library and manuscripts of his uncle Enea Silvio Piccolomini (Pope Pius II). The Renaissance façade of the Libreria Piccolomini with two arches (entrance contained within one arch) is by the Sienese artist Marrina; the fresco of the 'Coronation of Pope Pius III' above is by Pinturicchio (1504). Frescos on the inner walls (1502–09) showing ten scenes from the life of Pius II are also by Pinturicchio. The Three Graces are a Roman copy after Praxiteles, the carved lecterns are by Barili (1496) and there are interesting choral books. The *Piccolomini altar* (beside and to the left of the Libreria Piccolomini), a three-storey Renais-

Cathedral library, 'The Three Graces'

sance structure with niches, was begun by A.Bregno in 1503. The niche figures of St.Peter, St.Paul and St.Pius are by Michelangelo (1504). The Madonna and Child in the upper middle niche was carved by the young J. della Quercia in *c*. 1400. The *Cappella di S.Ansano* (left transept) contains the Gothic marble *monument to Cardinal Riccarda Petroni* by T. di Camaino (1318). On the floor, there is the bronze tombstone commemorating Bishop Giovanni Pecci by Donatello (1427). The Renaissance *Cappella di S.Giovanni Battista* (left transept, opposite the Cappella di S.Ansano) was built by Giovanni di Stefano in 1482 for the arm reliquary of John the Baptist. Apart from the *frescos* dating from 1505 by Pinturicchio (showing scenes from the life of John the Baptist and portraits of Alberto Aringhieri, by whom the chapel was built), the chapel also has a

font from the workshop of A.Federighi (1484), a statue of St.Catherine of Alexandria by Neroccio (1487), and a bronze statue of John the Baptist by Donatello (1457).

The *marble high altar* in the choir is by B.Peruzzi (not later than 1532), while the bronze tabernacle dating from 1467 is by Vecchieta. The pillars in the choir have eight bronze angels by Beccafumi (1550), who also decorated the apse with frescos including a depiction of Paradise. The round *stained-glass window* in the apse, which has scenes from the life of the Virgin Mary designed by Duccio, dates from 1288 and is the oldest stained-glass church window of its kind in Italy.

The *Cappella Chigi* was built in 1661 and named after Pope Alexander VII who had it built. It is also known as the *Cappella del Voto* after a painting of the Virgin Mary which dates from the 13C and is probably by Guido da Siena. Most of the chapel's decorations, including the altar, the statues of Mary Magdalene and St.Jerome, and the tabernacle, are by G.L.Bernini.

Baptistery of S.Giovanni (Piazza S.Giovanni): The baptistery dates from 1316 and supports the extension of the cathedral choir on the steep downward slope of the hill; being beneath the cathedral apse it could be described as the crypt. The clearly articulated but incomplete façade with three portals was probably built by Giacomo di Mino di Neri Pellicciaio as late as 1382. Massive pillars supporting the cathedral choir divide the interior into nave and two aisles. Walls and Gothic vaults have *frescos* by Vecchietta and his assistants from the mid 15C. The hexagonal *font* (1417) was designed by J. della Quercia, who also carved the marble ciborium (1429) on a pillar in the middle of the font. Various artists had a share in decorating this magnificent master-

Baptistery, font (Ghiberti) ▷

piece which is transitional in style between Gothic and early Renaissance. The six gilded bronze reliefs on the font are by J. della Quercia (driving Zacharias out of the Temple) 1428–9, Giovanni di Turino (birth of the Baptist and his teaching) 1427, L.Ghiberti (baptism of Christ John the Baptist's imprisonment) and Donatello (Herod's banquet). These reliefs are separated by statuettes by Goro di Neroccio, Giovanni di Turino and Donatello ('Faith' and 'Hope').

S.Agostino (Prato di S.Agostino): This Augustinian church with colon-

naded portico and a 14C apse, was altered in the 15C and restored in the 18C. The single-aisled, well-lit interior was redesigned in baroque style by Vanvitelli in 1755. The *Crucifixion* (second altar on the right) is by Perugino (1506). Next to this is the Cappella Piccolomini which has a *fresco* (Maestà) by A.Lorenzetti (1340–8), a dramatic depiction of the Massacre of the Innocents (1483) by Matteo di Giovanni, the painting 'Legend of Agostino Novello' (*c.* 1330) by Simone Martini, and the 'Adoration of the Magi' by Sodoma (*c.* 1520) on the marble altar.

S.Francesco (Piazza S.Francesco): Begun in 1326 to a design by A. di Agnolo on a T-shaped ground plan and finished in 1475; altered in baroque style in 1655. The campanile was built in 1765. The brick façade with its neo-Gothic portal and rose window dates from 1894–1913. The single-aisled interior has two transepts and a square apse around which black-and-white transverse strips have been painted. The *Crucifixion* fresco in the first chapel to the left of the apse is by P.Lorenzetti (*c.* 1330), while the frescos in the third chapel to the left of the apse are the work of his brother Ambrogio (painted at the same time). Also of interest are the monument to Cristoforo Felici by U. da Cortona (1462; 2nd chapel to the right of the apse) the four-arched window in the apse, and the banners of several guilds on the walls.

Siena, S.Francesco 1 On the walls are banners of the craftsmen's guilds of the Republic of Siena 2 Monument to Tolomei family (13C) 3 Monument to Cristoforo Felici by U. da Cortona (1462) 4 'Madonna and Child' by A.Vanni 5 Remnants of a monument of Francesco di Giorgio Martini 6 Detached fresco by P.Lorenzetti (c. 1331, 'Crucifixion') 7 Detached frescos by A.Lorenzetti (c. 1331, 'St.Louis of Anjou', 'Martyrdom of the first Franciscan monks in Ceuta') 8 Frescos from the Lorenzetti school

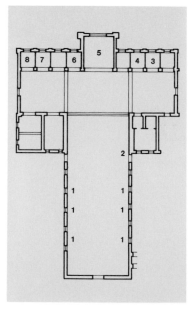

Oratorio di S.Bernardino (opposite the monastery of the church of S.Francesco): 15C building on the site where St.Bernardine's gave his passionate and sentimental sermons. The lower oratory includes a 'Madonna and Child with Saints' by Brescianino, and statues of St.Bernardine and St.Catherine.

S.Domenico (Piazza S.Domenico): A brick building begun in 1226. The campanile (reduced in height in the

18C) and transept were added in the 14C. The crypt beneath the transept, supports the latter and is known as 'Chiesa di Morte' (burial place). The *Cappella di S.Caterina* dating from 1488 (right side wall) has a reliquary of 1940 containing the head of the Saint who is buried in the church of S.Maria sopra Minerva in Rome; the marble tabernacle was designed by Giovanni di Stefano (1466). The chapel itself has *frescos* by Sodoma (1526) and a wall painting in oils by F.Vanni (1593) on the right wall.- There is a marble tabernacle with angels and a candlestick by G. da Maiano (*c.* 1475) on the high altar in the choir, which itself has three chapels on each side of it. Those chapels to the left have works by Matteo and Benvenuto di Giovanni (15C). The first chapel on the right has a painting of God the Father by Sodoma, the second chapel on the right has tombstones of German students from the 16&17C and a holy-water stoup by J. della Quercia at the entrance. The brick crypt has a nave, two aisles, and a painted crucifix by Sano di Pietro (*c.* 1460). The *cloister*, added to the right of the church in 1325, is decorated with *frescos* by L.Memmi (*c.* 1340) and A.Vanni (*c.* 1360).

S.Maria dei Servi (Piazza Alessandro Manzoni): The basilica, begun in the 13C, has an incomplete façade. The nave was vaulted and altered in Renaissance style in 1473–1528 to a design by B.Peruzzi. The sturdy, battlemented 13C Romanesque campanile has four rows of arched windows which increase in number the further up the building they are. Gothic transept and apse. The nave, divided up by granite columns, sanctuary and four chapels were redesigned in Renaissance style. On the second altar in the right aisle, there is the 'Madonna del Bardone' by Coppo di Marcolvaldo (1261) and the 'Massacre of the Innocents' by Matteo di Giovanani (*c.* 1470). The second chapel of the right transept has 'Madonna del Popolo' by L.Memmi (1317) and a fresco of the 'Massacre of the Innocents' by P.Lorenzetti (*c.* 1335).

Chiesa di Fontegiusta (near Via Camollia): A brick structure from 1482–4 on a square ground plan to a design by F. di C.Fedeli. The marble frame of the main portal is by Urbano

Siena, S.Domenico 1 Holy-water stoup by J. della Quercia 2 Cappella delle Volte; fresco by A.-Vanni (c. 1380, 'St.Catherine'), a true-to-life portrait of St.Catherine; paintings by C.Gambarelli (c. 1605) and A.Casolani (1587) 3 Altarpiece by Giovanni di Paolo (c. 1460, 'S.Bernardino') 4 Cappella di S.Caterina; marble tabernacle by Giovanni di Stefano (1466); reliquary (1940) with the head of St.Catherine; frescos by Sodoma (1526, 'Stories from the life of St.Catherine') and F.Vanni (1593, 'Healing of a possessed woman') 5 Tombstones of German students of Siena University in the 16&17C 6 'Virgin Mary between St.John the Baptist and St.Jerome' by Matteo di Giovanni (c. 1470) 7 Marble ciborium and candlestick angel by G. da Maiano (c. 1475) on the high altar 8 Altarpiece by F. di Giorgio Martini ('Nativity') 9 Panel painting by Matteo di Giovanni (c. 1480, 'St.Barbara between Angels and Saints', 'Adoration of the Magi') and Benvenuto di Giovanni (1483, 'Virgin Mary with Saints')

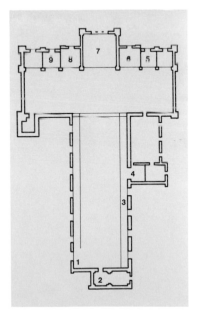

da Cortona (1489). The interior has a nave and two aisles, and includes a fresco (1528) by B.Peruzzi (left side wall), and a marble tabernacle on the high altar (*c.* 1515) by Marrina, who also designed the bronze ciborium on the third altar on the right.

S.Maria di Provenzano (Piazza Provenzano): Built by Flaminoi del Turco in 1594 in honour of the terracotta of the Madonna at the high altar. The church has a straight, white façade and a tall dome. The Madonna originally belonged to Provenzano Salvani who in 1260 led the Sienese to victory over Florence at Montaperti.

S.Spirito (Via dei Pispini): A Renaissance church (1498) with a Romanesque façade. The portal was built by Peruzzi in 1519; the massive dome is by Cozzarelli (1508). Single-aisled interior with frescos by Sodoma (first chapel on right, known as the Spanish chapel), 'Coronation of the Virgin' by Beccafumi (third chapel on right), 'Coronation of the Virgin' by Pacchia, a painted Cross by Sano di Pietro (both the latter in the third

chapel on left), and a terracotta crib by A. della Robbia (right of entrance).

S.Maria del Carmine (Via Mantellini): 14C church with rose window above the portal and a campanile; altered by B.Peruzzi in the early 16C. The church is named after the 'Madonna del Carmine' altarpiece in the apse. The single-aisled interior, with tall Gothic windows and painted roof truss, has 'Nativity of the Virgin' by Sodoma (sacrament chapel), an 'Annunciation' by A.Lorenzetti (next to sacrament chapel), and 'St.Michael' by Beccafumi (2nd altar on right).

Other churches: *S.Sebastiano in Valle Piatta* (to the right of and behind the Ospedale di S.Maria della Scala, Piazza del Duomo). Built by G.Ponzi in the early 16C with a Greek cross ground plan. *S.Pietro alla Magione* (Via Camollia) was founded in the 11C; Renaissance brick chapel to the right of the façade. The originally Romanesque *church of S.Cristoforo* (Piazza Tolomei) has a brick façade articulated by four col-

S.Maria dei Servi

umns; altered in 1720. The single-aisled interior has a 14C wooden cross encased in leather, 'St.Gregory' by Sano di Pietro, and 'Madonna and Child with Saints' by Pacchia. The **church of S.Pietro Ovile** (Piazza Provenzano) was rebuilt in 17503. Nave and two aisles. Painted Crucifix by Giovanni di Paolo (*c*. 1450) and a 15C copy of the 'Annunciation' by S.Martini (the original is in the Uffici in Florence). The *church of S.Stefano* (NE corner of the La Lizza park) was rebuilt in 1641 and has a large winged altar by A.Vanni (*c*. 1400) with paintings (1460) by Giovanni di Paolo and others in the predella. The small *church of S.Eugenio* (Via Pispini) has a Virgin Mary (c. 1470) by Matteo di Giovanni. The *church of S.Martino* (Via di Porrione) dates from 1537. The façade was built in 1613 by G.Fontana. Single-aisled interior, with a dome above the crossing. High altar by Marrina (1522), 'Nativity of Christ' (1523) by Beccafumi (3rd altar on left), and sculptures from the workshop of J. della Quercia.

Ospedale di S.Maria della Scala

(opposite the cathedral façade): This hospital, named after the cathedral staircase ('Scala') opposite, was built at the turn of the 14C. In the Sala del Pellegrinaio, Domenico di Bartolo (1440–3) and other 15&16C Sienese artists painted a fresco cycle depicting the hospital's work. Other paintings include: a fresco of 'Joachim and Ann' by Beccafumi (1512) in the second courtyard and 15C frescos by Vecchieta in the library. The *hospital church of S.Maria della Scala* is 15C, although it was originally built in 1252. Single-aisled interior with 15C bronze statue of Christ by Vecchieta.

House of St.Catherine (Vicolo del Tiratoio, beneath the church of S.Domenico): Catherine, daughter of Jacopo the dyer, was born on 25 March 1347. She is remembered for persuading Pope Gregory XI to return to Rome from his safe exile in Avignon in 1377. Since 1939 she has been the patron saint of Italy along with St.Francis. After her canonization in 1461, the house where she was born was converted into a shrine with oratories. The portico (Portico dei

Palazzo Sansedoni

Communi d'Italia) was built in 1941 by the Italian municipal authorities. The visitor passes through a small loggia (1533) designed by Pelori and enters the *upper oratory*, the former kitchen of the house, where remains of the stove can be seen. The coffered ceiling, the altar (B.Fungai), Renaissance pews, and 17 wall paintings of the Saint's life (16&17C), were added later. The *Oratorio delle Camere*, Catherine's former bedroom, contains the stone Catherine used as a pillow and a fresco cycle by A.Franchi (1896). The *Oratorio del Crocifisso* in the former garden houses the 13C crucifix in front of which Catherine received the stigmata in 1375. The lower oratory (1474), the *Oratorio di S.Caterina Fontebranda*, occupies the dyer's shop where her father worked.

Piazza del Campo: In the centre of Siena, at foot of the city's three hills. Often simply called *il Campo*, this piazza is among the most beautiful in the world, with its fan-like form which so cleverly fits the natural slope of the ground. All the buildings are in harmony with one another and the piazza unspoilt by the presence of any major streets which might disrupt the balance for only narrow corridors between the palaces and residences lead into the square. The Palazzo Pubblico itself blends well with the Campo's other buildings, being of roughly the same height and differing only in building material and some architectural details. The lofty *Torre del Mangia* symbolizes the freedom of the city, so important to Siena. Such a unique architectural harmony is the result of the efforts of a committee which had responsibility for the beauty of the city and was given all the necessary authority. Thus, for example, in 1370 the committee ordered the pulling down of a building projecting 40 centimetres from the line of the front of the buildings around the Campo. The *Fonte Gaia* (cheerful source), a rectangular well open to one side and

originally fed from an aqueduct, stands outside the Loggia della Mercanzia (in the middle of the top of the fan). Reliefs (1410–19) by J. della Quercia on the well walls have been replaced by copies by T.Sarrochi (1868; the originals are preserved in the Palazzo Pubblico).

Palazzo Pubblico (Piazza del Campo): Begun in 1297. The ground floor and first storey were complete by 1310, the three-storeyed central section and the right side wing by 1342, and the left side wing by 1680. 'Sienese arches' (a surbased arch below a double peaked arch) are visible above the doors and windows of the ground floor built in grey travertine ashlars. The rest of the palazzo is built in red brick and has two storeys of tripartite windows beneath double peaked arches. Side wings end in battlements above the second storey, while the central part has a further storey crowned with battlements and two bell gables. Between the two windows in the third storey a copper disc bears St.Bernardine's monogram of Christ. Two storeys immediately below this, on the second storey, there is the Medici's Grand Ducal coat-of-arms, while the black and white Sienese coat-of-arms (known as the Balzana) can be seen in the panels of the arches above the windows and doors.

The *Torre del Mangia* (1325–44; left corner of the palazzo) is 290 ft. high and was built by the brothers M. and F. di Rinaldi to a model by L.Memmi. The tower is named after the bell-ringer, whose nickname was 'Mangia Guadagni' (profit-eater). The main part of the tower is in red brick—like the upper storeys of the palazzo—punctured by air holes. The battlements, built in travertine and supported on brackets, are surmounted by a further battlemented tower in which there is a bell cast in 1666. In 1352–76, after the plague of

Palazzo Publico ▷

1348, the *Cappella Piazza* (at the foot of the tower) was built as an open Renaissance loggia. 14C niche figures; altar fresco by Sodoma (1539). The *rooms* inside the palazzo have valuable frescos and paintings. The *Coronation of the Virgin* (1445) by Sano di Pietro is in the ground floor vestibule, and in the room adjoining this on the right there is a *Resurrection* by Sodoma (1537). The Sala del Mappamondo, named after a world map (now lost) by A.Lorenzetti has several works by great artists: a fresco of *Madonna and Child between Apostles and Saints (Maestà)* to the left of the entrance by Simone Martini (1315), another monumental fresco by the same artist, *The Sienese commander-in-chief Guidoriccio da Fogliano riding to the siege of Montemassi* (1328) on the opposite wall; underneath the latter is an *Enthroned Virgin* by Sano di Pietro (probably *c.* 1260); Sienese Saints on the pillars are by Sodoma, Vecchieta and Sano di Pietro.

The Sala del Mappamondo is adjoined on its right by the Sala della Pace where A.Lorenzetti, painted the largest medieval fresco cycle to have a secular theme (1337–40). It depicts *Good and Bad Government* and *the effects of good government on town and country* (entrance) and *the effects of bad government* (opposite).

Frescos of (1407) in the 'Cappella' and 'Anticappella' (reached via the Sala del Mappamondo) are by Taddeo di Bartolo (the 'Life of the Virgin Mary' deserves special mention); the 'Holy Family and St.Leonard' at the high altar was painted by Sodoma (1535), while the inlay on the choir stalls was by Domenico di Niccolò (completed by 1428). The Sala del Concistoro has *vault frescos* by D.Beccafumi (1529–35) and a marble portal by B.Rossellino (1448). The *fresco cycle* (1407) of the 'Story of the life of Pope Alexander III' in the Sala dei Priori was painted by Spinello and Parri Aretino, while the ceiling frescos are by Martino di Bartolommeo (1408). The original figures and reliefs of the *Fonte Gaia* are the work of J. della Quercia and are preserved in the loggia on the top storey. The 'Madonna and Child' *fresco* opposite the

Palazzo Chigi-Saracini, ceiling

entrance wall is by A.Lorenzetti (1340). Frescos (1886–91) in the Sala Monumentale depict the most important political events during the rule of Vittorio Emanuele II.

Other rooms house the *Musco Civico* which has ceramics, coin and weapon collections, and various other objects of artistic merit.

Palazzo Sansedoni (Piazza del Campo): A three-storeyed building dating back to 1219 incorporating the base of a tower; extended by Agostino di Giovanni in 1339. In accordance with a decree of 1297, the windows of the curved façade which follows the curvature of the Campo were copied from the windows of the Palazzo Pubblico (tripartite windows below pointed arches).

Loggia della Mercanzia (Piazza del Campo): Gothic and Renaissance palazzo built in 1417–28 to plans by Sano di Matteo and formerly the seat of law courts dealing with commerce. The figures of saints on the pillars are by Vecchieta (outer ones) and A.Fe-

derighi (in the middle). The latter also carved five portraits of important Romans, including Cicero, on the right marble bench.

Palazzo del Capitano di Giustizia (Via del Capitano): A late-13C Gothic palace with narrow Sienese peaked arches above the doors and barred windows of the ground floor. The upper storey has a fine frieze of arches, and two-part windows under arches. In contrast to the ground floor, the upper storey is brick. (This use of two different building materials recurs regularly in Siena.

Palazzo Chigi-Saracini (Via di Città): Begun in the 12C, this palazzo has two rows of three-part windows below arches in typical Sienese style. The present building is mainly 14C. Like the façade, the battlemented corner tower is in two colours (the lower sections are grey, the upper parts are of red brick). The Accademia Musicale Chigiana, whose courses are of international repute, has been housed here since 1932. 13–

Cappella Piazza, niche figures. Right: Picture gallery, Virgin Mary from the del Riccio school

15C paintings and sculptures by Vecchietta, Matteo di Giovanni, Sodoma, Pinturicchio, S.Martini, J. della Quercia, Sassetta and others are on display in the rooms, including the concert hall and the music library.

Palazzo Piccolomini delle Papesse (Via di Città 128): Built for Caterina, Piccolomini, sister of Pope Pius II, in 1460–95 to a design by B.Rossellino. The palazzo is thought to be modelled on the Florentine Palazzo Rucellai and the Piccolomini palazzi in Siena and Pienza, (the model city of Pope Pius II).

Palazzo Salimbeni (Piazza Salimbeni): A 14C Gothic palazzo extended and restored in the late 19C. The second floor has six tripartite windows beneath Sienese arches and there are small blind arches below the battlements on top of the building. The *Palazzo Tantucci* (1548) by the Sienese architect Riccio stands on the left side of the piazza and adjoins the Palazzo Salimbeni at right angles. The early-Renaissance *Palazzo Spanocchi* (right side of the Piazza) was begun by G. da Maiano in *c.* 1470. It has rectangular windows on the ground floor, two rows of double-arched windows on the floors above and a fine courtyard with loggia. The 'Monte dei Paschi di Siena' is housed in these three palazzi. Founded in 1472, it is the oldest bank in Siena. A monument (1882) to Sallusto Bandini stands in the middle of the Piazza.

Palazzo Tolomei (Piazza Tolomei 11): A plain palazzo built between 1207 and 1265, with double windows below peaked arches on the upper storey, and a portal rebuilt in the 19C. It is the oldest family palazzo in Siena. A *she-wolf* by D.Arrighetti stands on an ancient column in the Piazza Tolomei.

Palazzo Piccolomini (Via Banchi di Sotto 52): This very lovely Renaissance palazzo (1469) with its impressive cornice was built to a design by B.Rossellino, who used as his model the Palazzo Rucellai in Florence. Today the *State Archive* is here. It contains Siena's most important documents (Papal Bulls, court documents, imperial decrees, writings by Pope Pius II, etc.) going back to 736. There are also book covers from the journals of the Biccherna (the Sienese fiscal court of law) dating from 1258–1659. These covers have decorations, mainly of biblical scenes, by D.Beccafumi, P. and A.Lorenzetti, Sano di Pietro, Taddeo di Bartolo, and others.

Loggia del Papa (Via di Pantasseto): The 'Pope's Loggia' was built by A.-Federighi in 1462 for Pope Pius II in honour of the Piccolomini family. This Renaissance building has an arcaded passage and a richly decorated attic.

Other palazzi: The *Palazzo Marsili* (Via di Città 132), with tripartite Gothic windows, was built by L. di B. Luponi (1458). The *Palazzo della Prefettura* (built in 1489 in the square to the right of the cathedral) was originally built by G.Petrucci and altered by B.Buontalenti in the 16C. The neo-Gothic *Archbishop's Palace* (1718–23) is to the left of the cathedral. The *Palazzo del Magnifico* (Via Pellegrini) was built for Pandolfo Petrucci, Signore di Siena (known as il Magnifico), in 1508 to the design of G.Cozzarelli. The Renaissance *Palazzo Pollini* by the architect and painter B.Perucci (1481–1536) is in the Via Pendola.

Pinacoteca Nazionale (Palazzo Buonsignori, Via S.Pietro 29): The 14C Gothic *Palazzo Buonsignori*, is a fine Sienese family palazzo. It has battlements and three-arched windows. The Pinacoteca Nazionale has been housed here since 1932. Its exhibits are mostly 12–16C Sienese paintings, but there are also Umbrian, Tuscan, Genoan, Flemish and

German works. All the important Sienese painters are represented here, with the exception of S.Martini. A chronological tour of the Pinacoteca begins on the second floor. It is advisable to obtain a catalogue, because the arrangement is altered from time to time by the inclusion of newly acquired works. Works of interest on the second floor include: the 'Madonna of the Franciscans' by Duccio di Buoninsegna and his workshop; 'St.Peter Enthroned' by Guido da Siena; a 'Madonna and Child' by the artist of Badia a Isola; an 'Annunciation' by A.Lorenzetti; 'Madonna Enthroned' by P.Lorenzetti; 'Madonna and Child' by L.Memmi; 'Annunciation' by Taddeo di Bartolo; 'Madonna with angels making music' by Domenico di Bartolo; and 'Crucifixion' by Giovanni di Paolo. On the first floor: 'Annunciation' by G. da Cremona; a 'St.Jerome' by A.Dürer; works by Pinturicchio, Beccafumi and Sodoma. The colonnaded courtyard has classical and medieval sculptures.

Museo dell'Opera Metropolitana (Duomo Nuovo, Piazza del Duomo): There are only a few remains of the new cathedral, which was begun in 1339 and halted when unfinished in 1355. The cathedral museum occupies three arches of the section intended to be the nave. The museum exhibits include original pieces and work which was never actually added to the building. On the ground floor there are originals (c. 1290) carved by G.Pisano for the cathedral façade, and also a relief by J. della Quercia. The *Maestà* (1311) by Duccio di Buoninsegna was on the cathedral's high altar until 1506, but today it is inc the Duccio room on the first floor of the museum. The originals on the reverse of the Maestà, and also the predella panels, have been detached and now appear alongside. The 'Nativity of the Virgin' by P.Lorenzetti (1342), 'Virgin Mary' from Crevole by Duccio (1283), and paintings by A.Lorenzetti Beccafumi and others, are on

display in the same room. There are also plans for the Duomo Nuovo, designs for floor mosaics and floor graffiti in the old cathedral (same floor), 12 wooden statues of Apostles by G.Mazzueli (2nd floor), and 'Virgin Mary with the large eyes' (1238; 3rd floor). The Sienese appealed to the latter Madonna (by an anonymous artist) for help and protection before the battle of Montaperti.

Museo Archeologico Nazionale (Via della Sapienza): Finds from the Neolithic, Etruscan, Greek and Roman periods, discovered in the area around Siena but also in Chiusi, Chianciano and the region around Monte Amiata, are on display here. There are urns from the Villanova culture, a terra sigillata vessel, Etruscan terracottas, Etruscan and Egyptian bronzes, and Etruscan, Italic and Roman coins.

Fonte Branda (Via S.Caterina, below S.Domenico): Mentioned in 1081 as a dyers' well. Its present 13C design by Giovanni di Stefano has three pointed arches above the basins with battlements on top.

Forte S.Barbara (in the NW of Siena): In 1560, after Siena had been incorporated into the Grand Duchy of Tuscany, Cosimo I built this massive rectangular brick fortress with four strong bastions at the corners. The plans were drawn up by Lanci. Today the fortress is part of the La Lizza park. Open-air plays are performed in the fortress courtyard. The 'Enoteca Italia' (wine-tasting rooms with old Italian vintage wines) occupy one of the bastions.

Also worth seeing: The brick *city wall*, with its splendid gates, which still surrounds Siena. Among the gatehouses are the 14C *Porta Camollia* (on the Via Camollia, in the NW), which was altered in 1604 and whose front resembles a castle. On the gate is the well-known welcome 'Cor magis tibi Sena pandit' ('Siena opens its heart to you entirely'). Other gates include the *Porta d'Ovile*, *Porta Romana* and the *Porta Pispini*. Among the many Sienese public fountains are the *Fonte Branda* (see above), the 13C *Fonte di Follonica* (below the Piazza S.Francesco), the enormous 14C *Fonte Nuovo* (Via Piank d'Ovile), and the 14C *Fonte di Pescaia* (below Porta Camollia). The *university* founded in the 13C, with 16C buildings, is in the Via Banchi di Sotto. The *Museo dell'Accademia del Fisiocritici* (at the end of Via S.Pietro, opposite S.Agostino) is a natural history museum with mineralogical and zoological exhibits. The *Via Sallustio Bandini*, with its many 13C houses, is the city's most typical medieval street.

Environs: Castello di Belcaro (5 km. SW): A *castle* stood here in the 12C but in *c.* 1520 it was converted into a summer villa with a loggia and a chapel (inside part of the former castle's wall passage) for the Sienese banker Turamini. Frescos by Peruzzi in some of the rooms were unfortunately repainted very badly in the 19C. There is a Madonna by Matteo di Giovanni in one of the rooms. St.Catherine lived here for a short time in the 14C.

Certosa di Pontignano (9 km. N.): Today the former Carthusian monastery (14C) is part of Siena University. Three cloisters date from the 14&15C. The church has frescos of the 'History of the Carthusians', and in the chapel there is a painting of 'St.Catherine under the Cross'.

Convento S.Bernardo dell'Osservenza (3 km. NE, on a hill above Siena): In the 12C there was a hermitage here and in the 13C a monastery was founded; St.Bernardine built the monastery a small church in *c.* 1425. In 1476, Pandolfo Petrucci (Signore di Siena) commissioned the architect G.Cozzarelli to enlarge the church. Badly damaged in 1944, it has since been rebuilt.The single-aisled interior

has eight side chapels and a choir crowned by a dome. Works by A. della Robbia include fine terracottas and stucco. The third chapel on the right has St.Bernardine's *reliquary shrine* (1454) by Francesco d'Antonio and 'Virgin Mary with Saints' by Sano di Pietro. 'Virgin Mary with Saints' in the fourth chapel on the right is by an anonymous artist known as Maestro dell'Osservanza (1436). The splendid *terracotta groups* of the 'Coronation of the Virgin Mary' and the 'Annunciation' (on the pillars supporting the triumphal arch) are by A. della Robbia. 'Virgin Mary with Angels' (first chapel on the left) is by Sano di Pietro; in the sacristy there is a Pietà by G.Cozzarelli. The monastery has a reconstruction of St.Bernardine's cell, along with associated items of interest like missals, objects in gold and coral, paintings, book illuminations, and sculptures (*Museo Aurelio Castelli*, to the right of the sacristy). There is also a head of Christ, carved by Landi di Pietro in 1337 (much damaged).

Eremo di Lecceto (6 km. W.): This Augustinian monastery, probably founded in the 4C or 5C, stands at a height of 1070 ft. in the middle of a dense wood. Its castle-like fortifications includes a tower which is probably later than the church (1317–44). Sienese *frescos* (*c.* 1400) on the church portico; cloisters from the 13C (columns in the arcades) and 15C (pillars). Some 4 km. to the NW of Eremo di Lecceto is **S.Leonardo al Lago**. The apse of the church attached to the 12C Augustinian hermitage was frescoed by L.Vanni (*c.* 1370). There is a rose window above the Romanesque portal in the façade.

Torri (17 km. S.): Today this 11C former Vallombrosan abbey is privately owned. It has a unique cloister whose arcades date from the time the abbey was built.

Siena, picture gallery, ' S.Paolo', 14C, by M. di Castello ▷

50060 Vallombrosa

Florence   p.138☐F 4

A town surrounded by dense pine and beech forests at the foot of Monte Secchieta (4755 ft.) in the N. of Pratomagno. Today it is a popular place for a day trip.

Vallombrosa monastery: The Florentine aristocrat Giovanni Gualberto Visdomini entered a hermitage below Monte Secchieta in 1015 and in 1038 he founded the Vallombrosan order here and established new, stricter Benedictine precepts (each monk was given the same tasks). The monastery increased in importance after the founder's canonization in 1193 and by the 15C the abbots of Vallombrosa had become powerful counts with large possessions. The monastery was suppressed in the 19C. Today it is occupied by a school of forestry and on occasion is used for cultural purposes. The few monks who still live here brew an excellent herb-favoured liqueur. A massive surrounding wall with a wrought-iron gate, 15C watchtower and 13C campanile combine to make the monastery look more like a castle. The single-aisled monastery church has a portico from 1644. Inside there are 16–18C *frescos, paintings* (mostly of scenes from the life of St.Gualberto) and 16C choir stalls and altars.

The dome is supported on eight columns. Interesting refectory and cloister.

Environs: Cascia (12 km. SW, above Reggello): The Pieve (1073) has capitals with carvings of men and animals. 7 km. to the S. of Cascia is *Pian di Scò*. The 12&13C Romanesque *church* has three apses and a frieze of arches. Columns with imaginatively designed capitals divide the interior into nave and two aisles.
Montemignaio (10 km. E.): A town surrounded by chestnut forests with a 13C late Romanesque *Pieve* in which there is a painting of the Virgin by R.Ghirlandaio, and a della Robbia terracotta. The *Castello Leone* built by the Guidi counts in *c.* 1100 survives as a ruin; walls, a well and the castle chapel's portico are visible.
Pontassieve (18 km. NE): Pontassieve, surrounded by slopes covered with vines and olive trees, is a centre for wine production. The 'Toscanello d'Oro', a fair for wine and agricultural produce, is held here in May. *Palazzo Sansoni*, the old *Ponte Mediceo*, and the 12C *Trebbio castle* outside the town are interesting.

55049 Viareggio

Lucca   p.134☐B 3

Viareggio, an elegant seaside resort, has a sandy beach 330 ft. wide and almost 7 km. long, with a slight downward slope. The town's very mild climate was probably one reason why Viareggio developed into a popular centre on the Riviera della Versilia from the mid-19C onwards. Lucca built a watchtower by the sea in 1171, and the first settlement developed around this in the 15C. Chiefly inhabited by fishermen, it became an important fishing port. There is a famous annual carnival procession, with enormous fantastic images and unique masks which are on view throughout the year in the halls on the

Viale Marco Polo. The 'Premio Viareggio' for literature, and another prize for journalism, are awarded in August.

Worth seeing: The former *Palazzo Comunale* (Piazza Mazzini) which houses the *Museo A.C. Blanc* and has prehistoric finds from the Viareggio region.

Environs: Torre del Lago Puccini (7 km. S.): This town is named after Giacomo Puccini (1858–1924), the composer from Lucca whose house is on Lago Massaciuccoli, 1 km. to the E. Puccini spent most of his time in the *Villa Puccini*, where he wrote much of his music. He is buried with his wife in a small chapel here. A small museum is devoted to him.

56058 Volterra

Pisa   p.134□D 5

There was a settlement here in the Villanova period (before the 8C BC), probably owing to the favourable location on a high mountain ridge above the Cecina and Era rivers. The Etruscan city of *Velathri* (c. 800 BC) was a member of the loosely connected but very influential confederation of twelve cities. The city experienced its heyday in the 4C BC, when it had enormous possessions extending to the Maremma coastal district, including the Isola Aethalia (Elba), and to the rivers Arno and Chiana. At that time the city and the surrounding country estates and wells were surrounded by walls 23620 ft. long and up to 36 ft. high. In the second Punic War, the municipium of *Volaterrae* supplied Rome, its federal ally, with shipbuilding materials and other equipment, and during the civil wars it withstood Sulla's siege for two years thanks to its massive walls. In the second half of the 13C the Free Community held its own against bishops and hostile neighbouring towns.

Vallombrosa, monastery church, ceiling fresco

In 1361 the Comune, which was split between Guelphs and Ghibellines, asked Florence for assistance, and from then on Volterra was ruled by Florence. Lorenzo il Magnifico besieged the city in 1472 and then built the enormous Rocca Nuova, thereby suppressing Volterra's urge to become a free community. In 1530 the city was incorporated into the Grand Duchy of Tuscany.

Today Volterra is known for its medieval buildings, Etruscan remains and alabaster working (alabaster is easy to work but also fragile) revived by Marcello Inghirami in the 18C. Alabaster was very popular with the Etruscans who used it for cinerary urns.

Cathedral (behind the Palazzo dei Priori): Begun in Romanesque style in 1120 and rebuilt in Pisan style from

1254 onwards. The blind arches and small round windows on the ground floor date from the time the cathedral was originally built, while the marble main portal with richly decorated frame and the gable with its colonnaded loggia and frieze of arches are both 13C. That side facing the Palazzo dei Priori was faced with black-and-white marble strips.

The *interior*, which has a nave and two aisles, was redesigned in 1580–4, when the columns were decorated with stucco imitating granite and the carved, gilded coffered *ceiling* (with busts of nine Saints from Volterra in the middle section) was added. The interior walls were painted with black-and-white stripes. Four columns resting on animal figures support the main body of the pulpit, which was re-assembled in the 17C from 12C parts (left aisle). The reliefs on the pulpit's rectangular parapet are probably by pupils of Guglielmo the Pisan. The marble ciborium at the high altar and two candlesticks with angels next to it are by Mino da Fiesole (1471). The Cappella dell'Addolorata (back of left aisle) has two mid-15C terracotta cribs and a 15C *fresco* of the Magi by B.Gozzoli. Other features include the monument to St.Octavian by R.Cioli (1522, left chapel in the right transept), a group of painted wooden figures showing the Deposition (13C, second chapel in the right transept), Gothic choir stalls and a bishop's seat dating from 1404, an Annunciation by Mariotto Albertinelli (1497, left aisle), and a 16C reliquary cupboard in the sacristy.

Baptistery (opposite the cathedral): A free-standing 13C building on an octagonal ground plan. The side towards the cathedral has a Romanesque portal and is faced with white and dark green marble strips. The other sides have tall windows and no marble facings.

The baptistery has a 16C dome, a font by A.Sansovino (1502) decorated with reliefs, altar decorations by Mino da Fiesole (*c.* 1500), and an Etruscan urn used as a holy-water stoup.

S.Francesco (Via S.Lino): This 13C church has been almost completely redesigned. Only the adjoining Cap-

Volterra, Palazzo dei Priori, façade decorated with coats-of-arms

pella della Croce di Giorno, begun in 1315, remains in its original form. This vaulted chapel has a *fresco cycle* (1410) by Cenni di Francesco showing the Legend of the Holy Cross (in imitation of the cycle by A.Gaddi in the church of S.Croce in Florence), and the Four Evangelists by Jacopo da Firenze (in the dome, also dating from 1410).

S.Michele (Piazza S.Michele): This 13C church has a Romanesque-Pisan façade (blind arcades) and a 14C marble Virgin Mary above the portal. The interior was redesigned in classical style in 1826.

Palazzo dei Priori (Piazza dei Priori): This palazzo (1208–54) in the city centre stands in one of the most beautiful squares in Italy and is the oldest building of its kind in Tuscany. Asymmetrical campanile. The ground floor is decorated with coats-of-arms. Five double windows beneath pointed arches are to be seen on the first floor; the second and third floors each have three double windows. Two stone lions, the symbols of Florentine

authority, can be seen on the corner pillars on the ground floor. The *Sala del Consiglio*, which has a groin vault and a fresco of the Annunciation (c. 1370), and the *Sala di Giustizia* with a wooden ceiling and interesting furniture, some of which is 15C, are both on the first floor.

The *Galleria Pittorica* on the second floor has paintings by local 14–17C Florentine and Sienese artists. These include: 'Deposition' by Rosso Fiorentino, 'Virgin Mary' by Taddeo di Bartolo, 'Redeemer with Saints' by D.Ghirlandaio, 'St.Sebastian' by Neri di Bicci, 'Annunciation' by L.Signorelli, and putti by Daniele da Volterra. Works by German and Flemish artists are also on display.

Palazzo Pretorio (Piazza dei Priori): This palazzo was in fact several palazzi which were joined together in the 13C. Some two arched windows under pointed arches. The crenellated *Torre del Podestà* is often called 'Torre del Porcellino' (porcellino = piglet), owing to the small figure of a pig on the upper right window.

Volterra, Fortezza

Palazzo Viti (Via di Sarti): Built in the 15C, and altered with a Renaissance façade in the 16C. In the courtyard there is a theatre (1819), complete with boxes. In the same street there is also the 16C *Palazzo Minucci*, probably built by A. da Sangallo the elder, and the 13C *Toscano tower house* built by Giovanni Toscano (on the corner with Via Matteotti).

Torre Buonparenti (Via Ricciarelli): An arch joins the 13C *tower house* of the Buonparenti family to the Torre-Casa Buonaguidi. Another *residential tower* belonging to the Buonparenti stands opposite.

Casa Ricciarelli (Via Ricciarelli): Small 'children's windows' with grilles can be seen underneath the windows.

Fortezza: An imposing Florentine stronghold on the highest hill in Volterra, it has been used as a prison since 1818. The Rocca Vecchia on the E. side, with its irregular ground plan, was built in 1343 for the Florentine

Volterra, Etruscan portal

Podestà 'Duke of Athens'. The square Rocca Nuova, with four corner towers and a round central tower known as 'Il Maschio', was built under Lorenzo il Magnifico from 1472 onwards. The elliptical central tower known as 'La Femmina' (the counterpart of the Maschio) in the Rocca Vecchia dates from the same time, as do the two parallel connecting walls which link the two castles and have a Gothic blind arcade.

Porta all'Arco or Arco Etrusco (Via Porta all'Arco): Remains of a gate from the Etruscan city wall include three posts built of ashlars and three well-weathered heads (which probably depict the three tutelary gods of Velathri). The Etruscan city wall dates from the 4C BC and it was 23,620 ft. long. Parts of the gate were used by the Romans in rebuilding the walls. The gate arches and the tunnel vault above the rising passageway are from the medieval city wall, which coincided with the Etruscan wall at this point. Another remnant of an Etruscan gate is seen at the Via Porta Diana, where two Etruscan gateposts built in yellowish ashlars support the medieval arches of the Porta Diana.

Roman theatre (in the N., reached by the Viale F.Ferrucci): Excavation of the *Anfiteatro di Vallebuona*, built at the time of Emperor Augustus, has been in progress since 1950. Names of Volterra's most important families are carved into some of the first-row seats. The remains of *thermal baths* (3C AD) have been uncovered beneath the theatre.

Museo Etrusco Guarnacci (Via Don Minzoni 11): This, the oldest museum of Etruscan art, was founded in 1761 by Mario Guarnacci who left his valuable collection to the city of Volterra. Over 600 cinerary urns, most of them alabaster, but some limestone and terracotta, are on display in several rooms arranged according to their decorations. Nearly all of them are from the Hellenistic period (4–1C BC) and thus it is not surprising that the reliefs were often based on Greek models. The lids, however, have typically Etruscan recumbent figures in which the head is usually exaggeratedly large compared with the rest of the body. One terracotta lid shows two recumbent peasants (2–1C BC). Among other exhibits there are prehistoric finds (11–8C BC), Roman floor mosaics, finds from the Roman theatre of Volterra, amphorae, vases (often with red or black figures), bronze statuettes (many with excessively long figures, including the 'Ombra della Sera', 24 in. in height), bronze mirrors, gold jewellery (including gold-leaf diadems), and Etruscan, Roman and Greek coins.

Museo Diocesano di Arte Sacra (Via Roma 1): This museum has been housed in the former bishops' palace since 1936 and its collection consists of art from Volterra cathedral and from churches near Volterra. There is a terracotta bust of St.Linus (a Pope from Volterra, successor to St.Peter) by A. della Robbia, a polychrome marble 'Madonna and Child' by N.Pisano, 'Enthroned Virgin between the two Johns' by Rosso Fiorentino (1521), a reliquary bust of St.Octavian (16C), and a 16C bronze crucifix by Giambologna. Other exhibits include Roman sarcophagi (1–3C AD), statues, liturgical vestments, and church utensils.

Le Balze (2 km. NW of the city centre): The oldest Etruscan burial grounds, the Lombard church of SS.Giusto e Clemente (four columns survive), and the monastery of S.Marco, all collapsed into this gorge at the end of Volterra. A new *church of S.Giusto* with a tall stone façade was built on staggered foundations in the 17&18C, but is now itself in danger of collapsing. The *Badia*, ruins of a Camaldolensian abbey founded in 1030, lie not far from this church, underneath the remains of the Etruscan walls. The Florentine artist Mascagni painted the fresco cycle of the 'Life of the missionaries Giusto and Clemente' in the refectory of the

Volterra, Fortezza

monastery (which cannot be visited). The cloister also survives.

Also worth seeing: The *church of S.Agostino* (Piazza XX. Settembre) has a 14C Crucifixion fresco and a 13C painted wooden Cross. The *church of S.Lino* (Via S. Lino) was built in *c.* 1480 in honour of Pope Linus. The 11C *church of S.Alessandro* (beneath Arco Etrusco) has a Romanesque portal and a modern portico. The *Fonte di Docciola* (1245), a rectangular basin beneath two pointed arches, can be seen in the Via di Docciola. Since 1967, two *temples* (2C BC) and a large *cistern*, the so-called Piscina, have been excavated W. of the Rocca Nuova. The medieval *city wall* still surrounds the city; surviving remains of the Etruscan wall are mainly in the N., outside the city.

Environs: Montecatini in Val di Cecina (15 km. W.): The former *castle* of the bishops of Volterra passed to the Belforti family in the 14C. The 14C tower survives, along with some remains of the castle. This tower has black-and-white stripes at its base. An angel by Mino da Fiesole, and several terracottas from the della Robbia workshop, are to be found in the Romanesque-Pisan *parish church* (1361). The *Palazzo Pretorio* with its colonnaded hall, and an old *cistern*, are also to be seen.

Pomarance (22.5 km. S.): A medieval town with the Romanesque *parish church of S.Giovanni*.

List of towns (△) which are given a main entry in the text, and of towns (→) which are dealt with under a different heading

Abbadia a Isola → Poggibonsi
Abbadia San Salvatore △
Abbazia di Farneta → Cortona
Abbazia di Monte Oliveto Maggiore
→ Buonconvento
Abbazia di S.Antimo → Montalcino
Abetone → Cutigliano
Anghiari → Sansepolcro
Ansedonia (Cosa) → Orbetello
Antella, L' → Florence
Arcidosso → Abbadia San Salvatore
Arezzo △
Arliano → Lucca
Artimiono → Prato
Asciano → Buonconvento
Azzano → Pietrasanta

Badia di Ripoli → Florence
Badia Prataglia → Poppi
Bagni di Lucca → Barga
Bagnone → Pontremoli
Barberino di Mugello → Borgo San
Lorenzo
Barberino Val d'Elsa → Poggibonsi
Barga △
Bibbiena △
Borgo a Mozzano → Barga
Borgo San Lorenzo △
Buggiano → Pescia
Buonconvento △

Cafaggiolo → Borgo San Lorenzo
Calci → Pisa
Camaiore → Pietrasanta
Camaldoli → Poppi
Campiglia Marittima → Piombino
Campo Cecina → Carrara
Camucia → Cortona
Capalbio → Orbetello
Capraia → Elba
Caprese Michelangelo → Bibbiena
Careggi → Prato
Carmignano → Prato
Carrara △
Cascia → Vallombrosa

Castagneto-Carducci → Cecina
Castellina in Chianti → Poggibonsi
Castello di Belcaro → Siena
Castello di Brolio → Poggibonsi
Castello di Romena → Poppi
Castelnuova di Garfagnana → Barga
Castelfiorentino → Certaldo
Castelvecchio Pascoli → Barga
Castelvecchio → Pescia
Castiglioncello → Cecina
Castiglion Fiorentino → Cortona
Castiglione della Pescaia △
Castiglione di Garfagnana → Barga
Castiglione d'Orcia → Pienza
Cecina △
Cerreto Guidi → Empoli
Certaldo △
Certosa di Pisa → Pisa
Certosa di Pontignano → Siena
Cetona → Chiusi
Chianciano → Montepulciano
Chianciano Terme → Montepulciano
Chiusdino → Massa Marittima
Chiusi △
Civitella in Val di Chiana → Monte
San Savino
Colle di Val d'Elsa → Poggibonsi
Collodi → Pescia
Colonnata, marble quarries of →
Carrara
Comeana → Prato
Convento Monte Senario → Borgo
San Lorenzo
Convento S.Bernardo
dell'Osservanza → Siena
Convento S.Vivaldo → Certaldo
Cortona △
Cutigliano △

Dicomano → Borgo San Lorenzo
Diecimo → Barga

Elba △
Empoli △
Eremo di Lecceto → Siena

Fiesole △
Figline Valdarno → San Giovanni
  Valdarno
Firenze △
Fivizzano → Pontremoli
Florence △
Follonica → Massa Marittima
Forte dei Marmi → Massa
Fosdinovo → Carrara

Gaiole in Chianti → Poggibonsi
Galluzzo → Florence
Gavinana → Cutigliano
Gavorrano → Massa Marittima
Gorgona → Livorno
Greve → Poggibonsi
Gropina → San Giovanni Valdarno
Grosseto △

Impruneta △
Incisa in Val d'Arno → San Giovanni
  Valdarno
Isola del Giglio → Orbetello
Isola di Giannutri → Orbetello
Istia d'Ombrone → Grosseto

La Verna, monastery → Bibbiena
La Villa → Barga
Licciana Nardi → Pontremoli
Livorno △
Loro Ciuffenna → San Giovanni
  Valdarno
Lucca △
Lucignano → Monte San Savino

Magliano in Toscana → Grosseto
Marciana → Elba
Marciana Marina → Elba
Marina di Cecina → Cecina
Marina di Massa → Massa
Marina di Pietrasanta → Pietrasanta
Marlia → Lucca
Marsiliana → Orbetello
Massa △
Massa Marittima △
Meleto → Poggibonsi
Monsummano Terme → Pescia
Montalcino △
Montecarlo, Convento di → San
  Giovanni Valdarno
Montecatini in Val di Cecina →
  Volterra
Montecatini Terme → Pescia
Montecatini Val di Nievole → Pescia

Montecchio Vesponi → Cortona
Montecristo → Elba
Montelupo Fiorentino → Empoli
Montemignaio → Vallombrosa
Montepulciano △
Monterchi → Sansepolcro
Monteriggioni → Poggibonsi
Monte San Savino △
Montevarchi → San Giovanni
  Valdarno
Monticchiello → Pienza

Orbetello △

Paganico → Grosseto
Panzano → Poggibonsi
Pescia △
Piancastagnaio → Abbadia San
  Salvatore
Pian di Scò → Vallombrosa
Pienza △
Pietrasanta △
Pieve di Cellole → San Gimignano
Pieve S.Appiano → Poggibonsi
Pieve S.Cresci → Borgo San Lorenzo
Pieve S.Pietro di Romena → Poppi
Piombino △
Pisa △
Pistoia △
Pitigliano △
Poggibonsi △
Poggio a Caiano → Prato
Poggio Buco → Pitigliano
Pomarance → Volterra
Pontassieve → Vallombrosa
Pontremoli △
Poppi △
Populonia → Piombino
Port'Ercole → Orbetello
Porte S.Stefano → Orbetello
Porto Azzuro → Elba
Portoferraio → Elba
Prato △
Pratolino → Prato
Punta Ala → Castiglione della Pescaia

Radda in Chianti → Poggibonsi
Rigoli → Lucca
Rio nell'Elba → Elba
Rocca d'Orcia → Pienza
Roccalbegna → Abbadia San
  Salvatore
Roselle Scavi → Grosseto
Rosignano-Marittimo → Cecina

San Casciano in Val di Pesa →
   Impruneta
San Cassiano → Barga
San Galgano → Massa Marittima
San Gimignano △
San Giovanni a Corazzano → San
   Miniato
San Giovanni Valdarno △
San Godenzo → Borgo San Lorenzo
San Guido Bolgheri → Cecina
San Leonardo al Lago → Siena
San Lucchese → Poggibonsi
San Marcello Pistoiese → Cutigliano
San Martino a Mensola → Firenze
San Miniato △
San Piero a Grado → Pisa
San Piero a Sieve → Borgo San
   Lorenzo
San Quirico d'Orcia → Pienza
Sansepolcro △
Santa Fiora → Abbadia San Salvatore
Sant'Agata → Borgo San Lorenzo
Santa Anna in Comprena → Pienza
Santuario di Montenero → Livorno
Sarteano → Chiusi
Saturnia → Pitigliano
Scarlino → Massa Marittima
Scarperia → Borgo San Lorenzo
Seggiano → Abbadia San Salvatore
Segromigno → Lucca
Seravezza → Pietrasanta
Serravalle → Pescia
Sestino → Sansepolcro
Sesto Fiorentino → Prato

Settignano → Firenze
Siena △
Sinalunga → Monte San Savino
Sorano → Pitigliano
Sovana → Pitigliano
Sovara → Sansepolcro
Staggia → Poggibonsi
Stia → Poppi
Strada → Poppi
Suvereto → Cecina

Talamone → Orbetello
Terranuova Bracciolini → San
   Giovanni Valdarno
Torre del Lago Puccini → Viareggio
Torri → Siena
Trebbio → Borgo San Lorenzo

Uzzano → Pescia

Valdicastello Carducci → Pietrasanta
Vallombrosa △
Vetulonia → Castiglione della Pescaia
Viareggio △
Vicchio → Borgo San Lorenzo
Vicopisano → Pisa
Villa Basilica → Pescia
Villafranca in Lunigiana →
   Pontremoli
Villa Gamberaia → Firenze
Villa I Tatti → Firenze
Villamagna → Firenze
Vinci → Empoli
Volterra △

San Casciano in Val di Pesa → Impruneta
San Cassiano → Barga
San Galgano → Massa Marittima
San Gimignano △
San Giovanni a Corazzano → San Miniato
San Giovanni Valdarno △
San Godenzo → Borgo San Lorenzo
San Guido Bolgheri → Cecina
San Leonardo al Lago → Siena
San Lucchese → Poggibonsi
San Marcello Pistoiese → Cutigliano
San Martino a Mensola → Firenze
San Miniato △
San Piero a Grado → Pisa
San Piero a Sieve → Borgo San Lorenzo
San Quirico d'Orcia → Pienza
Sansepolcro △
Santa Fiora → Abbadia San Salvatore
Sant'Agata → Borgo San Lorenzo
Santa Anna in Comprena → Pienza
Santuario di Montenero → Livorno
Sarteano → Chiusi
Saturnia → Pitigliano
Scarlino → Massa Marittima
Scarperia → Borgo San Lorenzo
Seggiano → Abbadia San Salvatore
Segromigno → Lucca
Seravezza → Pietrasanta
Serravalle → Pescia
Sestino → Sansepolcro
Sesto Fiorentino → Prato

Settignano → Firenze
Siena △
Sinalunga → Monte San Savino
Sorano → Pitigliano
Sovana → Pitigliano
Sovara → Sansepolcro
Staggia → Poggibonsi
Stia → Poppi
Strada → Poppi
Suvereto → Cecina

Talamone → Orbetello
Terranuova Bracciolini → San Giovanni Valdarno
Torre del Lago Puccini → Viareggio
Torri → Siena
Trebbio → Borgo San Lorenzo

Uzzano → Pescia

Valdicastello Carducci → Pietrasanta
Vallombrosa △
Vetulonia → Castiglione della Pescaia
Viareggio △
Vicchio → Borgo San Lorenzo
Vicopisano → Pisa
Villa Basilica → Pescia
Villafranca in Lunigiana → Pontremoli
Villa Gamberaia → Firenze
Villa I Tatti → Firenze
Villamagna → Firenze
Vinci → Empoli
Volterra △